X-O MANOWAR

AT WAR WITH
UNITY

ROBERT VENDITTI | CARY NORD | VICENTE CIFUENTES | ULISES ARREOLA

CONTENTS

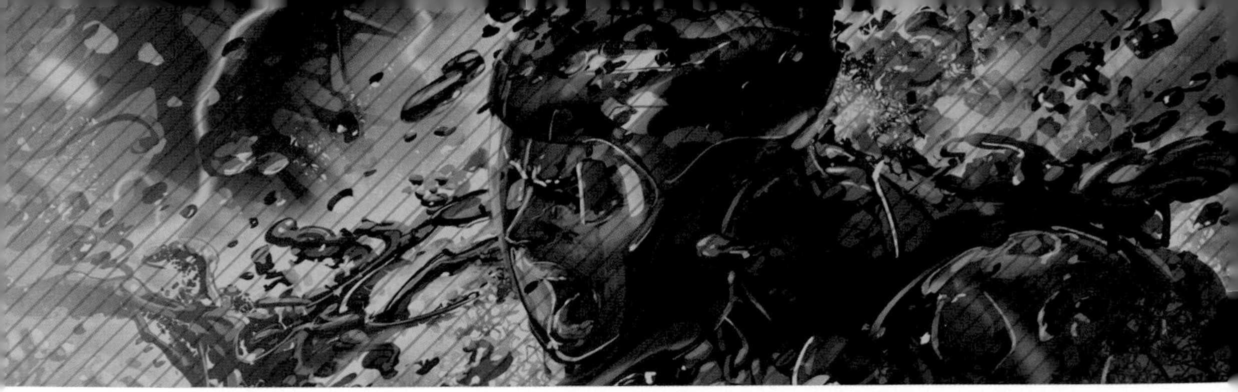

Collection Cover Art: Clayton Crain

VALIANT.

Peter Cuneo
Chairman

Dinesh Shamdasani
CEO and Chief Creative Officer

Gavin Cuneo
CFO and Head of Strategic Development

Fred Pierce
Publisher

Warren Simons
VP Executive Editor

Walter Black
VP Operations

Hunter Gorinson
Director of Marketing, Communications
& Digital Media

Atom! Freeman
Sales Manager

Travis Escarfullery
Production and Design Manager

Alejandro Arbona
Associate Editor

Josh Johns
Assistant Editor

Peter Stern
Operations Manager

Robert Meyers
Operations Coordinator

Ivan Cohen
Collection Editor

Steve Blackwell
Collection Designer

Rian Hughes/Device
Trade Dress and Book Design

Russell Brown
President, Consumer Products,
Promotions and Ad Sales

Jason Kothari
Vice Chairman

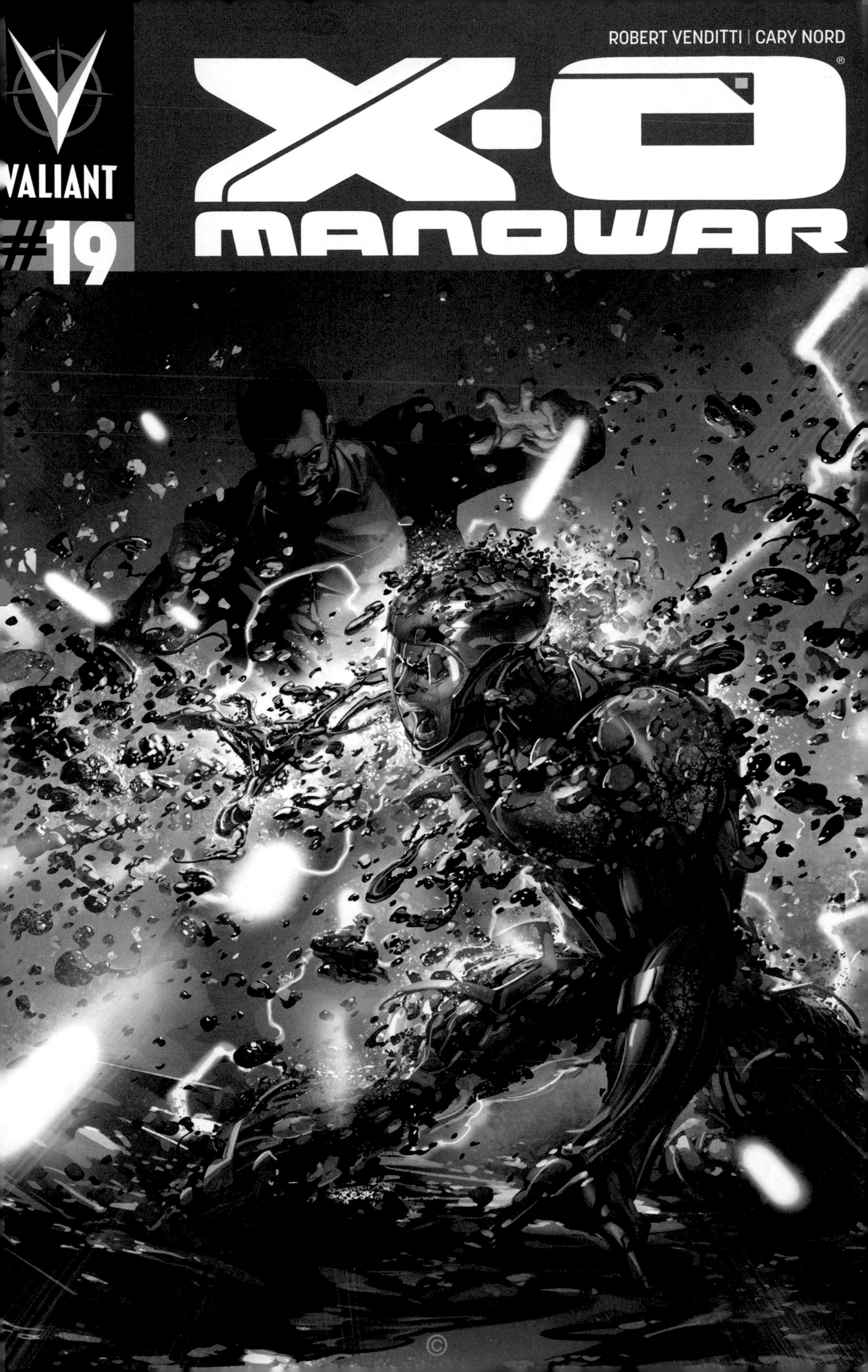
VALIANT
#19
ROBERT VENDITTI | CARY NORD
X-O
MANOWAR

PREVIOUSLY IN...

UNITY

Aric of Dacia, heir to the Visigoth throne, was enslaved by brutal alien conquerors called the Vine. Held captive for years, Aric escaped taking with him the Vine's most powerful weapon – Shanhara, the X-O Manowar armor. Seeking vengeance, Aric decimated the Vine homeworld and freed the last of his people. Now, displaced 1,600 years into the modern day, Aric leads his people back to Earth to reclaim the lost Visigoth homeland...

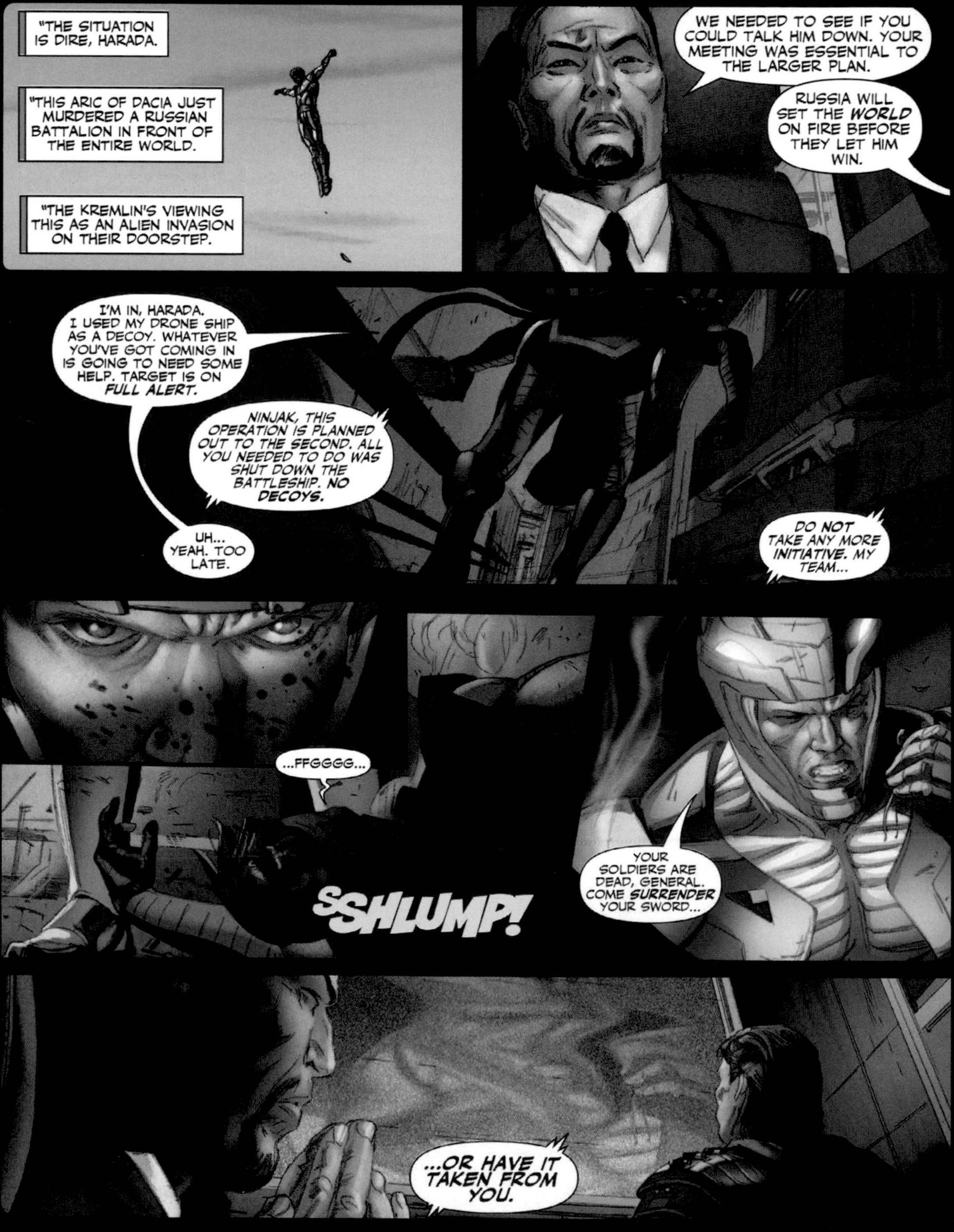
"THE SITUATION IS DIRE, HARADA.
"THIS ARIC OF DACIA JUST MURDERED A RUSSIAN BATTALION IN FRONT OF THE ENTIRE WORLD.
"THE KREMLIN'S VIEWING THIS AS AN ALIEN INVASION ON THEIR DOORSTEP.
WE NEEDED TO SEE IF YOU COULD TALK HIM DOWN. YOUR MEETING WAS ESSENTIAL TO THE LARGER PLAN.
RUSSIA WILL SET THE WORLD ON FIRE BEFORE THEY LET HIM WIN.
I'M IN, HARADA. I USED MY DRONE SHIP AS A DECOY. WHATEVER YOU'VE GOT COMING IN IS GOING TO NEED SOME HELP. TARGET IS ON FULL ALERT.
NINJAK, THIS OPERATION IS PLANNED OUT TO THE SECOND. ALL YOU NEEDED TO DO WAS SHUT DOWN THE BATTLESHIP. NO DECOYS.
UH... YEAH. TOO LATE.
DO NOT TAKE ANY MORE INITIATIVE. MY TEAM...
...FFGGGG...
SSHLUMP!
YOUR SOLDIERS ARE DEAD, GENERAL. COME SURRENDER YOUR SWORD...
...OR HAVE IT TAKEN FROM YOU.

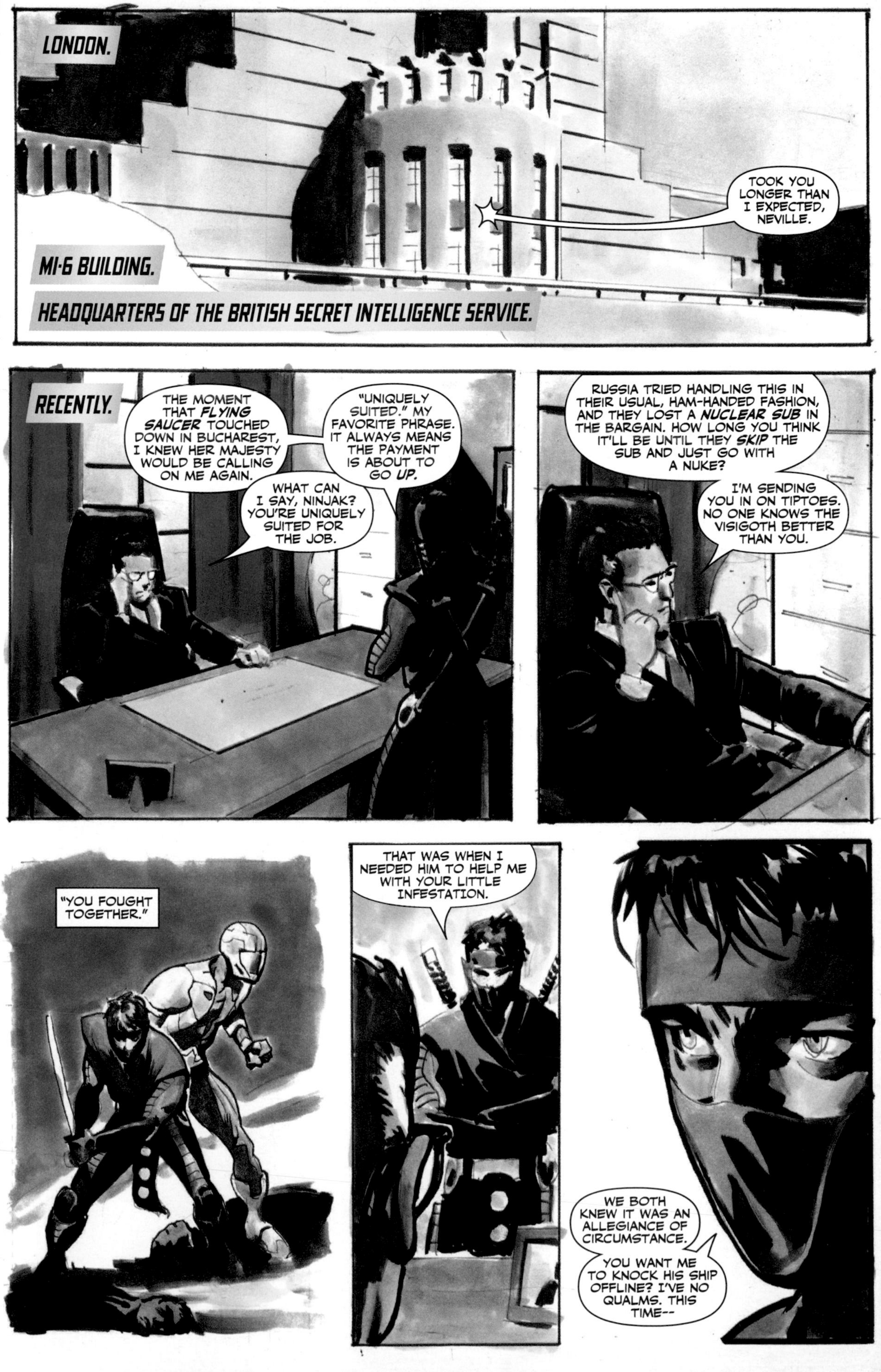
LONDON.
TOOK YOU LONGER THAN I EXPECTED, NEVILLE.
MI-6 BUILDING.
HEADQUARTERS OF THE BRITISH SECRET INTELLIGENCE SERVICE.
RECENTLY.
THE MOMENT THAT FLYING SAUCER TOUCHED DOWN IN BUCHAREST, I KNEW HER MAJESTY WOULD BE CALLING ON ME AGAIN.
WHAT CAN I SAY, NINJAK? YOU'RE UNIQUELY SUITED FOR THE JOB.
"UNIQUELY SUITED." MY FAVORITE PHRASE. IT ALWAYS MEANS THE PAYMENT IS ABOUT TO GO UP.
RUSSIA TRIED HANDLING THIS IN THEIR USUAL, HAM-HANDED FASHION, AND THEY LOST A NUCLEAR SUB IN THE BARGAIN. HOW LONG YOU THINK IT'LL BE UNTIL THEY SKIP THE SUB AND JUST GO WITH A NUKE?
I'M SENDING YOU IN ON TIPTOES. NO ONE KNOWS THE VISIGOTH BETTER THAN YOU.
"YOU FOUGHT TOGETHER."
THAT WAS WHEN I NEEDED HIM TO HELP ME WITH YOUR LITTLE INFESTATION.
WE BOTH KNEW IT WAS AN ALLEGIANCE OF CIRCUMSTANCE.
YOU WANT ME TO KNOCK HIS SHIP OFFLINE? I'VE NO QUALMS. THIS TIME--

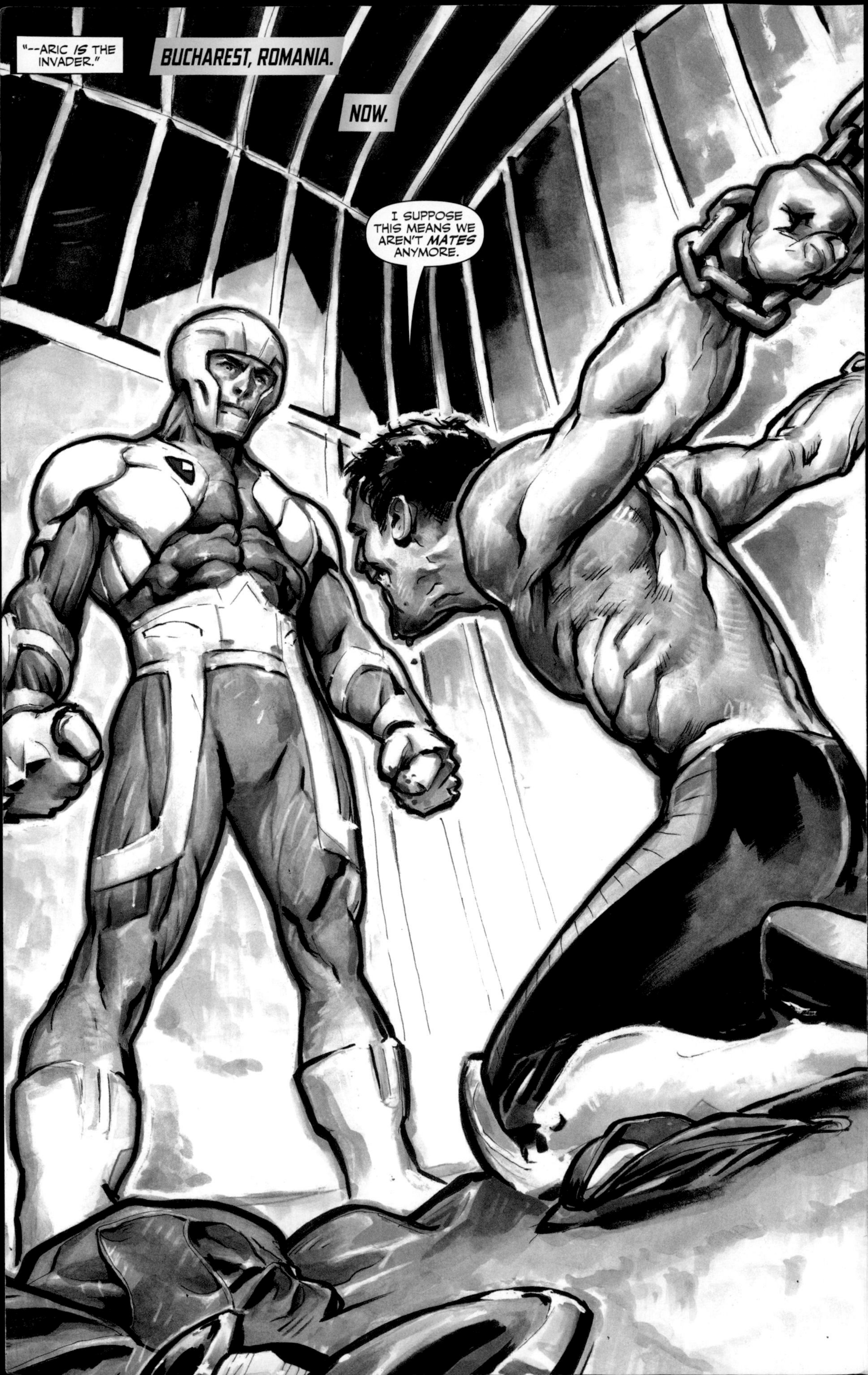
"--ARIC IS THE INVADER."
BUCHAREST, ROMANIA.
NOW.
I SUPPOSE THIS MEANS WE AREN'T MATES ANYMORE.

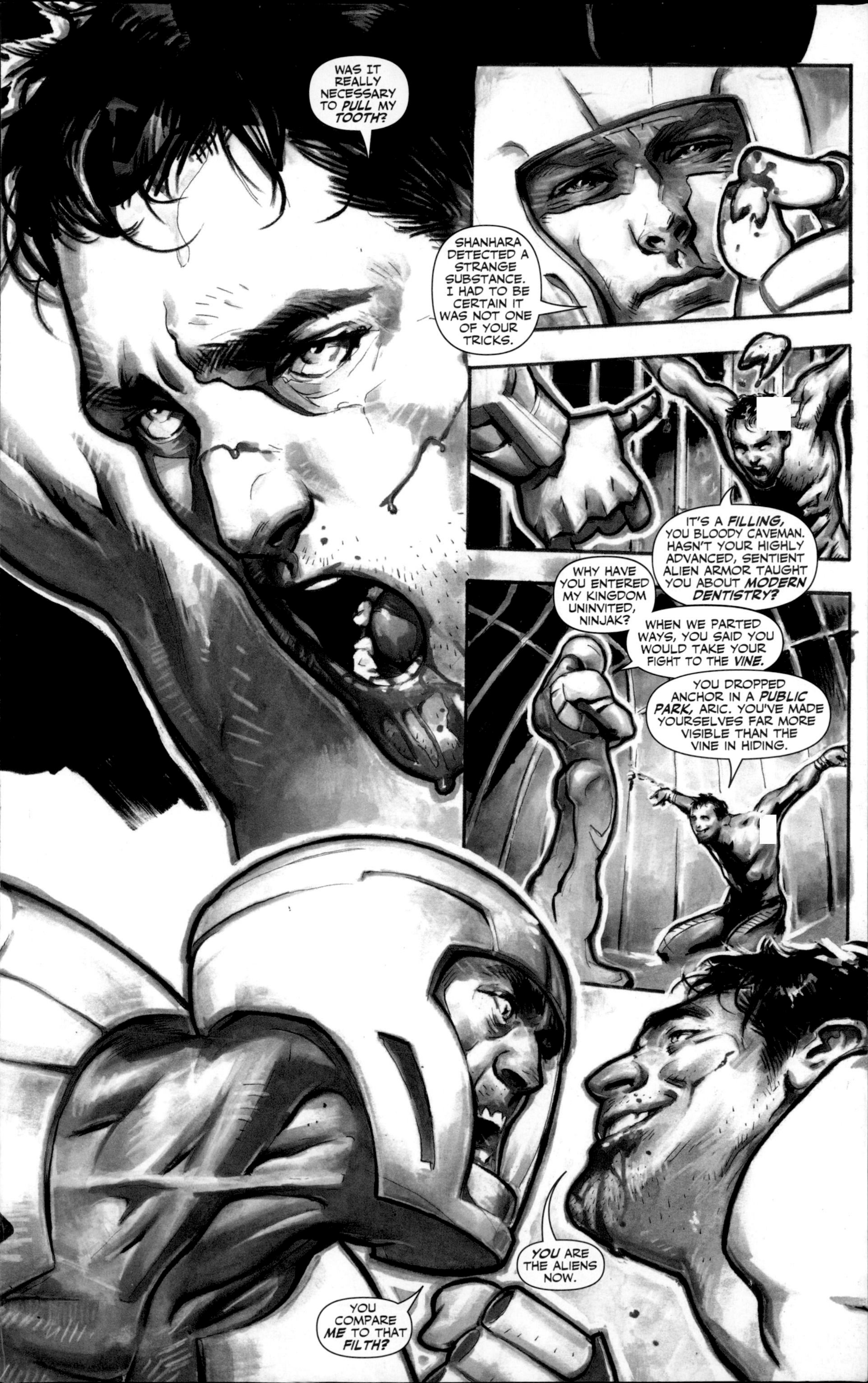
WAS IT REALLY NECESSARY TO *PULL* MY *TOOTH?*
SHANHARA DETECTED A STRANGE SUBSTANCE. I HAD TO BE CERTAIN IT WAS NOT ONE OF YOUR TRICKS.
IT'S A *FILLING,* YOU BLOODY CAVEMAN. HASN'T YOUR HIGHLY ADVANCED, SENTIENT ALIEN ARMOR TAUGHT YOU ABOUT *MODERN DENTISTRY?*
WHY HAVE YOU ENTERED MY KINGDOM UNINVITED, NINJAK?
WHEN WE PARTED WAYS, YOU SAID YOU WOULD TAKE YOUR FIGHT TO THE *VINE.*
YOU DROPPED ANCHOR IN A *PUBLIC PARK,* ARIC. YOU'VE MADE YOURSELVES FAR MORE VISIBLE THAN THE VINE IN HIDING.
YOU ARE THE ALIENS NOW.
YOU COMPARE *ME* TO THAT *FILTH?*

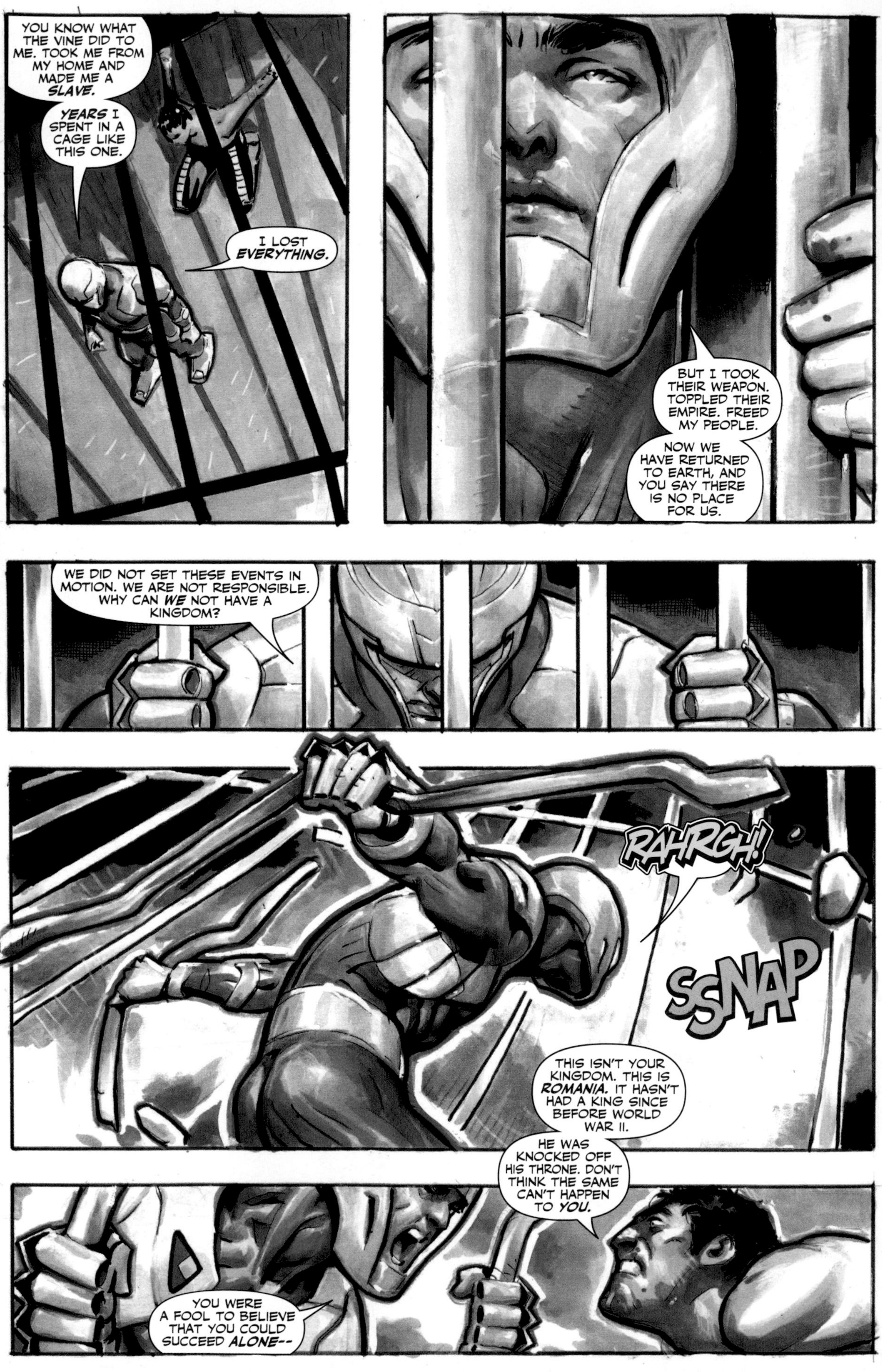

YOU KNOW WHAT THE VINE DID TO ME. TOOK ME FROM MY HOME AND MADE ME A SLAVE.
YEARS I SPENT IN A CAGE LIKE THIS ONE.
I LOST EVERYTHING.
BUT I TOOK THEIR WEAPON. TOPPLED THEIR EMPIRE. FREED MY PEOPLE.
NOW WE HAVE RETURNED TO EARTH, AND YOU SAY THERE IS NO PLACE FOR US.
WE DID NOT SET THESE EVENTS IN MOTION. WE ARE NOT RESPONSIBLE. WHY CAN WE NOT HAVE A KINGDOM?
RAHRGH!
SSNAP
THIS ISN'T YOUR KINGDOM. THIS IS ROMANIA. IT HASN'T HAD A KING SINCE BEFORE WORLD WAR II.
HE WAS KNOCKED OFF HIS THRONE. DON'T THINK THE SAME CAN'T HAPPEN TO YOU.
YOU WERE A FOOL TO BELIEVE THAT YOU COULD SUCCEED ALONE--

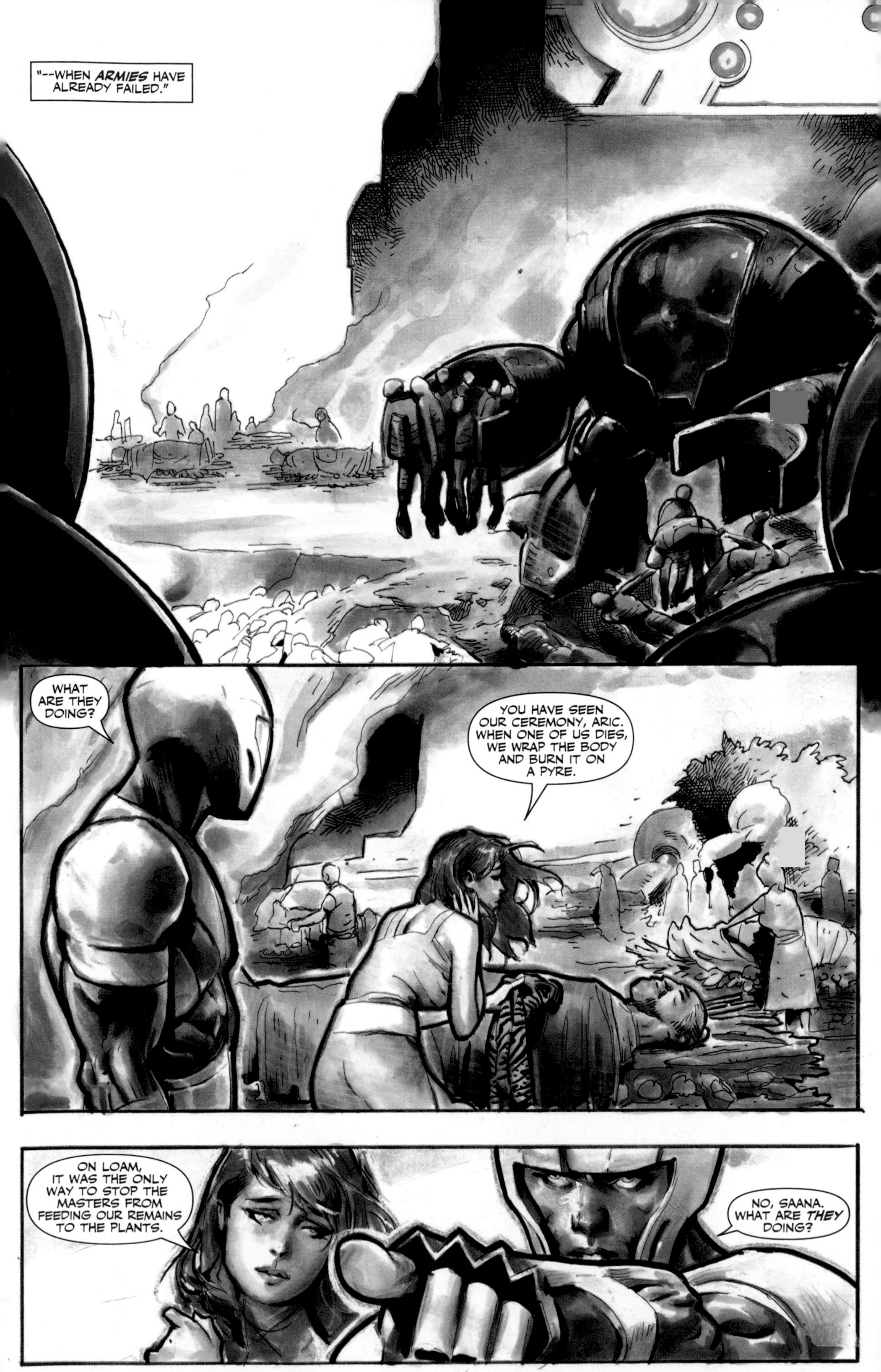
"--WHEN ARMIES HAVE ALREADY FAILED."
WHAT ARE THEY DOING?
YOU HAVE SEEN OUR CEREMONY, ARIC. WHEN ONE OF US DIES, WE WRAP THE BODY AND BURN IT ON A PYRE.
ON LOAM, IT WAS THE ONLY WAY TO STOP THE MASTERS FROM FEEDING OUR REMAINS TO THE PLANTS.
NO, SAANA. WHAT ARE THEY DOING?

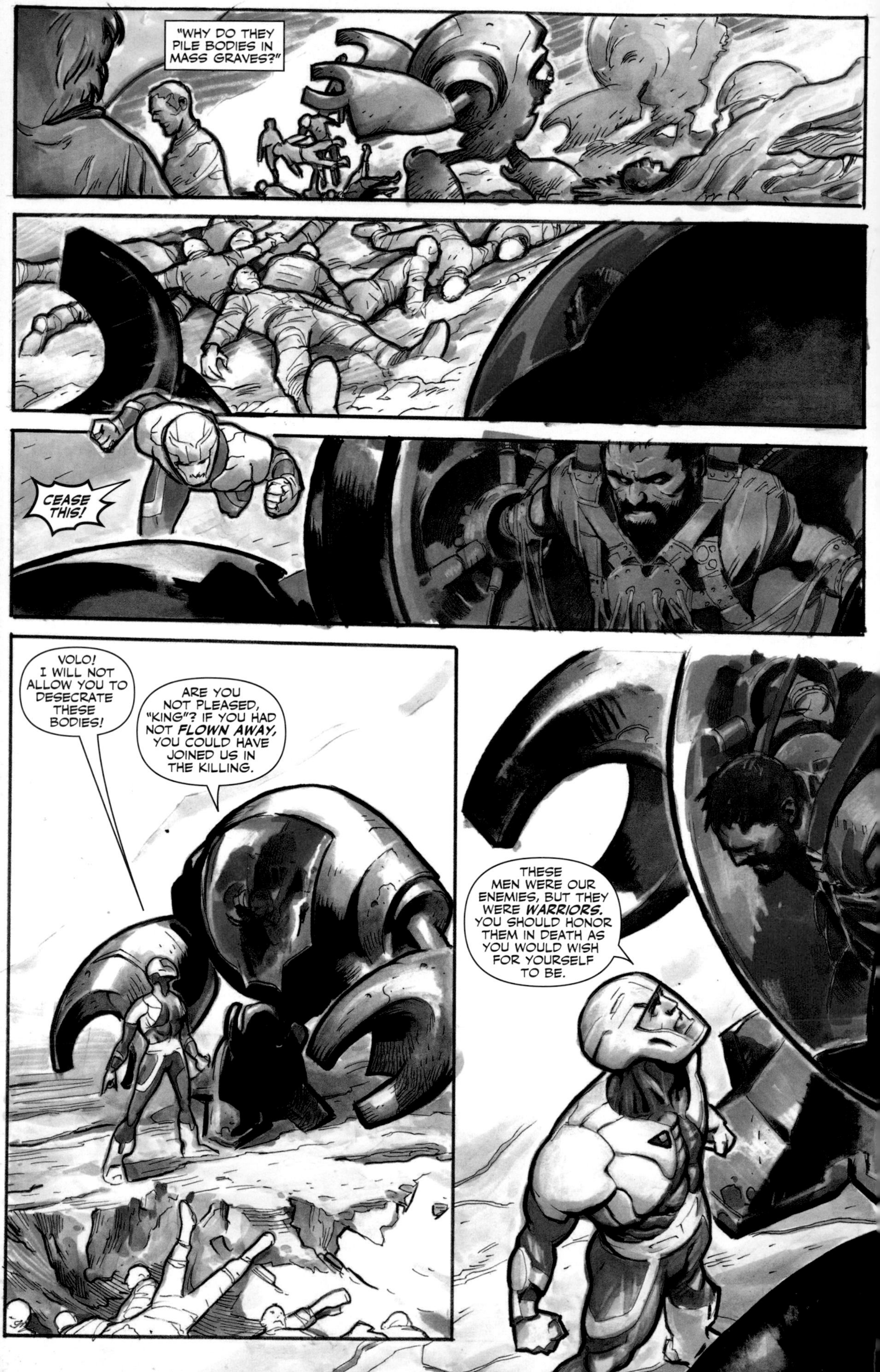
"WHY DO THEY PILE BODIES IN MASS GRAVES?"
CEASE THIS!
VOLO! I WILL NOT ALLOW YOU TO DESECRATE THESE BODIES!
ARE YOU NOT PLEASED, "KING"? IF YOU HAD NOT FLOWN AWAY, YOU COULD HAVE JOINED US IN THE KILLING.
THESE MEN WERE OUR ENEMIES, BUT THEY WERE WARRIORS. YOU SHOULD HONOR THEM IN DEATH AS YOU WOULD WISH FOR YOURSELF TO BE.

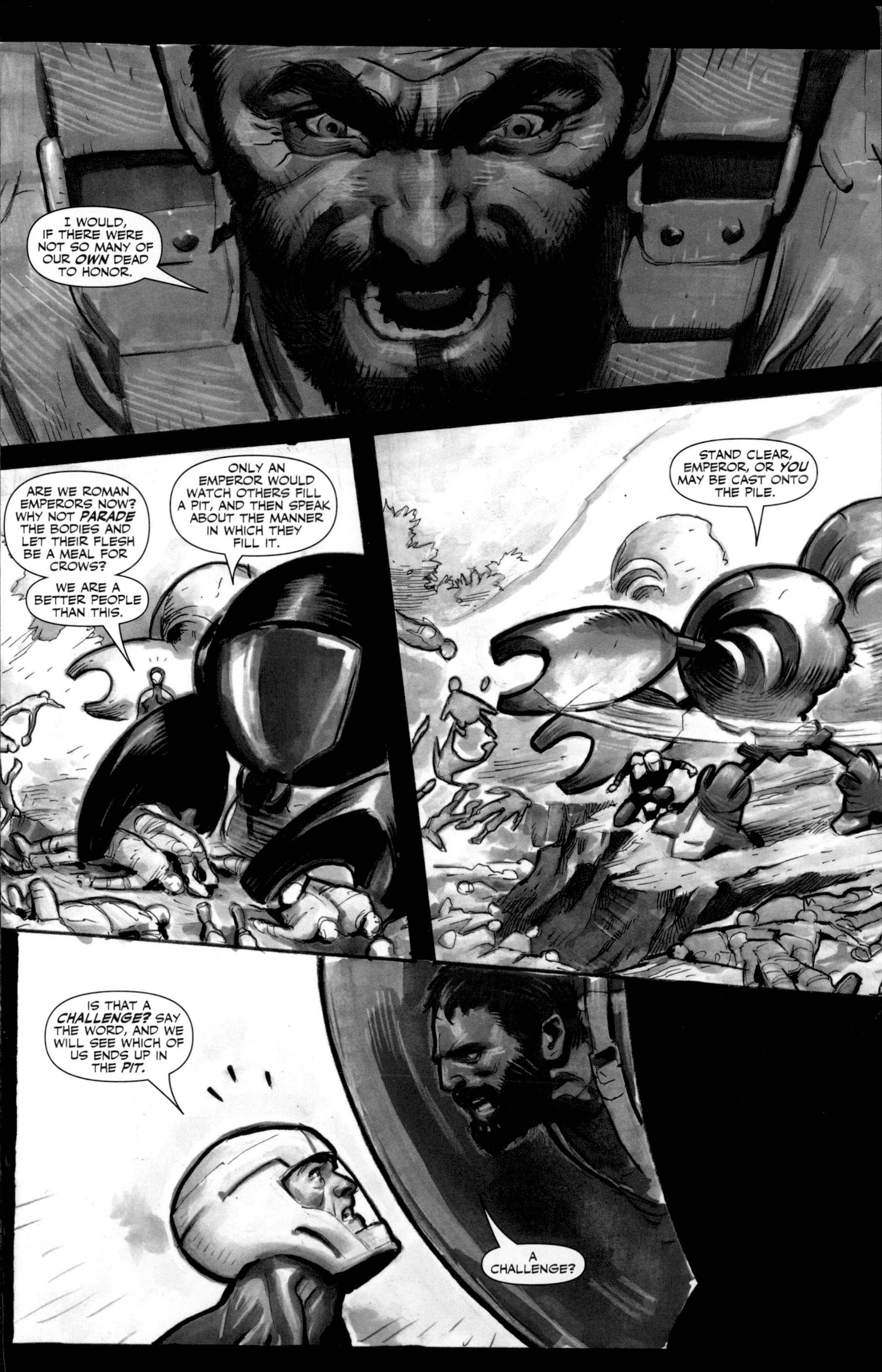
I WOULD, IF THERE WERE NOT SO MANY OF OUR OWN DEAD TO HONOR.
ARE WE ROMAN EMPERORS NOW? WHY NOT PARADE THE BODIES AND LET THEIR FLESH BE A MEAL FOR CROWS?
WE ARE A BETTER PEOPLE THAN THIS.
ONLY AN EMPEROR WOULD WATCH OTHERS FILL A PIT, AND THEN SPEAK ABOUT THE MANNER IN WHICH THEY FILL IT.
STAND CLEAR, EMPEROR, OR YOU MAY BE CAST ONTO THE PILE.
IS THAT A CHALLENGE? SAY THE WORD, AND WE WILL SEE WHICH OF US ENDS UP IN THE PIT.
A CHALLENGE?

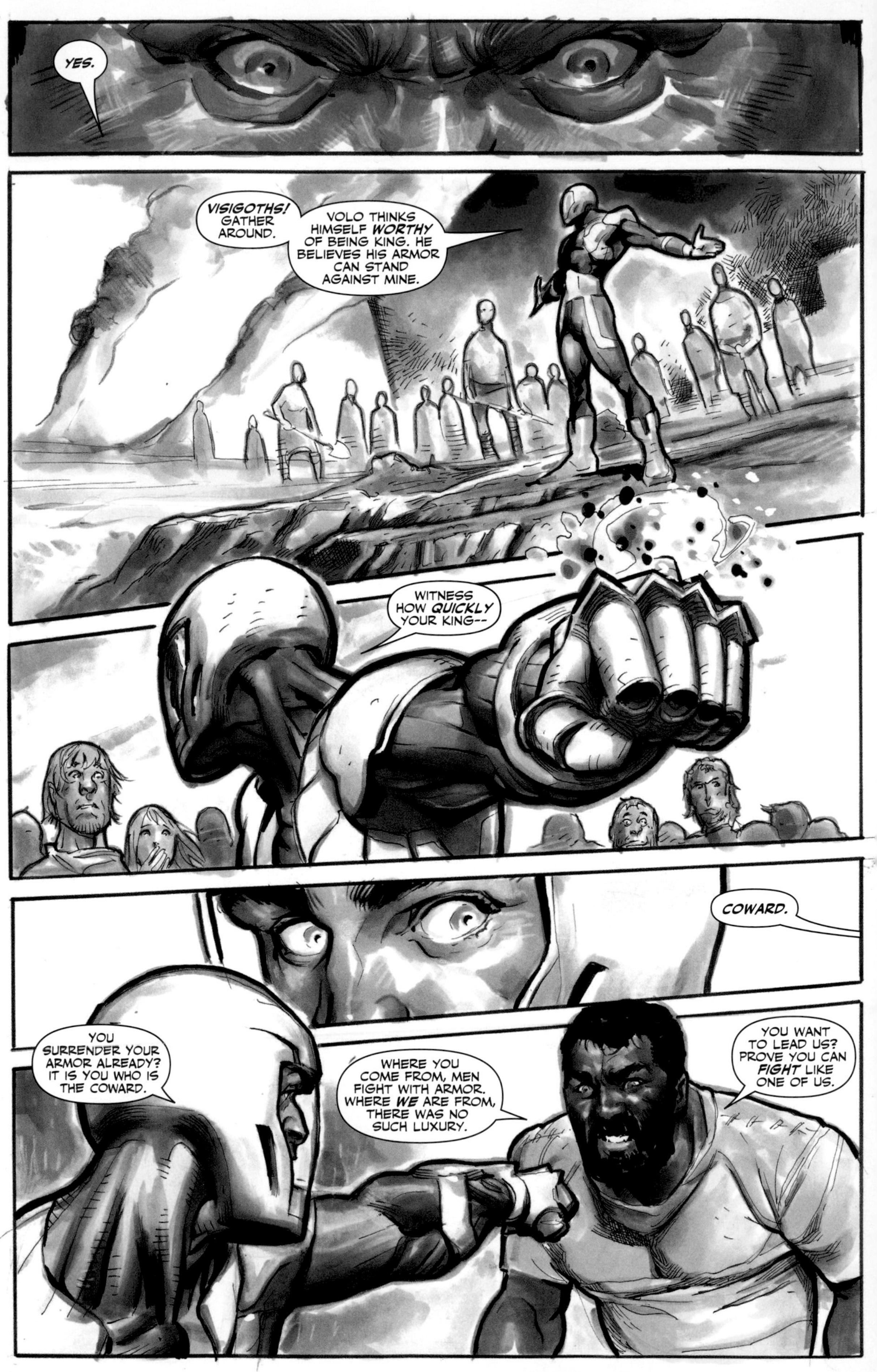
YES.
VISIGOTHS! GATHER AROUND.
VOLO THINKS HIMSELF WORTHY OF BEING KING. HE BELIEVES HIS ARMOR CAN STAND AGAINST MINE.
WITNESS HOW QUICKLY YOUR KING--
COWARD.
YOU SURRENDER YOUR ARMOR ALREADY? IT IS YOU WHO IS THE COWARD.
WHERE YOU COME FROM, MEN FIGHT WITH ARMOR. WHERE WE ARE FROM, THERE WAS NO SUCH LUXURY.
YOU WANT TO LEAD US? PROVE YOU CAN FIGHT LIKE ONE OF US.

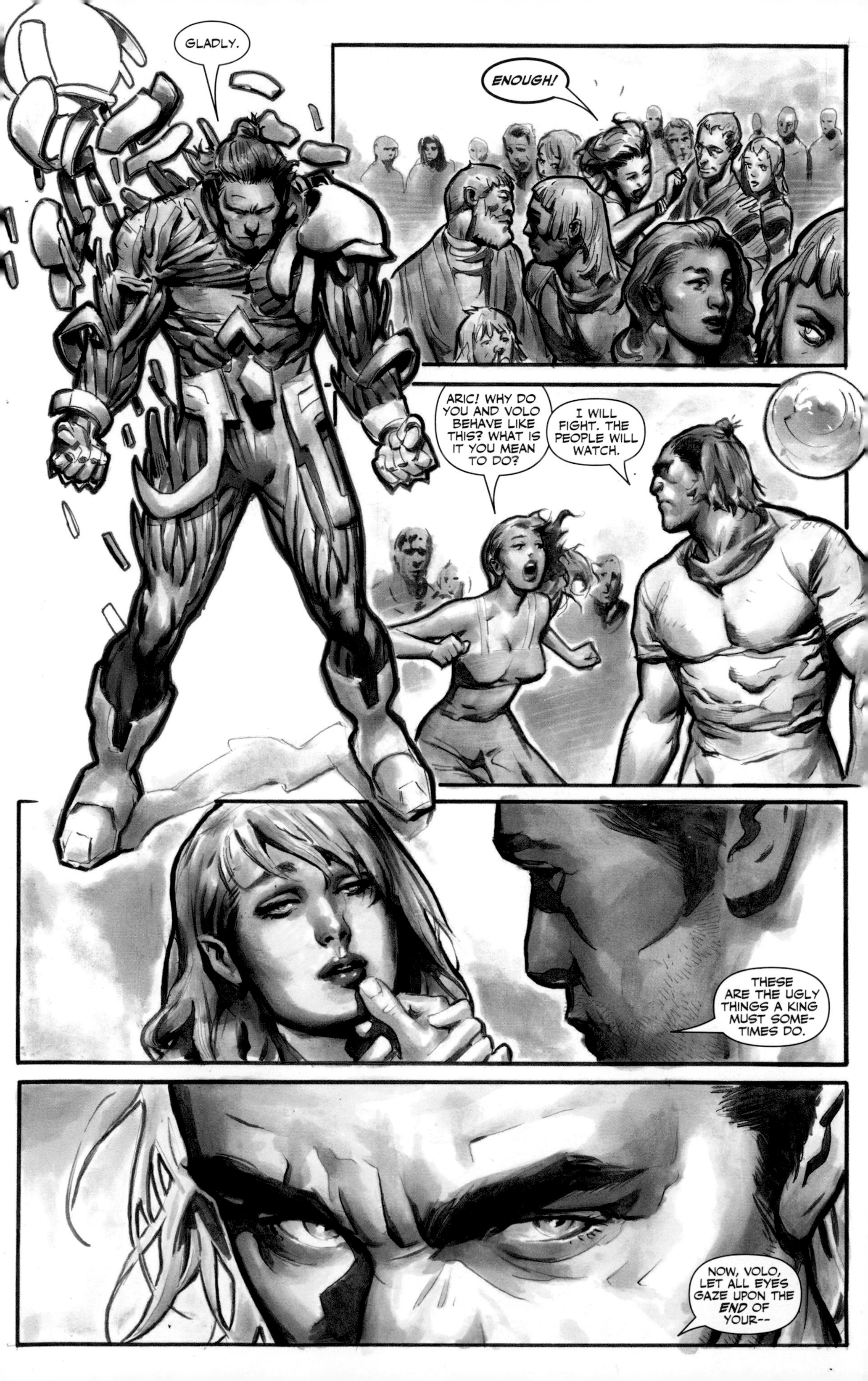
GLADLY.
ENOUGH!
ARIC! WHY DO YOU AND VOLO BEHAVE LIKE THIS? WHAT IS IT YOU MEAN TO DO?
I WILL FIGHT. THE PEOPLE WILL WATCH.
THESE ARE THE UGLY THINGS A KING MUST SOME-TIMES DO.
NOW, VOLO, LET ALL EYES GAZE UPON THE *END* OF YOUR--

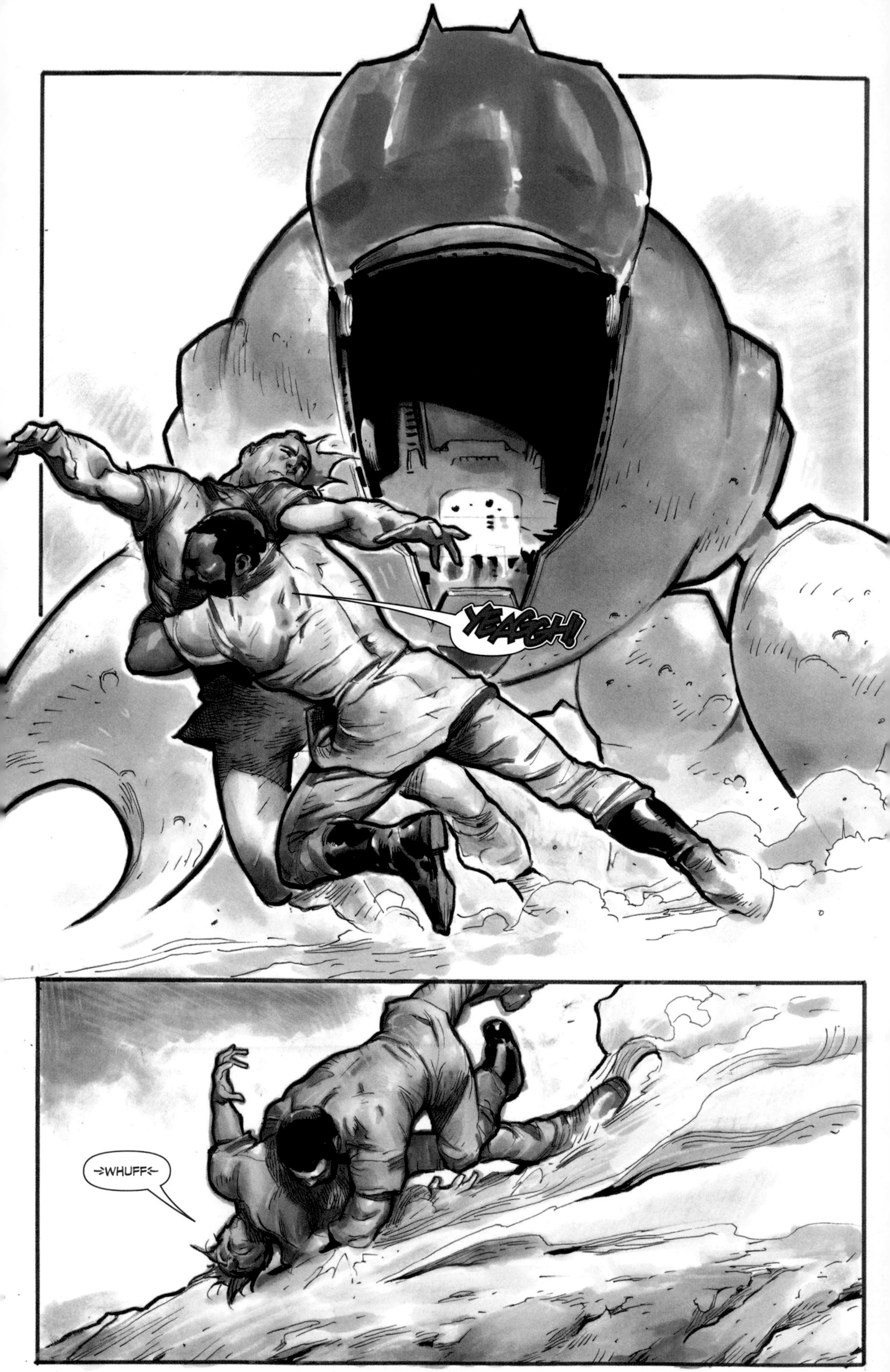
YEAGGH!
WHUFF

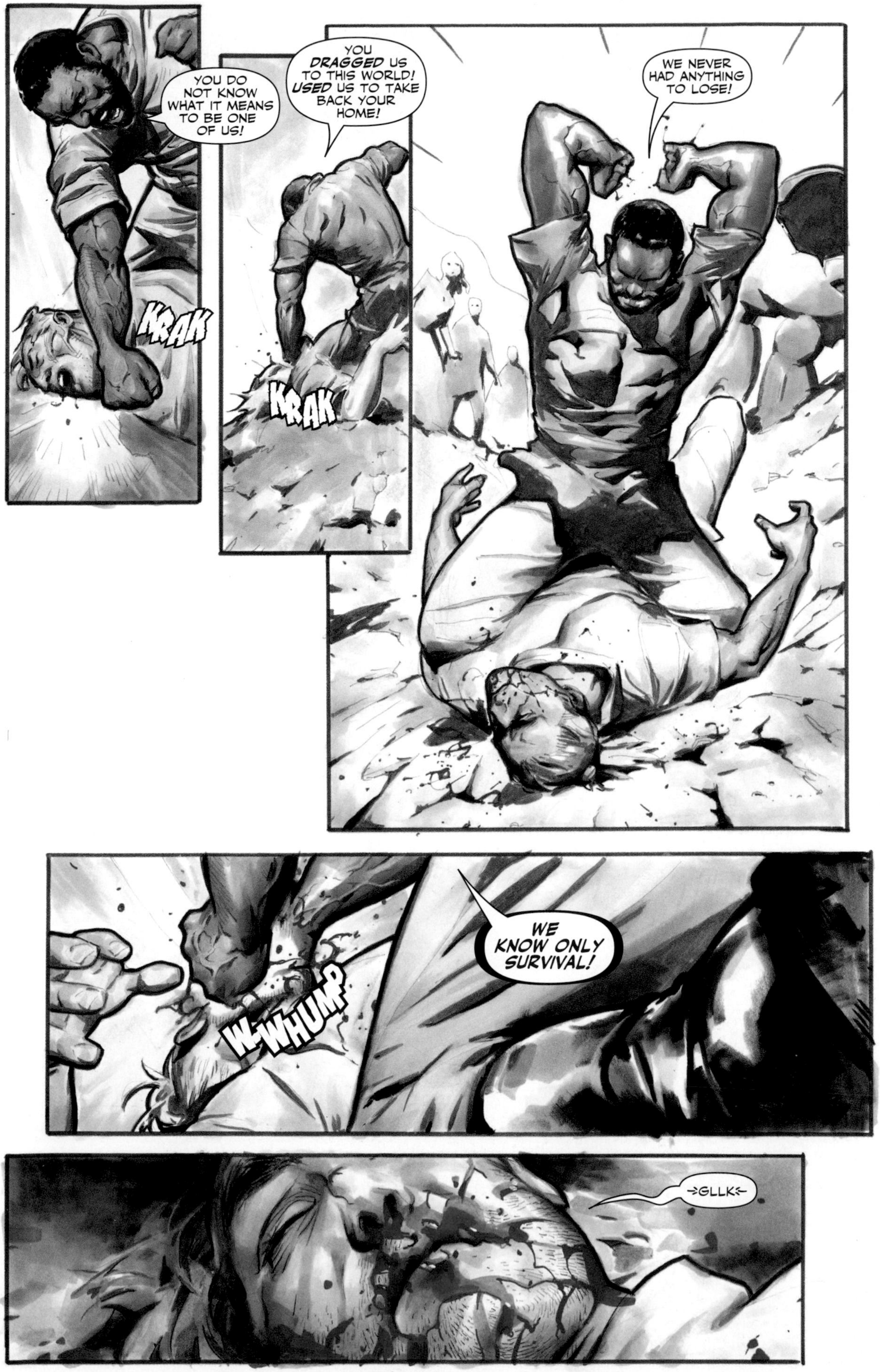
YOU DO NOT KNOW WHAT IT MEANS TO BE ONE OF US!
KRAK
YOU DRAGGED US TO THIS WORLD! USED US TO TAKE BACK YOUR HOME!
KRAK
WE NEVER HAD ANYTHING TO LOSE!
WE KNOW ONLY SURVIVAL!
W-WHUMP
GLLK

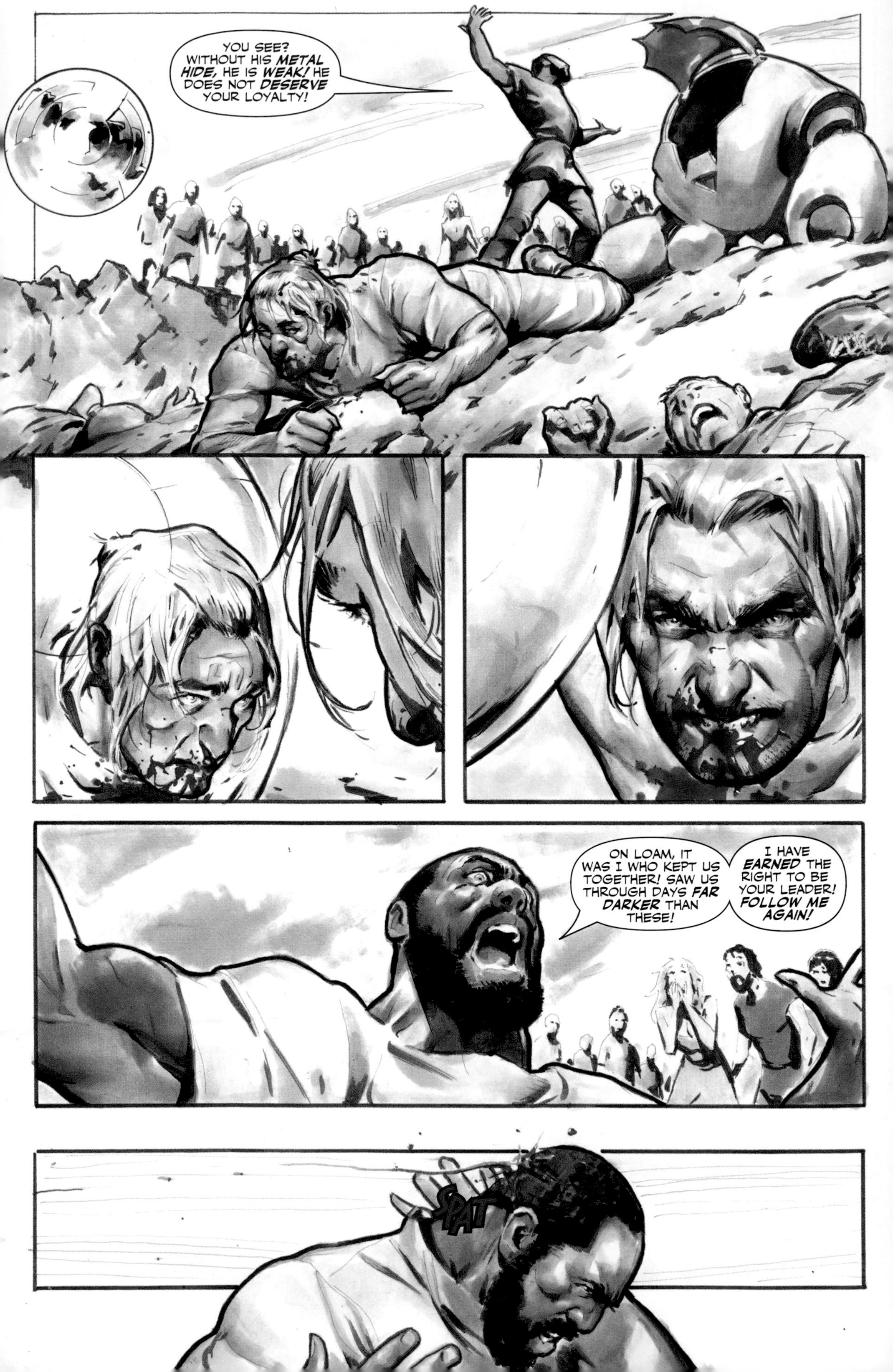
YOU SEE? WITHOUT HIS METAL HIDE, HE IS WEAK! HE DOES NOT DESERVE YOUR LOYALTY!
ON LOAM, IT WAS I WHO KEPT US TOGETHER! SAW US THROUGH DAYS FAR DARKER THAN THESE!
I HAVE EARNED THE RIGHT TO BE YOUR LEADER! FOLLOW ME AGAIN!
SPAT

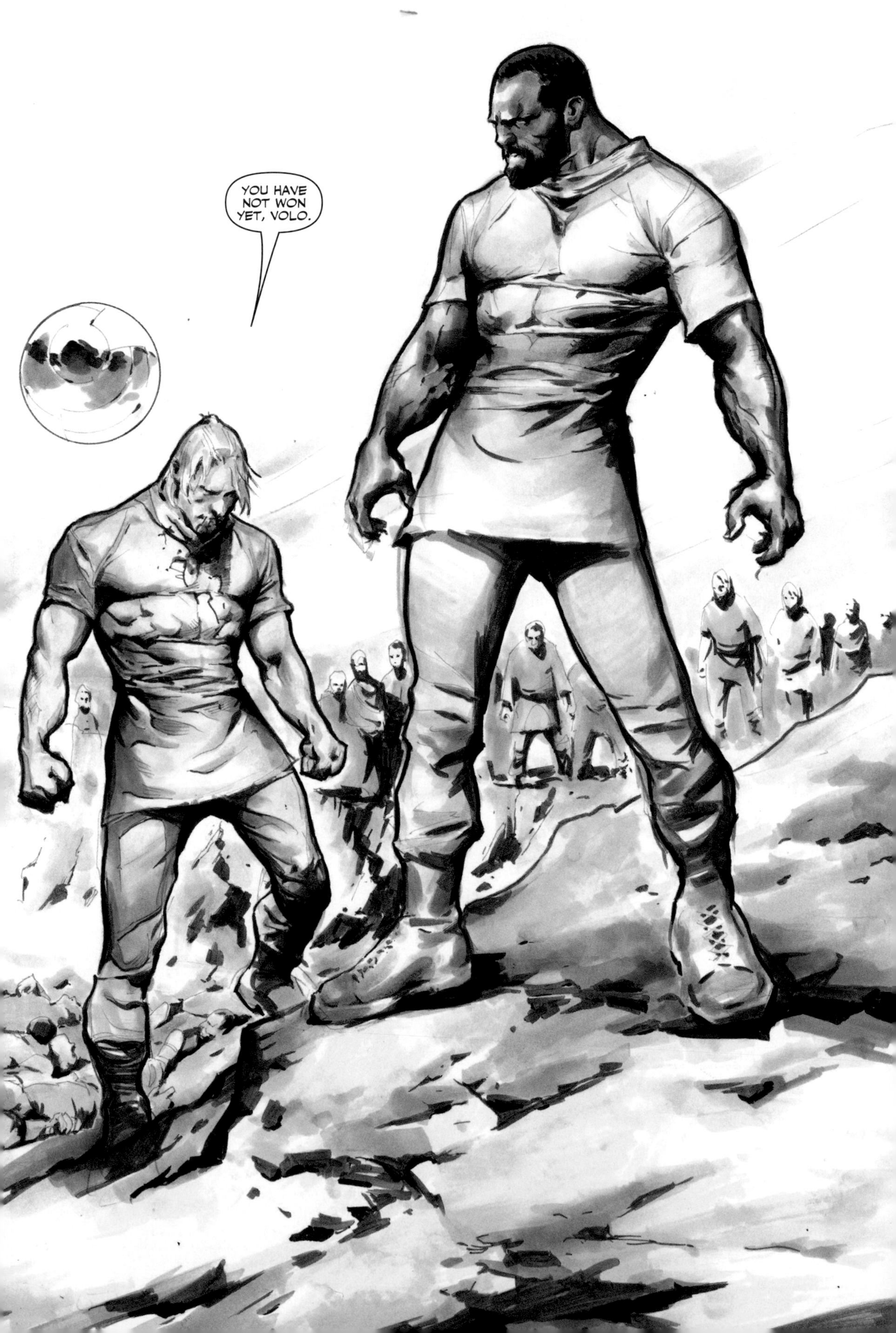
YOU HAVE NOT WON YET, VOLO.

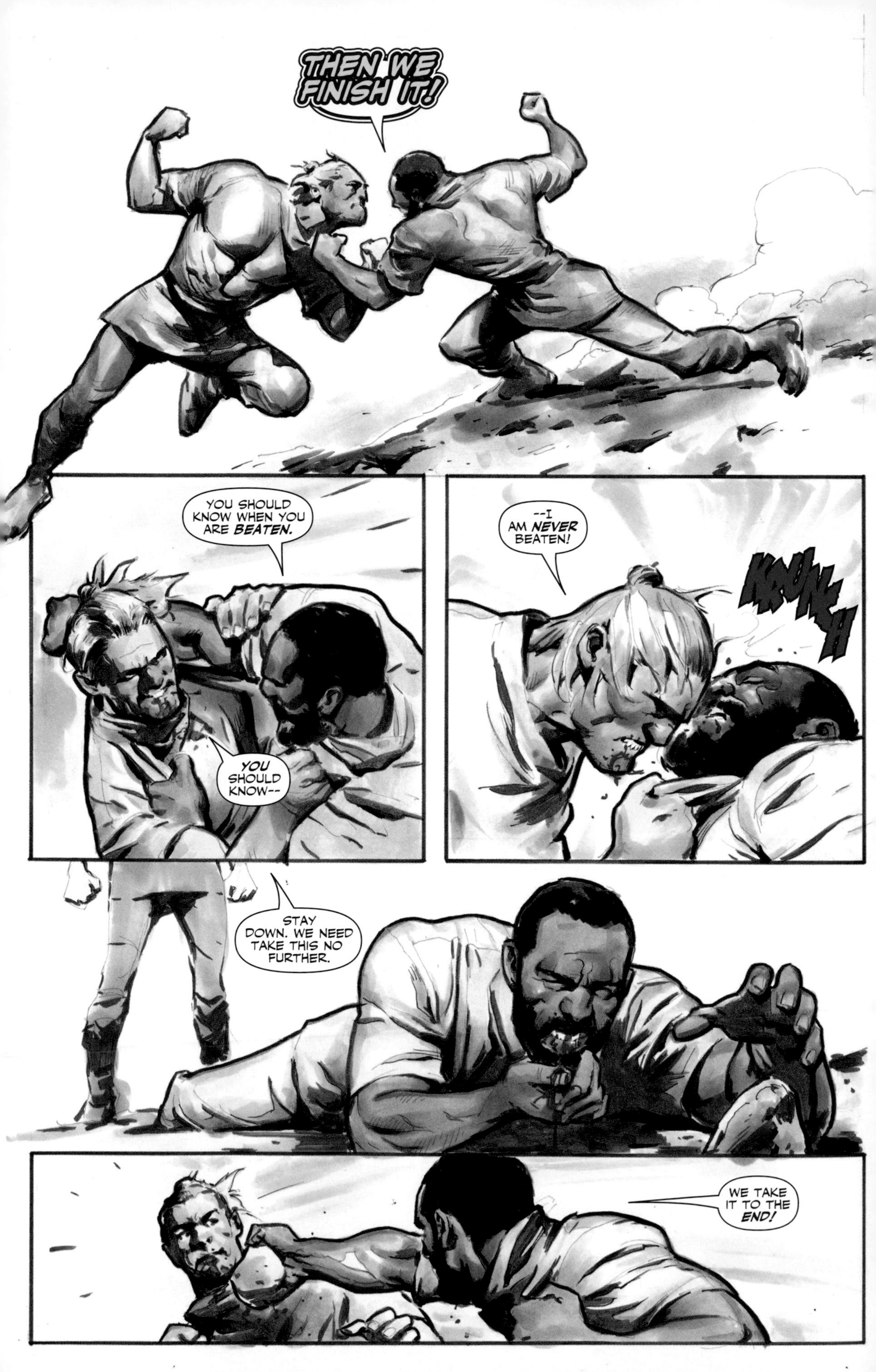
THEN WE FINISH IT!
YOU SHOULD KNOW WHEN YOU ARE BEATEN.
YOU SHOULD KNOW--
--I AM NEVER BEATEN!
KRUNCH
STAY DOWN. WE NEED TAKE THIS NO FURTHER.
WE TAKE IT TO THE END!

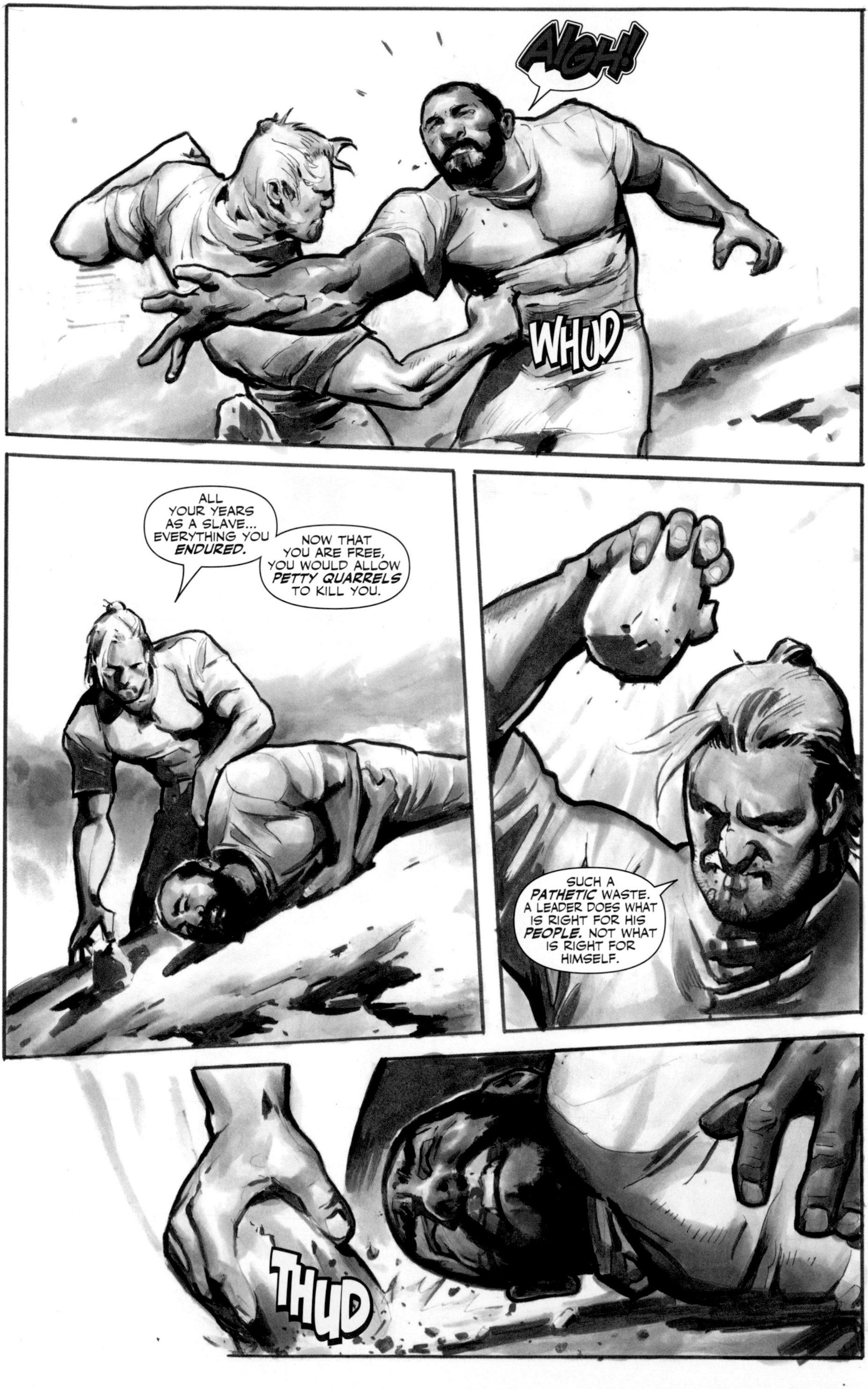
AIGH!
WHUD
ALL YOUR YEARS AS A SLAVE... EVERYTHING YOU ENDURED.
NOW THAT YOU ARE FREE, YOU WOULD ALLOW PETTY QUARRELS TO KILL YOU.
SUCH A PATHETIC WASTE. A LEADER DOES WHAT IS RIGHT FOR HIS PEOPLE. NOT WHAT IS RIGHT FOR HIMSELF.
THUD

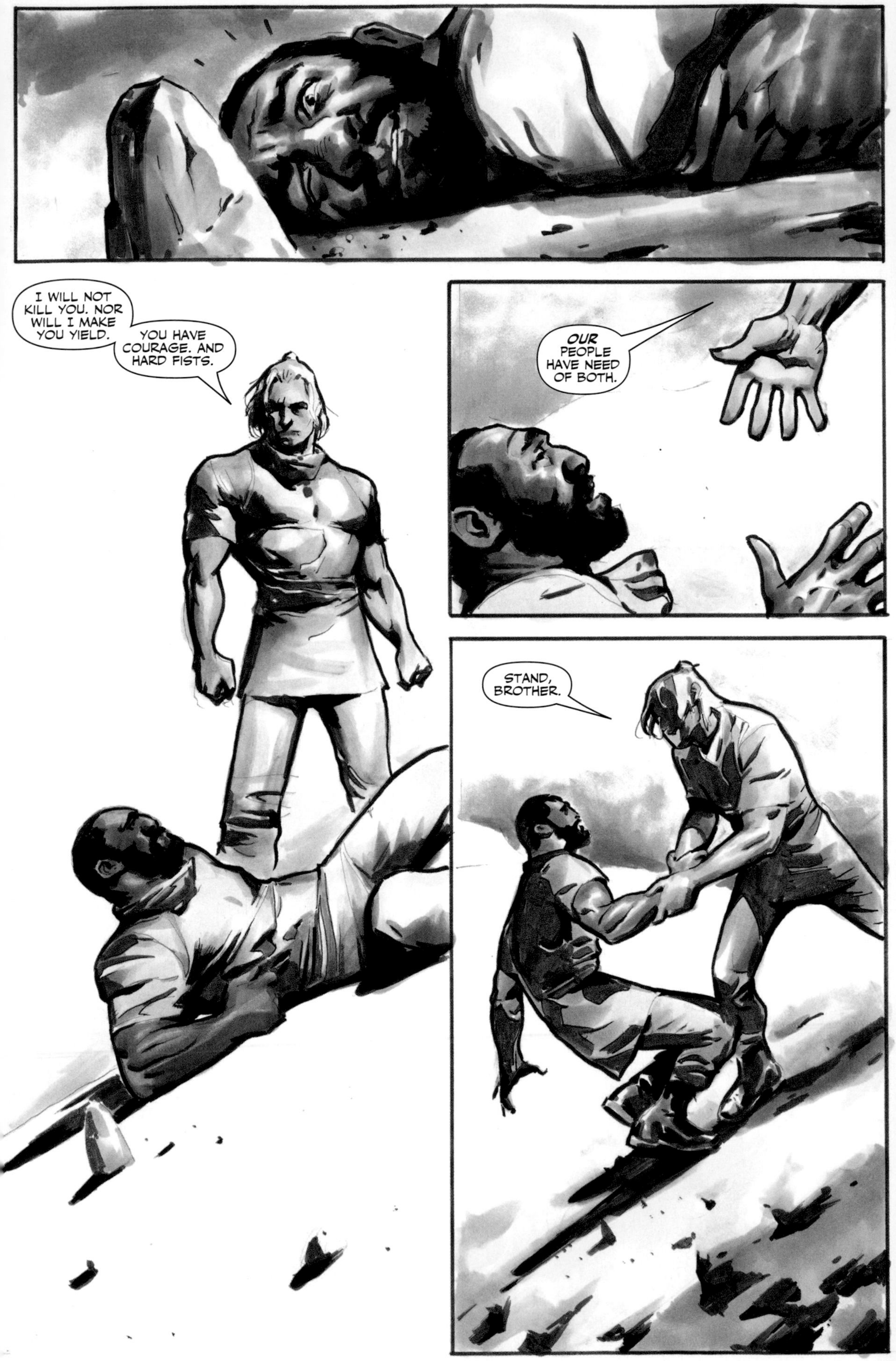
I WILL NOT KILL YOU. NOR WILL I MAKE YOU YIELD.
YOU HAVE COURAGE. AND HARD FISTS.
OUR PEOPLE HAVE NEED OF BOTH.
STAND, BROTHER.

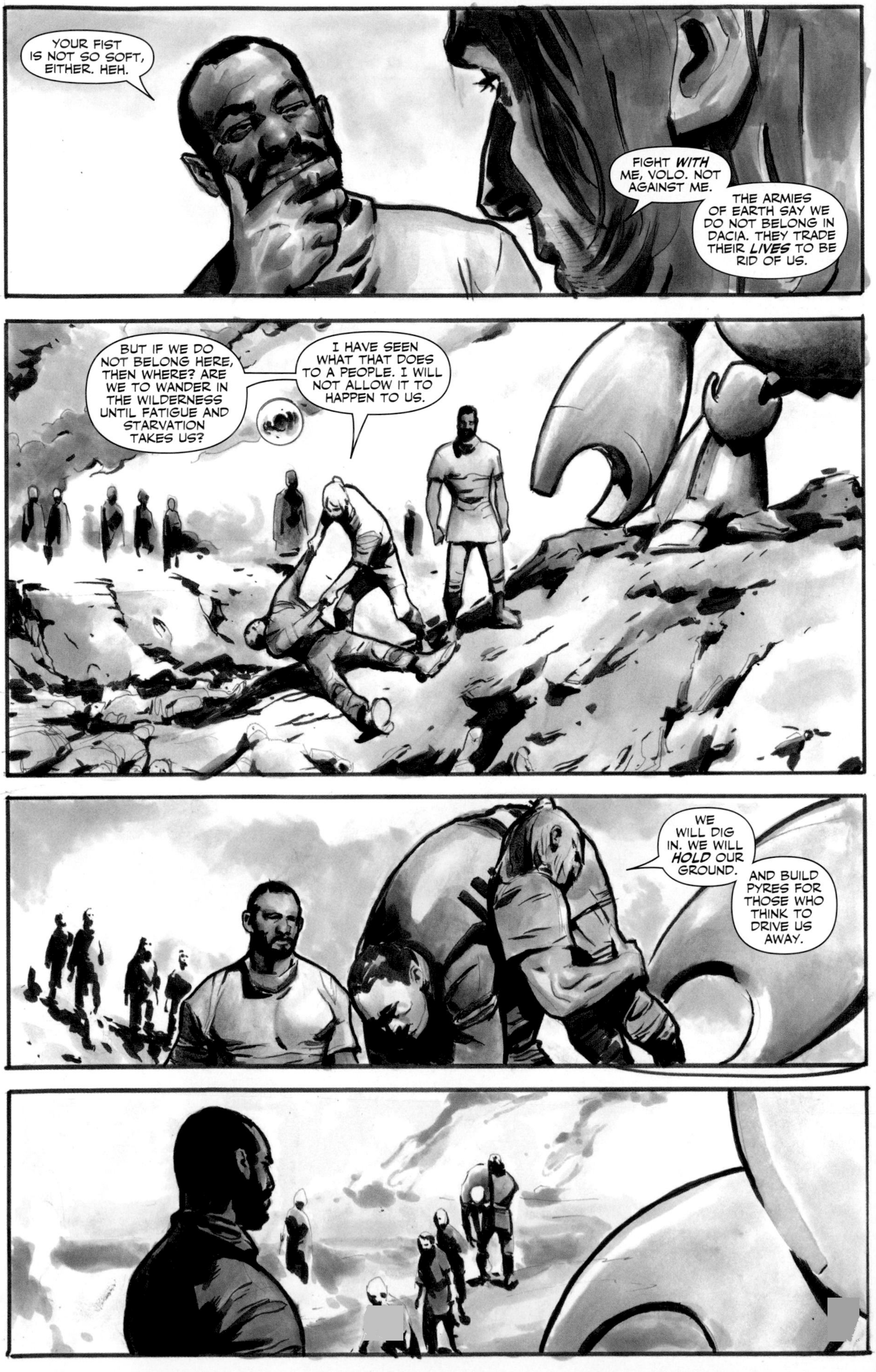
YOUR FIST IS NOT SO SOFT, EITHER. HEH.
FIGHT *WITH* ME, VOLO. NOT AGAINST ME.
THE ARMIES OF EARTH SAY WE DO NOT BELONG IN DACIA. THEY TRADE THEIR *LIVES* TO BE RID OF US.
BUT IF WE DO NOT BELONG HERE, THEN WHERE? ARE WE TO WANDER IN THE WILDERNESS UNTIL FATIGUE AND STARVATION TAKES US?
I HAVE SEEN WHAT THAT DOES TO A PEOPLE. I WILL NOT ALLOW IT TO HAPPEN TO US.
WE WILL DIG IN. WE WILL *HOLD* OUR GROUND.
AND BUILD PYRES FOR THOSE WHO THINK TO DRIVE US AWAY.

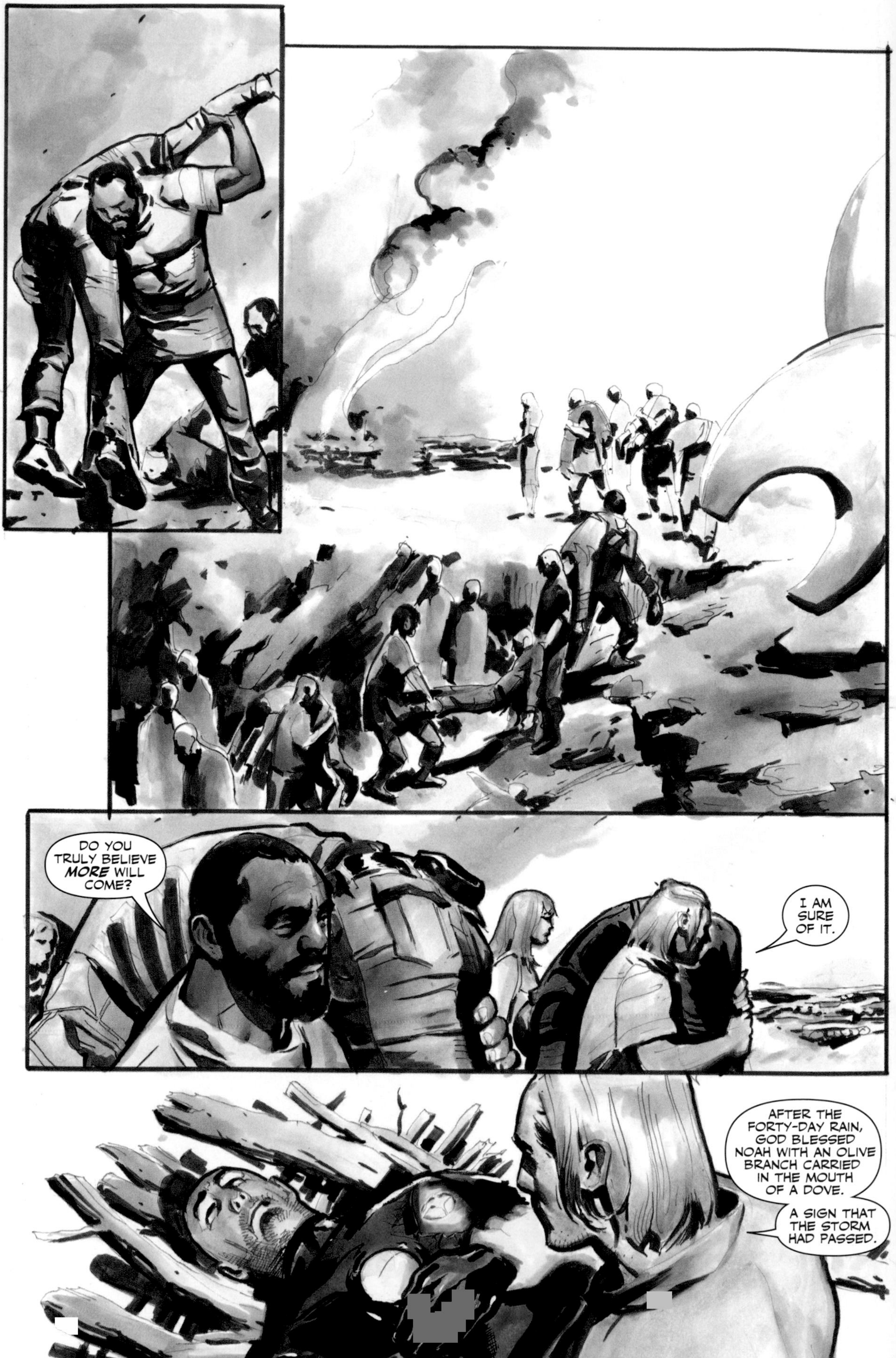
DO YOU TRULY BELIEVE MORE WILL COME?
I AM SURE OF IT.
AFTER THE FORTY-DAY RAIN, GOD BLESSED NOAH WITH AN OLIVE BRANCH CARRIED IN THE MOUTH OF A DOVE.
A SIGN THAT THE STORM HAD PASSED.

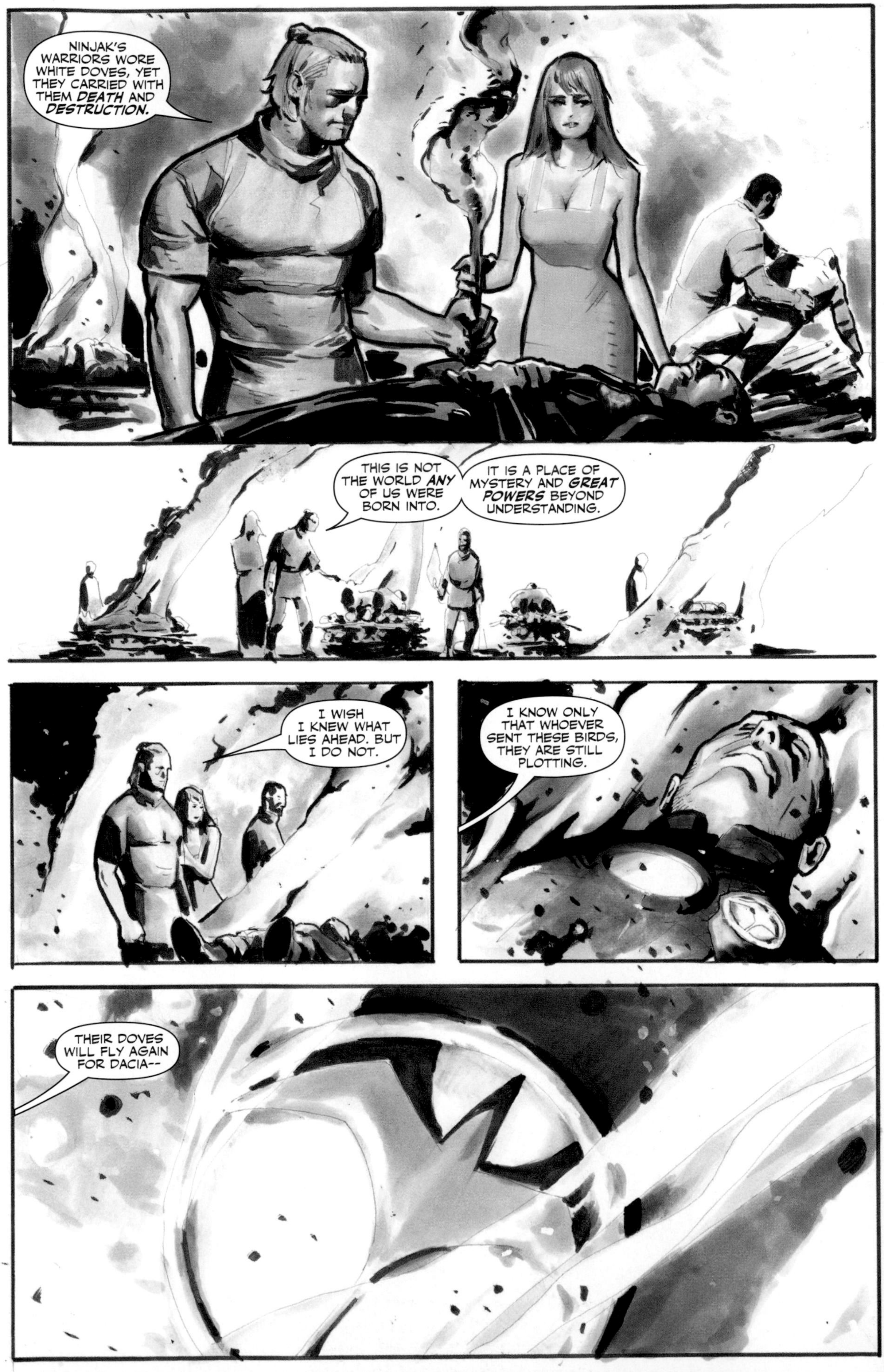
NINJAK'S WARRIORS WORE WHITE DOVES, YET THEY CARRIED WITH THEM DEATH AND DESTRUCTION.
THIS IS NOT THE WORLD ANY OF US WERE BORN INTO.
IT IS A PLACE OF MYSTERY AND GREAT POWERS BEYOND UNDERSTANDING.
I WISH I KNEW WHAT LIES AHEAD. BUT I DO NOT.
I KNOW ONLY THAT WHOEVER SENT THESE BIRDS, THEY ARE STILL PLOTTING.
THEIR DOVES WILL FLY AGAIN FOR DACIA--

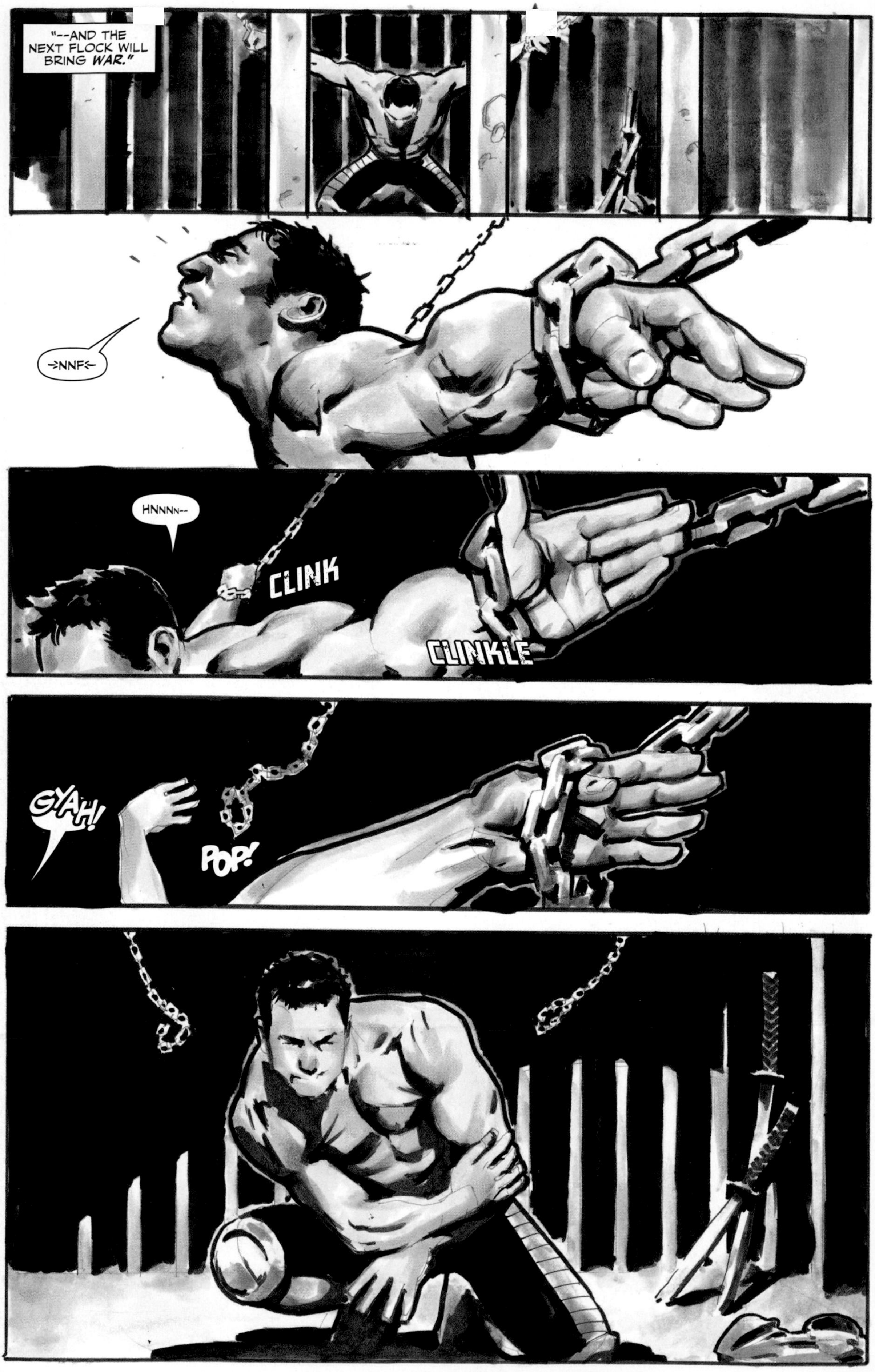
"--AND THE NEXT FLOCK WILL BRING WAR."
NNF
HNNNN--
CLINK
CLINKLE
GYAH!
POP!

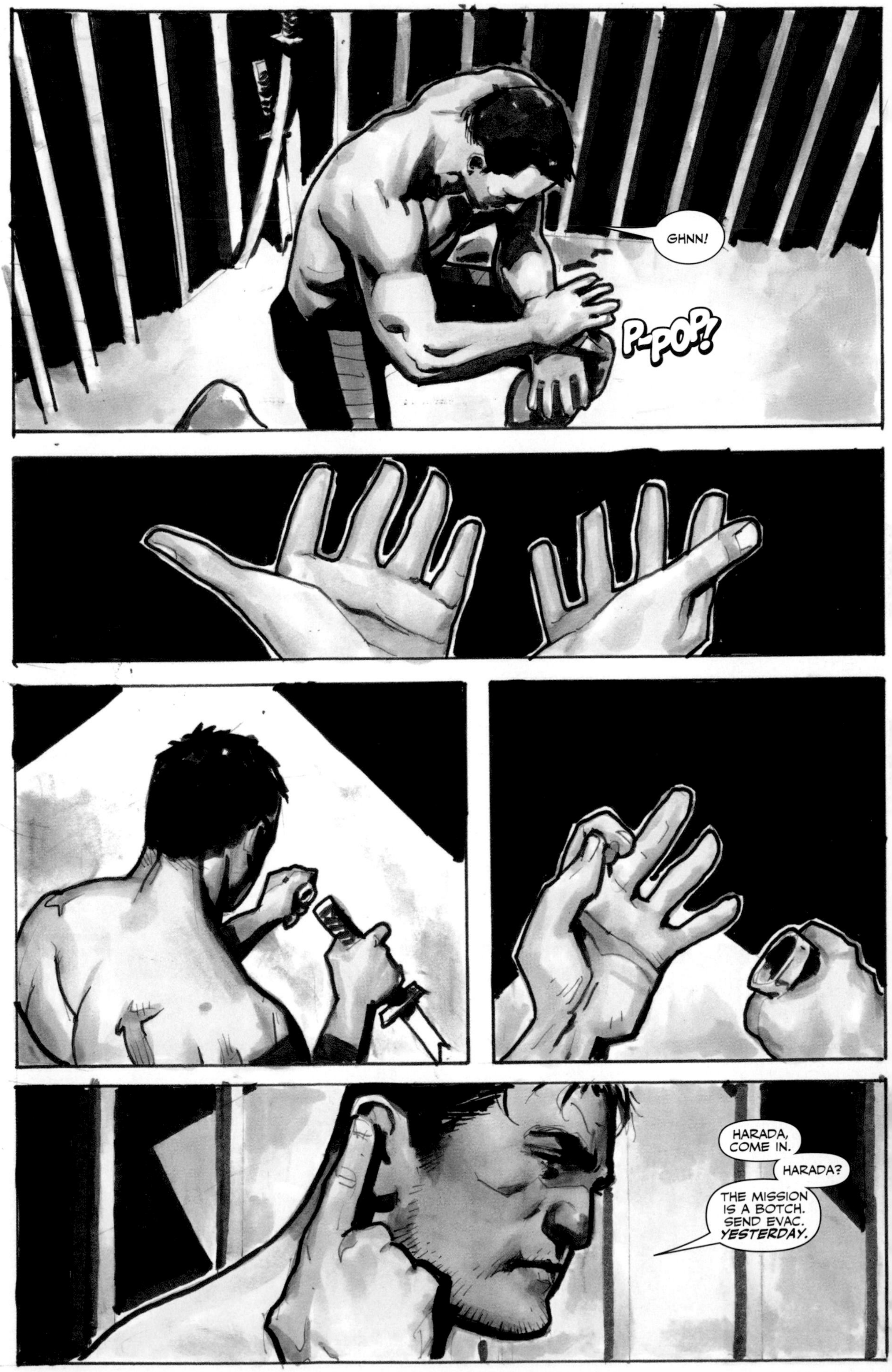
GHNN!
P-POP!
HARADA, COME IN.
HARADA?
THE MISSION IS A BOTCH. SEND EVAC. *YESTERDAY.*

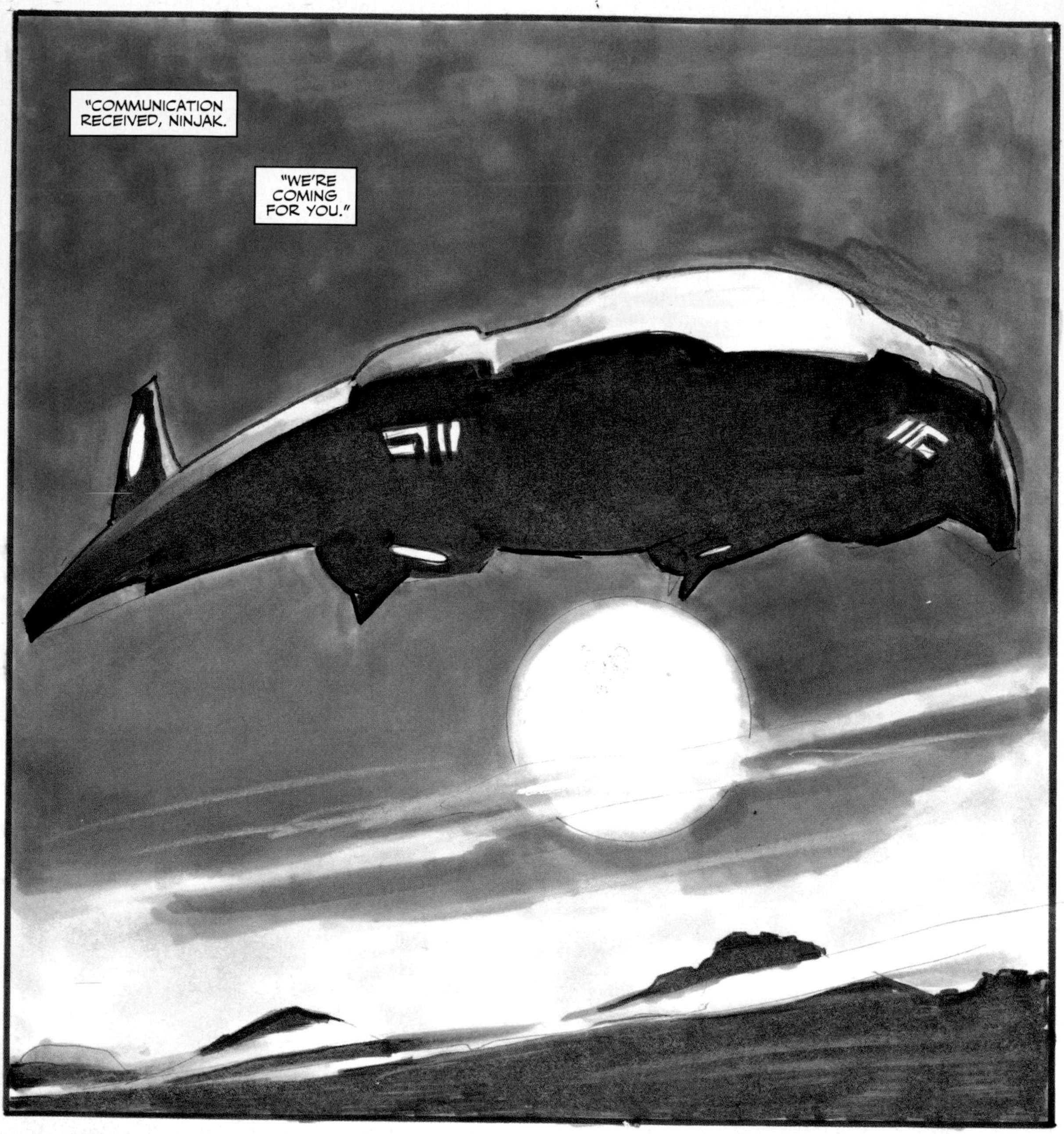
"COMMUNICATION RECEIVED, NINJAK.
"WE'RE COMING FOR YOU."

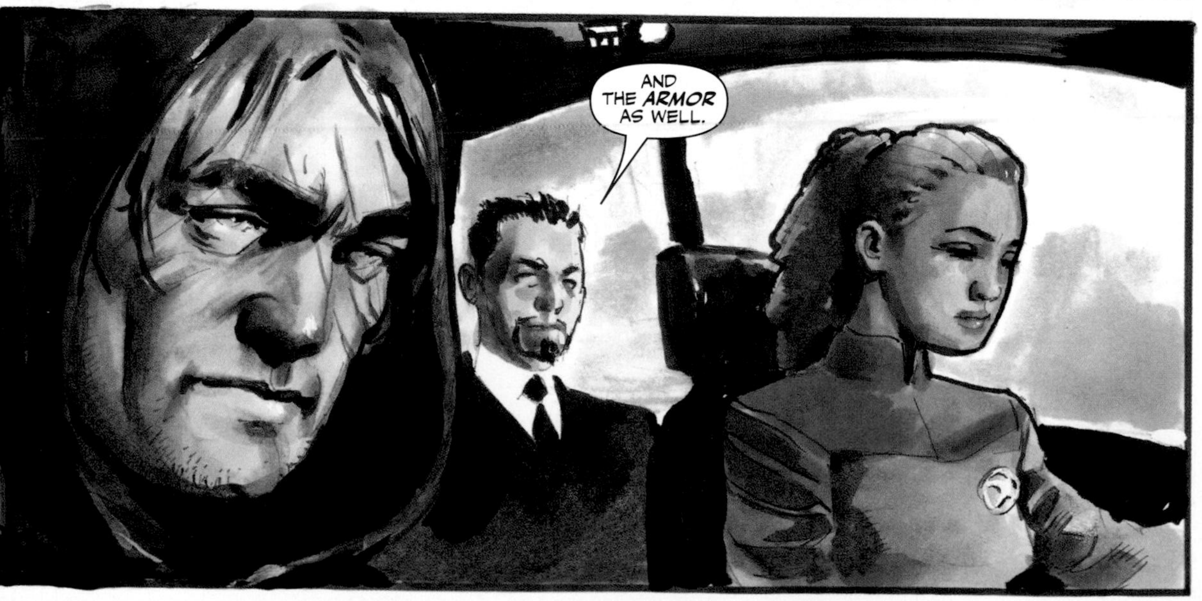
AND THE ARMOR AS WELL.

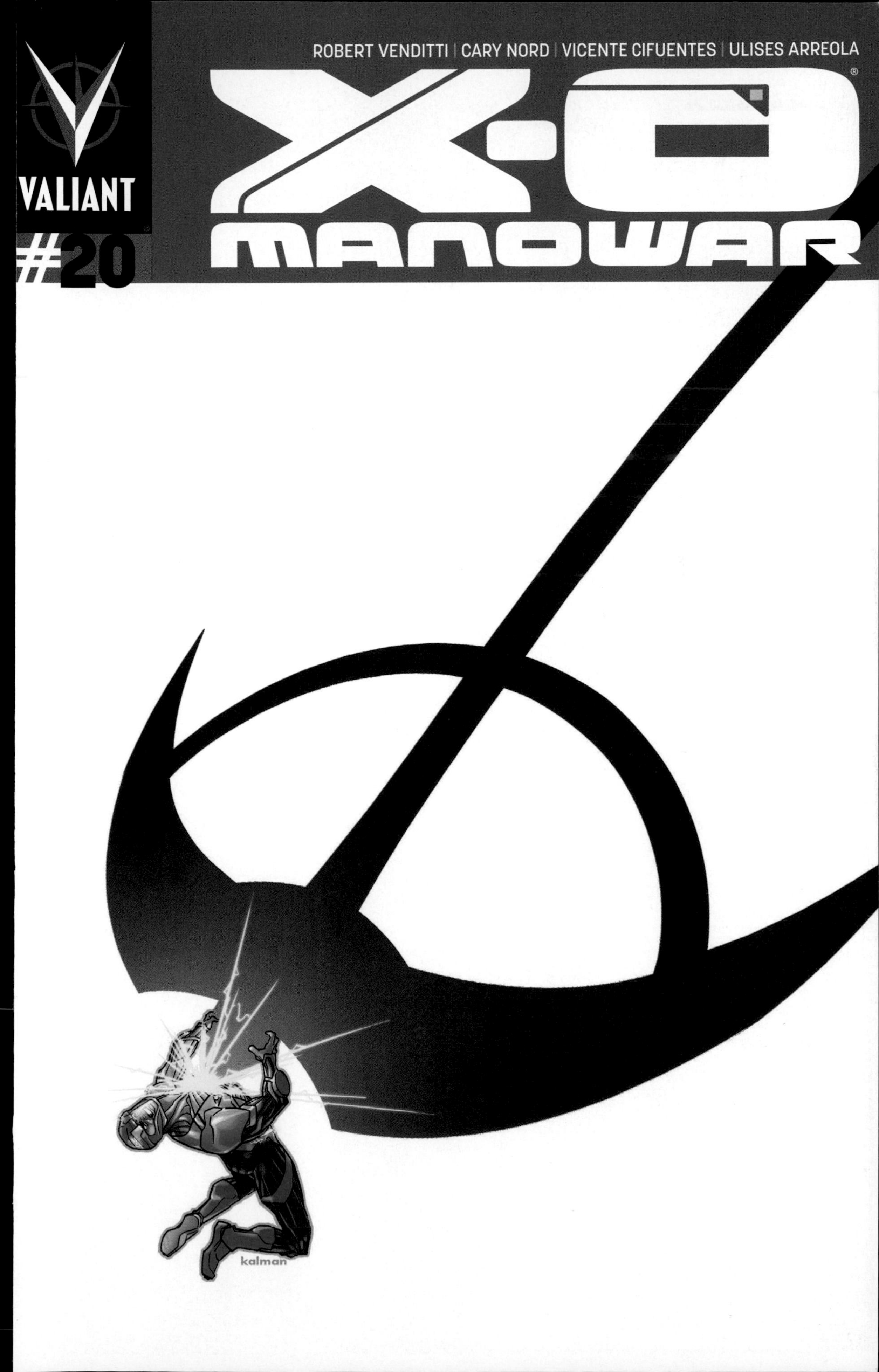
VALIANT
#20
ROBERT VENDITTI | CARY NORD | VICENTE CIFUENTES | ULISES ARREOLA
X-O MANOWAR
kalman

PREVIOUSLY IN...

UNITY

Ninjak, the world's deadliest secret agent; Livewire, the Harbinger Foundation's most formidable teletechnopath; and the 10,000-year-old champion, the Eternal Warrior; brought together by billionaire philanthropist and omega-level psionic Toyo Harada, together they are UNITY!

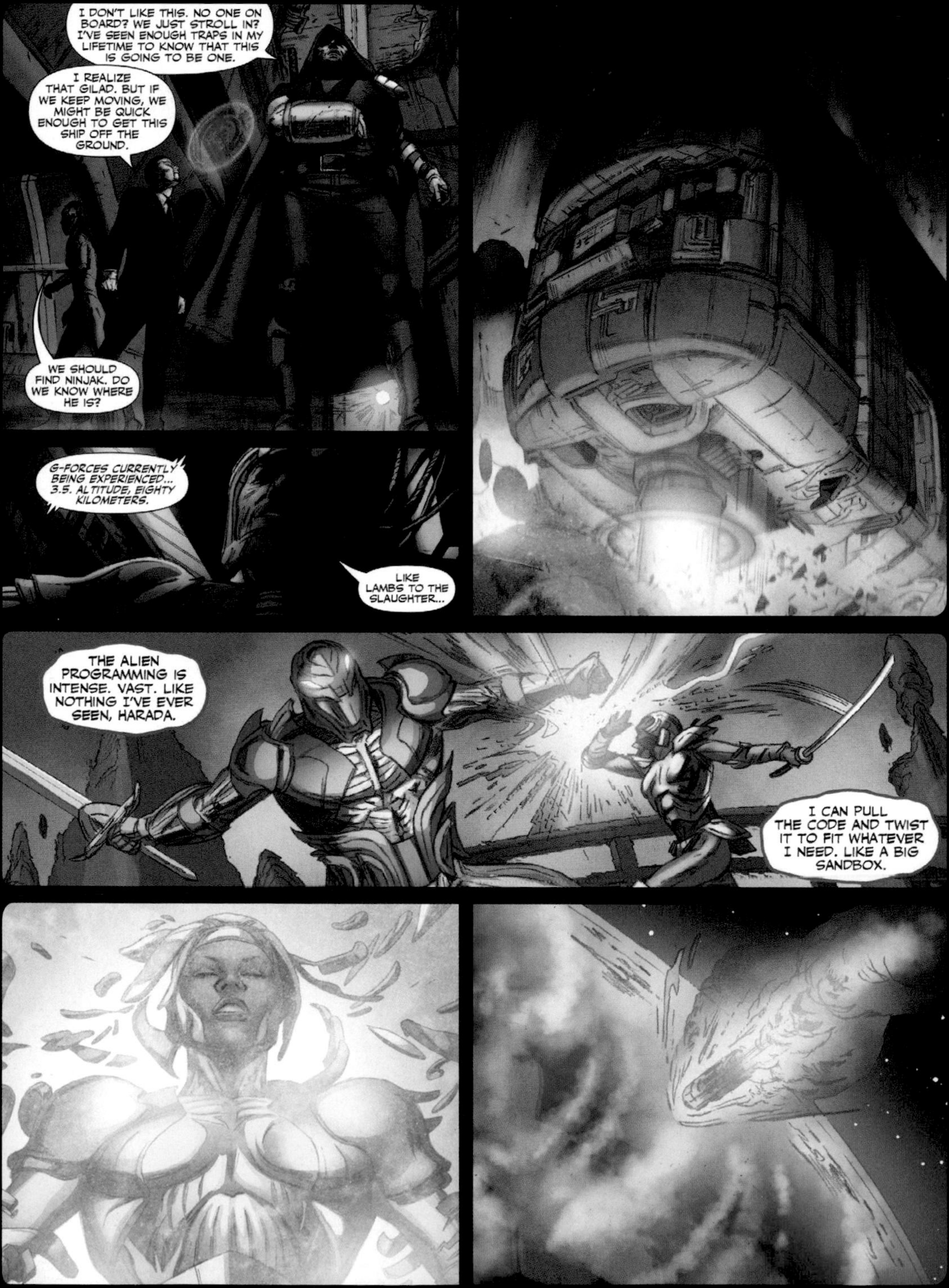
I DON'T LIKE THIS. NO ONE ON BOARD? WE JUST STROLL IN? I'VE SEEN ENOUGH TRAPS IN MY LIFETIME TO KNOW THAT THIS IS GOING TO BE ONE.
I REALIZE THAT GILAD. BUT IF WE KEEP MOVING, WE MIGHT BE QUICK ENOUGH TO GET THIS SHIP OFF THE GROUND.
WE SHOULD FIND NINJAK. DO WE KNOW WHERE HE IS?
G-FORCES CURRENTLY BEING EXPERIENCED... 3.5. ALTITUDE, EIGHTY KILOMETERS.
LIKE LAMBS TO THE SLAUGHTER...
THE ALIEN PROGRAMMING IS INTENSE. VAST. LIKE NOTHING I'VE EVER SEEN, HARADA.
I CAN PULL THE CODE AND TWIST IT TO FIT WHATEVER I NEED. LIKE A BIG SANDBOX.

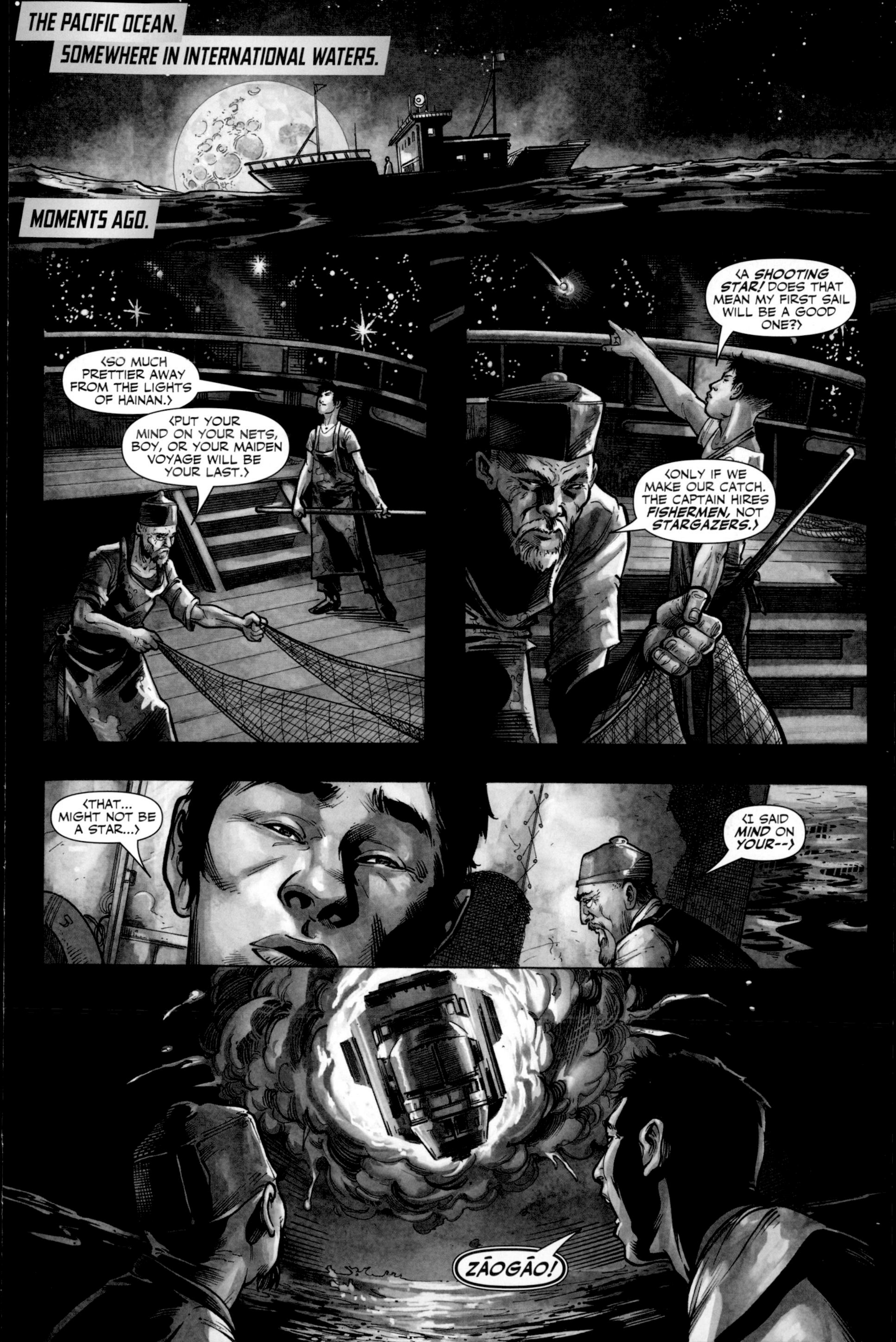
THE PACIFIC OCEAN.
SOMEWHERE IN INTERNATIONAL WATERS.
MOMENTS AGO.
‹SO MUCH PRETTIER AWAY FROM THE LIGHTS OF HAINAN.›
‹PUT YOUR MIND ON YOUR NETS, BOY, OR YOUR MAIDEN VOYAGE WILL BE YOUR LAST.›
‹A SHOOTING STAR! DOES THAT MEAN MY FIRST SAIL WILL BE A GOOD ONE?›
‹ONLY IF WE MAKE OUR CATCH. THE CAPTAIN HIRES FISHERMEN, NOT STARGAZERS.›
‹THAT... MIGHT NOT BE A STAR...›
‹I SAID MIND ON YOUR--›
ZĀOGĀO!

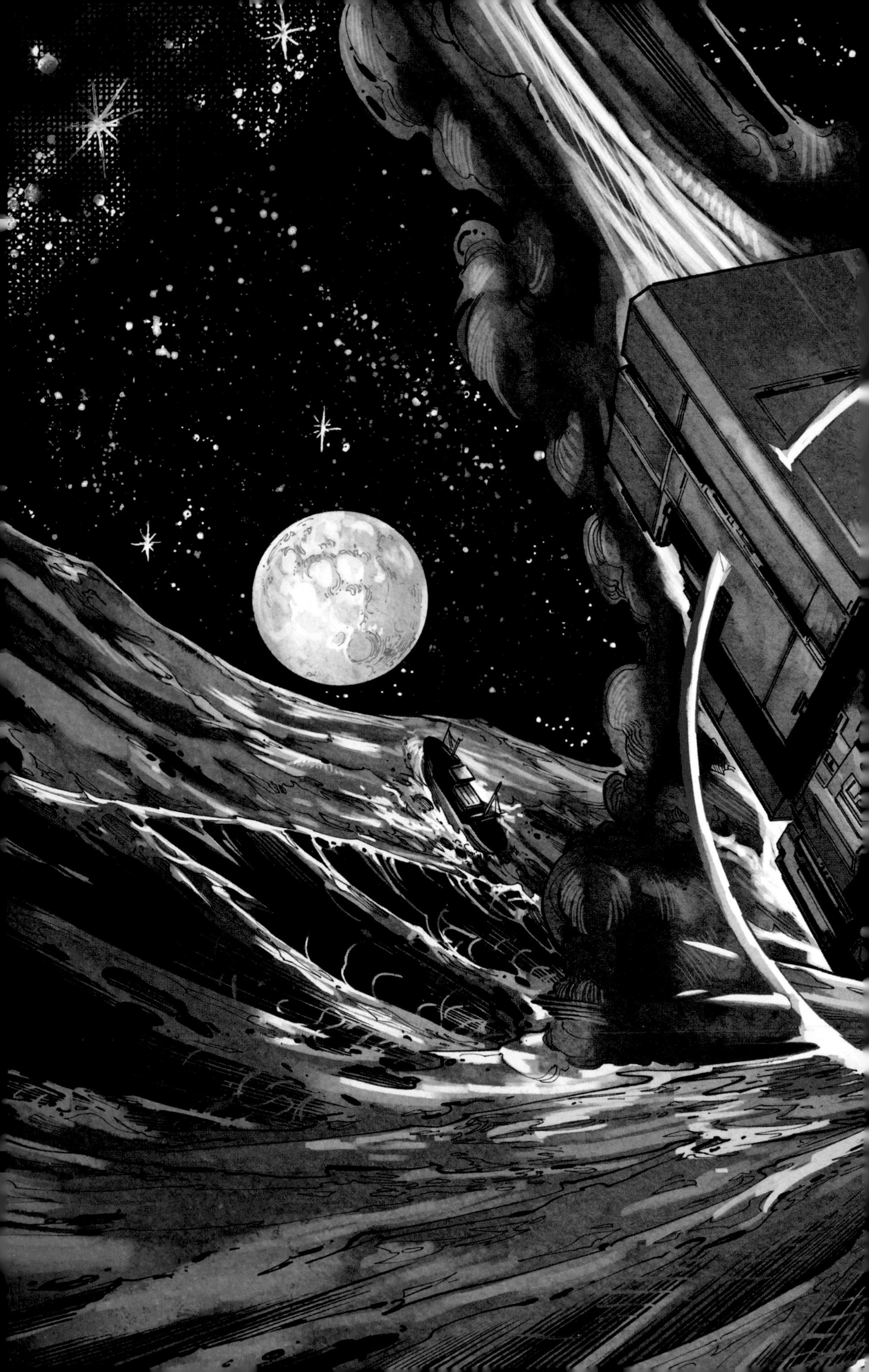

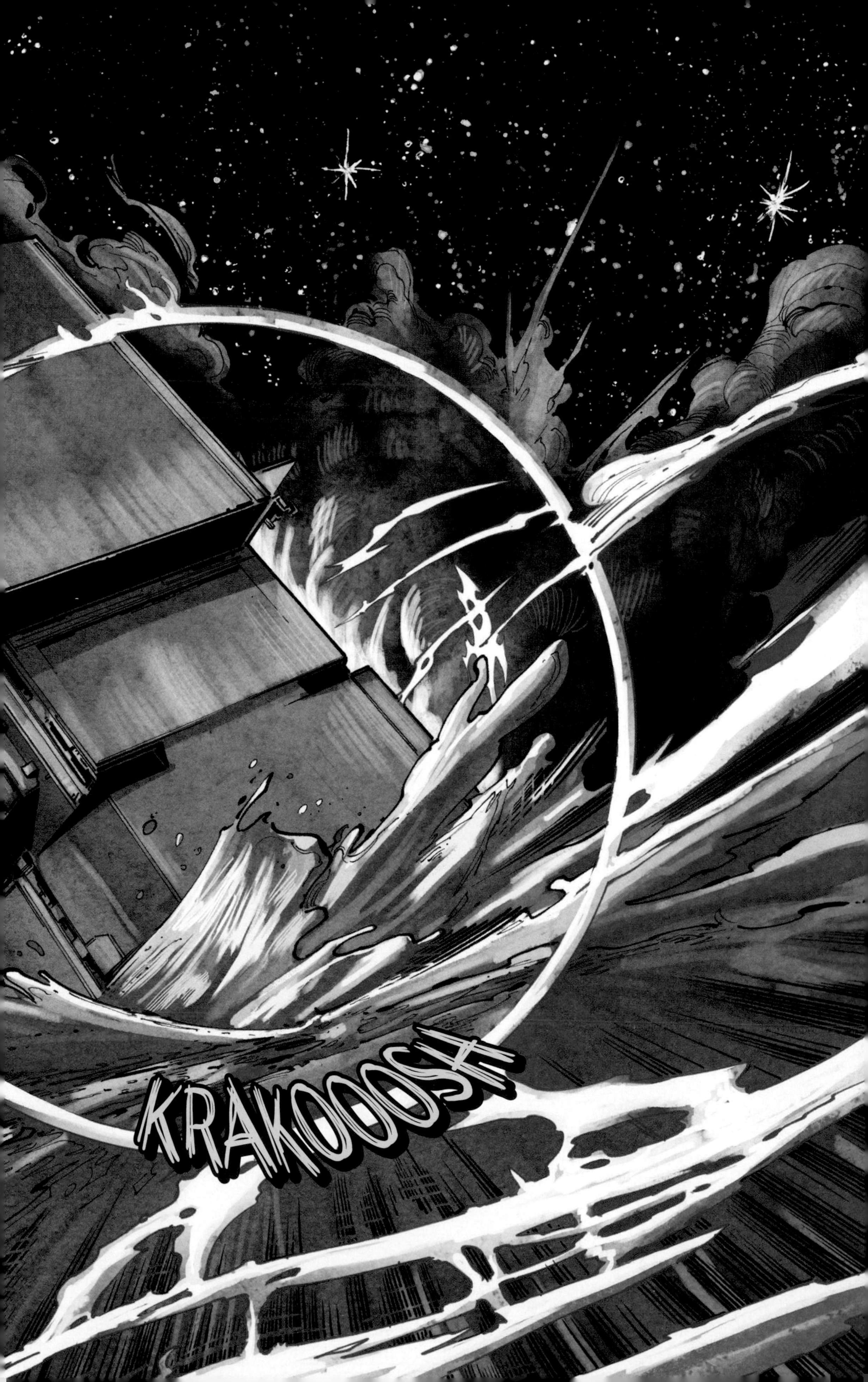
KRAKOOOSH

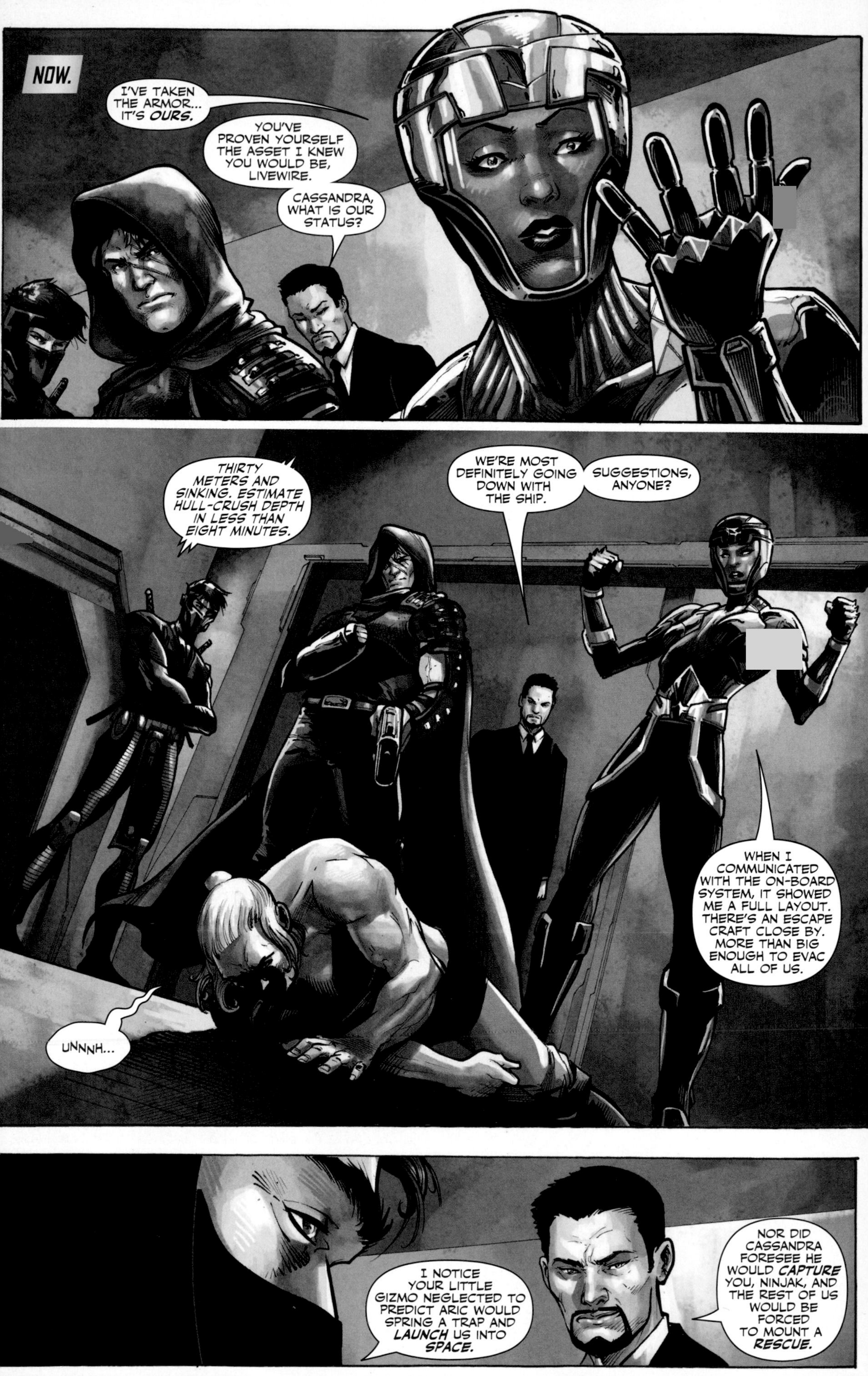
NOW.
I'VE TAKEN THE ARMOR... IT'S OURS.
YOU'VE PROVEN YOURSELF THE ASSET I KNEW YOU WOULD BE, LIVEWIRE.
CASSANDRA, WHAT IS OUR STATUS?
THIRTY METERS AND SINKING. ESTIMATE HULL-CRUSH DEPTH IN LESS THAN EIGHT MINUTES.
WE'RE MOST DEFINITELY GOING DOWN WITH THE SHIP.
SUGGESTIONS, ANYONE?
WHEN I COMMUNICATED WITH THE ON-BOARD SYSTEM, IT SHOWED ME A FULL LAYOUT. THERE'S AN ESCAPE CRAFT CLOSE BY. MORE THAN BIG ENOUGH TO EVAC ALL OF US.
UNNNH...
I NOTICE YOUR LITTLE GIZMO NEGLECTED TO PREDICT ARIC WOULD SPRING A TRAP AND LAUNCH US INTO SPACE.
NOR DID CASSANDRA FORESEE HE WOULD CAPTURE YOU, NINJAK, AND THE REST OF US WOULD BE FORCED TO MOUNT A RESCUE.

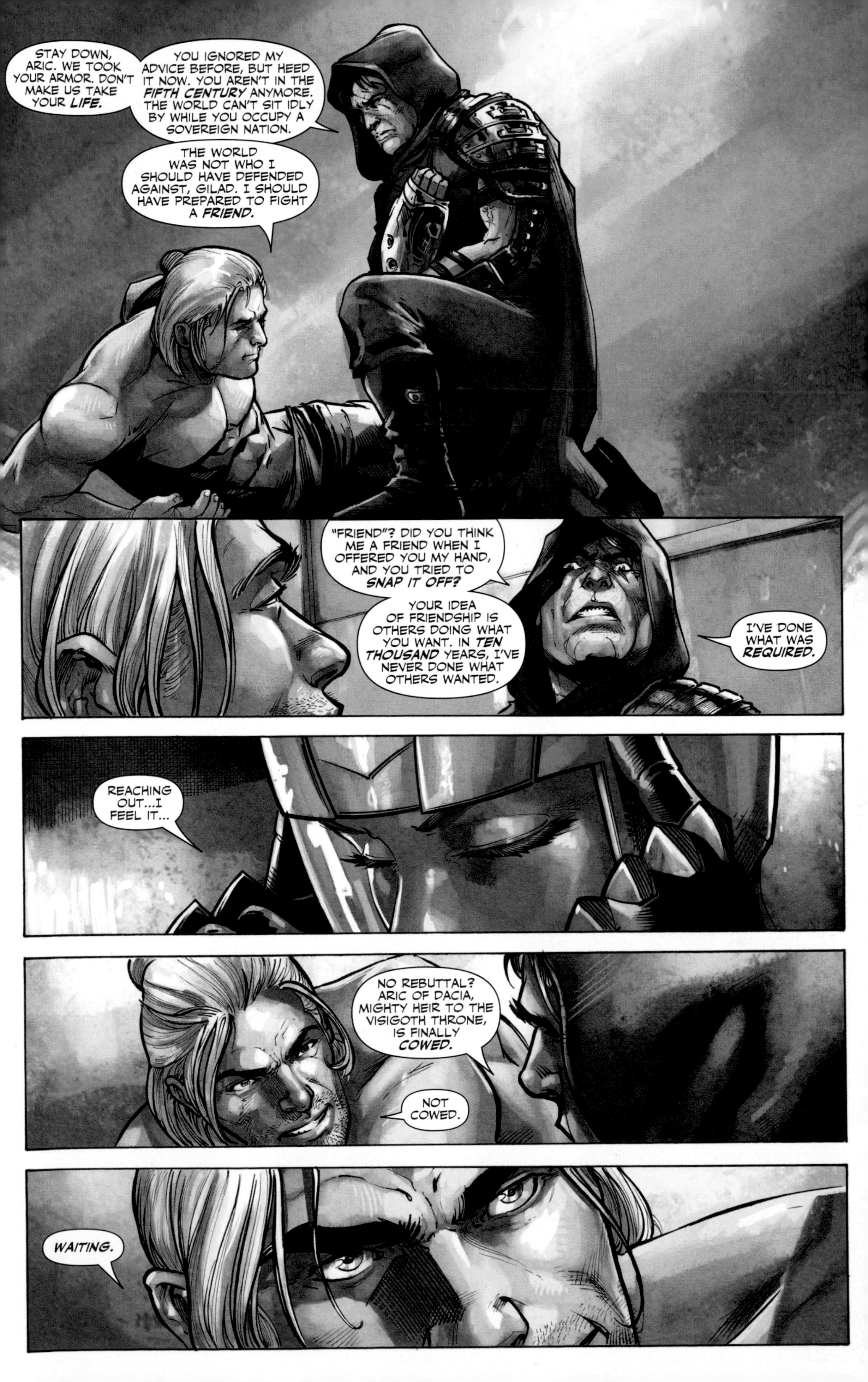
STAY DOWN, ARIC. WE TOOK YOUR ARMOR. DON'T MAKE US TAKE YOUR LIFE.
YOU IGNORED MY ADVICE BEFORE, BUT HEED IT NOW. YOU AREN'T IN THE FIFTH CENTURY ANYMORE. THE WORLD CAN'T SIT IDLY BY WHILE YOU OCCUPY A SOVEREIGN NATION.
THE WORLD WAS NOT WHO I SHOULD HAVE DEFENDED AGAINST, GILAD. I SHOULD HAVE PREPARED TO FIGHT A FRIEND.
"FRIEND"? DID YOU THINK ME A FRIEND WHEN I OFFERED YOU MY HAND, AND YOU TRIED TO SNAP IT OFF?
YOUR IDEA OF FRIENDSHIP IS OTHERS DOING WHAT YOU WANT. IN TEN THOUSAND YEARS, I'VE NEVER DONE WHAT OTHERS WANTED.
I'VE DONE WHAT WAS REQUIRED.
REACHING OUT...I FEEL IT...
NO REBUTTAL? ARIC OF DACIA, MIGHTY HEIR TO THE VISIGOTH THRONE, IS FINALLY COWED.
NOT COWED.
WAITING.

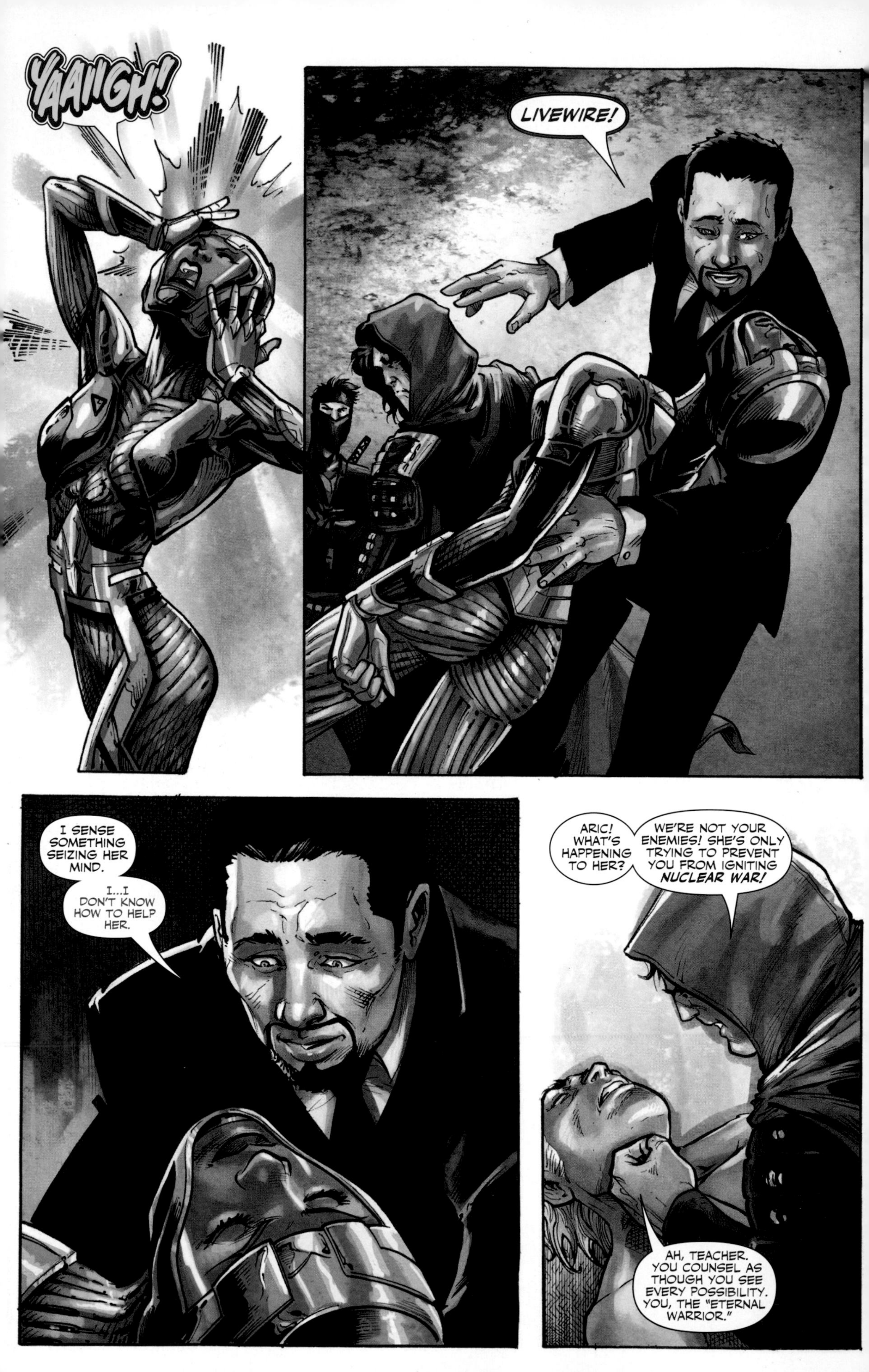
YAAIIGH!
LIVEWIRE!
I SENSE SOMETHING SEIZING HER MIND.
I...I DON'T KNOW HOW TO HELP HER.
ARIC! WHAT'S HAPPENING TO HER?
WE'RE NOT YOUR ENEMIES! SHE'S ONLY TRYING TO PREVENT YOU FROM IGNITING NUCLEAR WAR!
AH, TEACHER. YOU COUNSEL AS THOUGH YOU SEE EVERY POSSIBILITY. YOU, THE "ETERNAL WARRIOR."

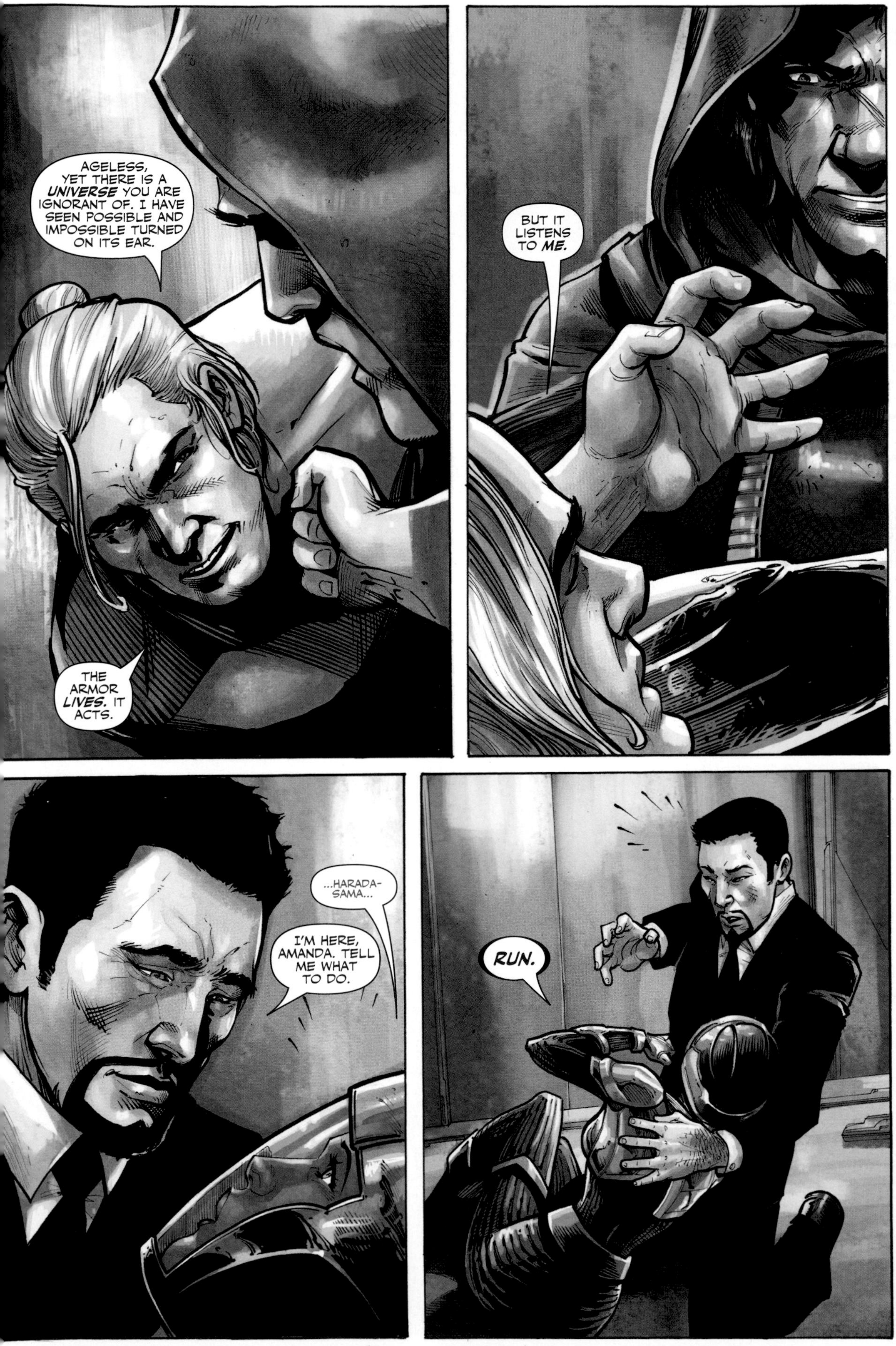
AGELESS, YET THERE IS A UNIVERSE YOU ARE IGNORANT OF. I HAVE SEEN POSSIBLE AND IMPOSSIBLE TURNED ON ITS EAR.
THE ARMOR LIVES. IT ACTS.
BUT IT LISTENS TO ME.
...HARADA-SAMA...
I'M HERE, AMANDA. TELL ME WHAT TO DO.
RUN.

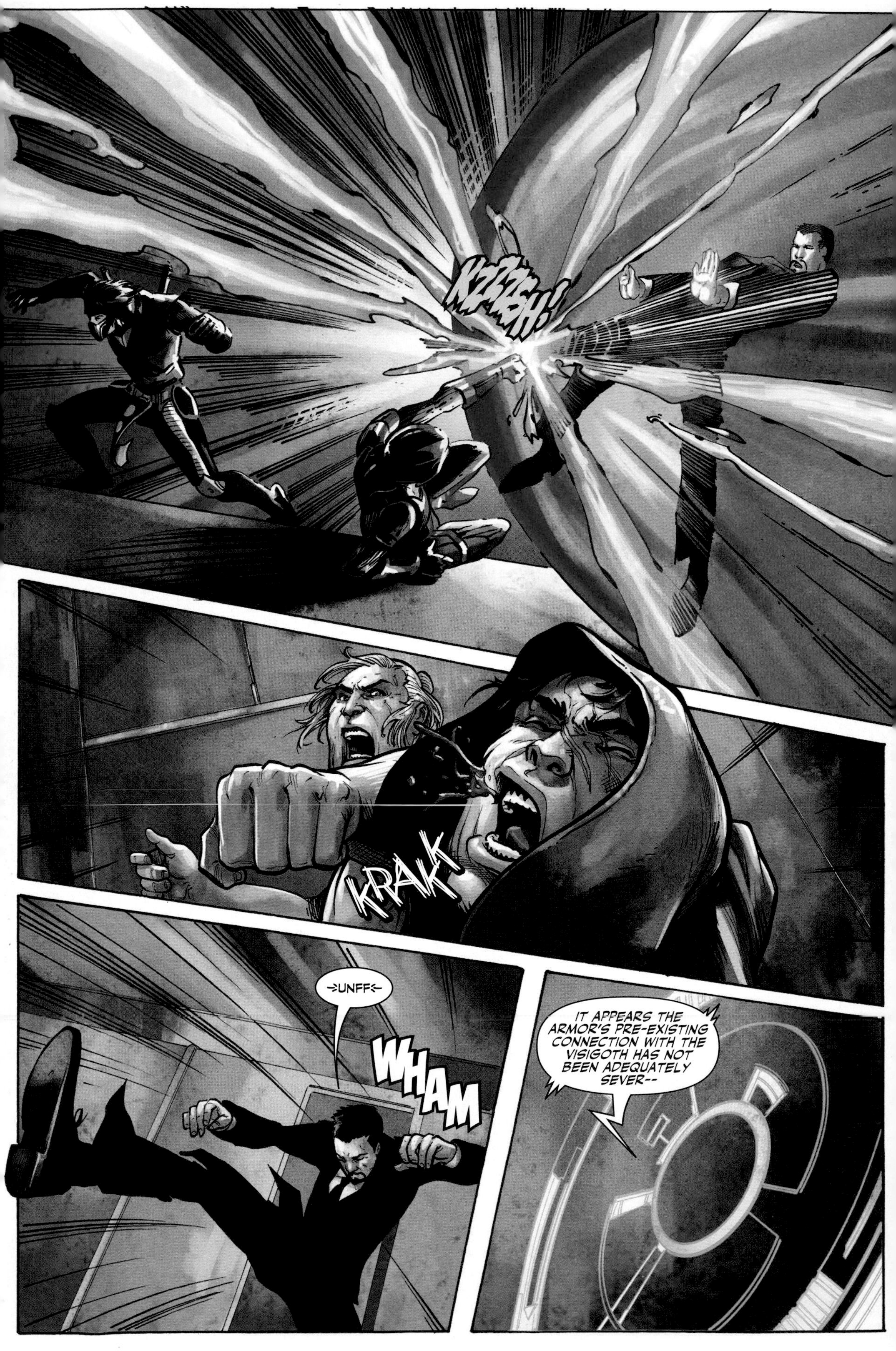
KZZZSH!
KRAK
-UNFF-
WHAM
IT APPEARS THE ARMOR'S PRE-EXISTING CONNECTION WITH THE VISIGOTH HAS NOT BEEN ADEQUATELY SEVER--

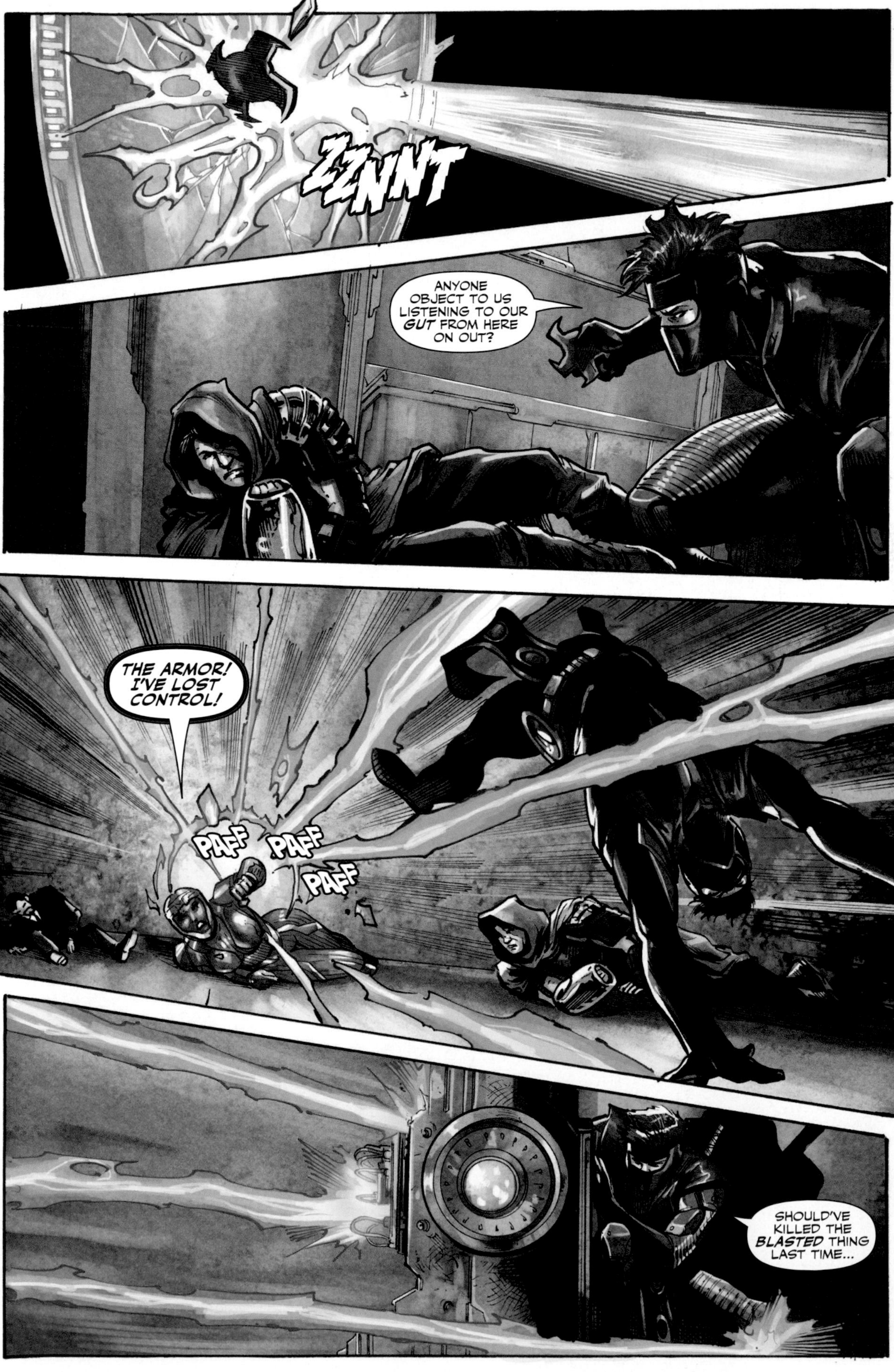
ZZNNT
ANYONE OBJECT TO US LISTENING TO OUR GUT FROM HERE ON OUT?
THE ARMOR! I'VE LOST CONTROL!
PAFF
PAFF
PAFF
SHOULD'VE KILLED THE BLASTED THING LAST TIME...

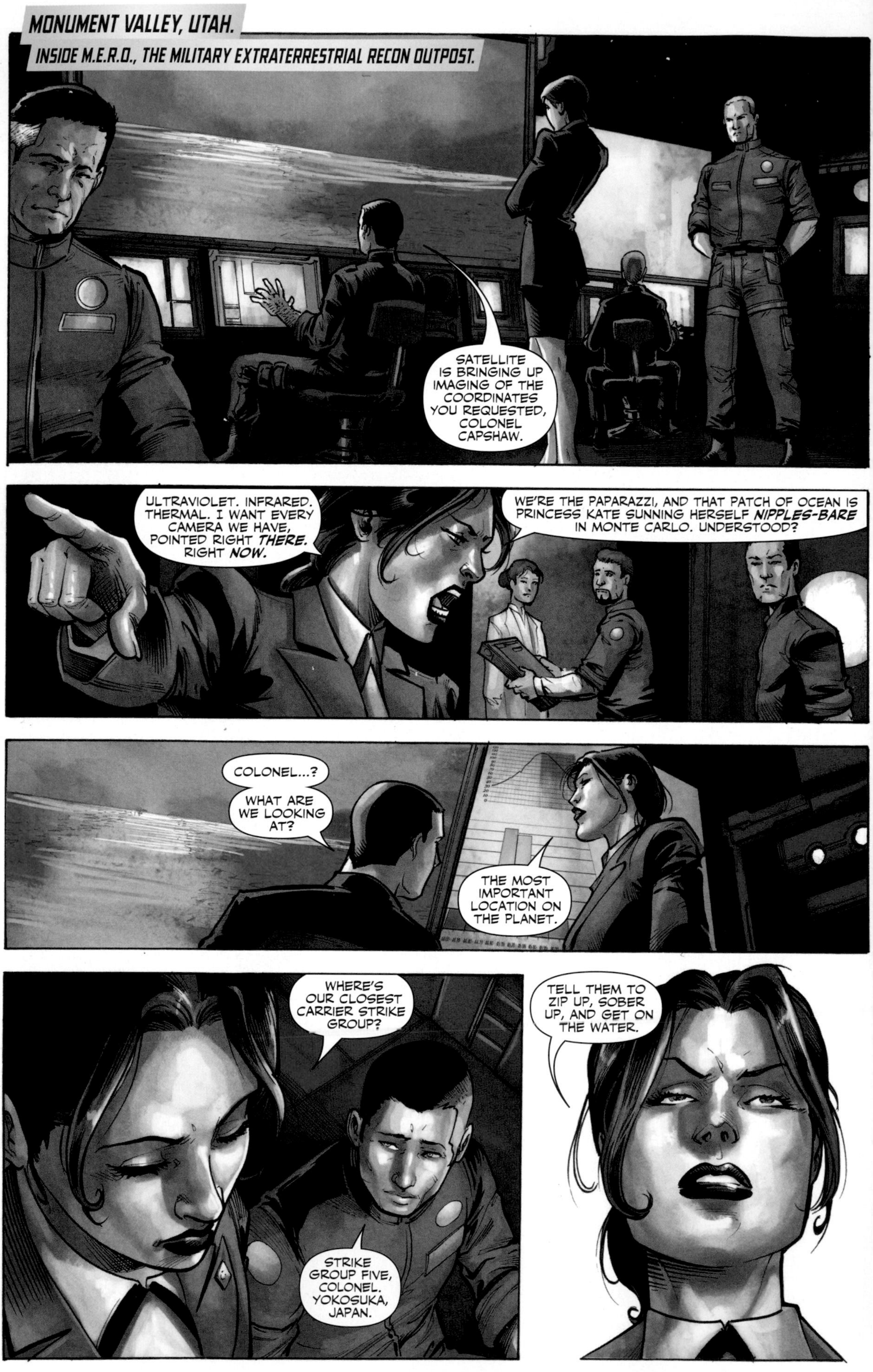
MONUMENT VALLEY, UTAH.
INSIDE M.E.R.O., THE MILITARY EXTRATERRESTRIAL RECON OUTPOST.
SATELLITE IS BRINGING UP IMAGING OF THE COORDINATES YOU REQUESTED, COLONEL CAPSHAW.
ULTRAVIOLET. INFRARED. THERMAL. I WANT EVERY CAMERA WE HAVE, POINTED RIGHT THERE. RIGHT NOW.
WE'RE THE PAPARAZZI, AND THAT PATCH OF OCEAN IS PRINCESS KATE SUNNING HERSELF NIPPLES-BARE IN MONTE CARLO. UNDERSTOOD?
COLONEL...?
WHAT ARE WE LOOKING AT?
THE MOST IMPORTANT LOCATION ON THE PLANET.
WHERE'S OUR CLOSEST CARRIER STRIKE GROUP?
STRIKE GROUP FIVE, COLONEL. YOKOSUKA, JAPAN.
TELL THEM TO ZIP UP, SOBER UP, AND GET ON THE WATER.

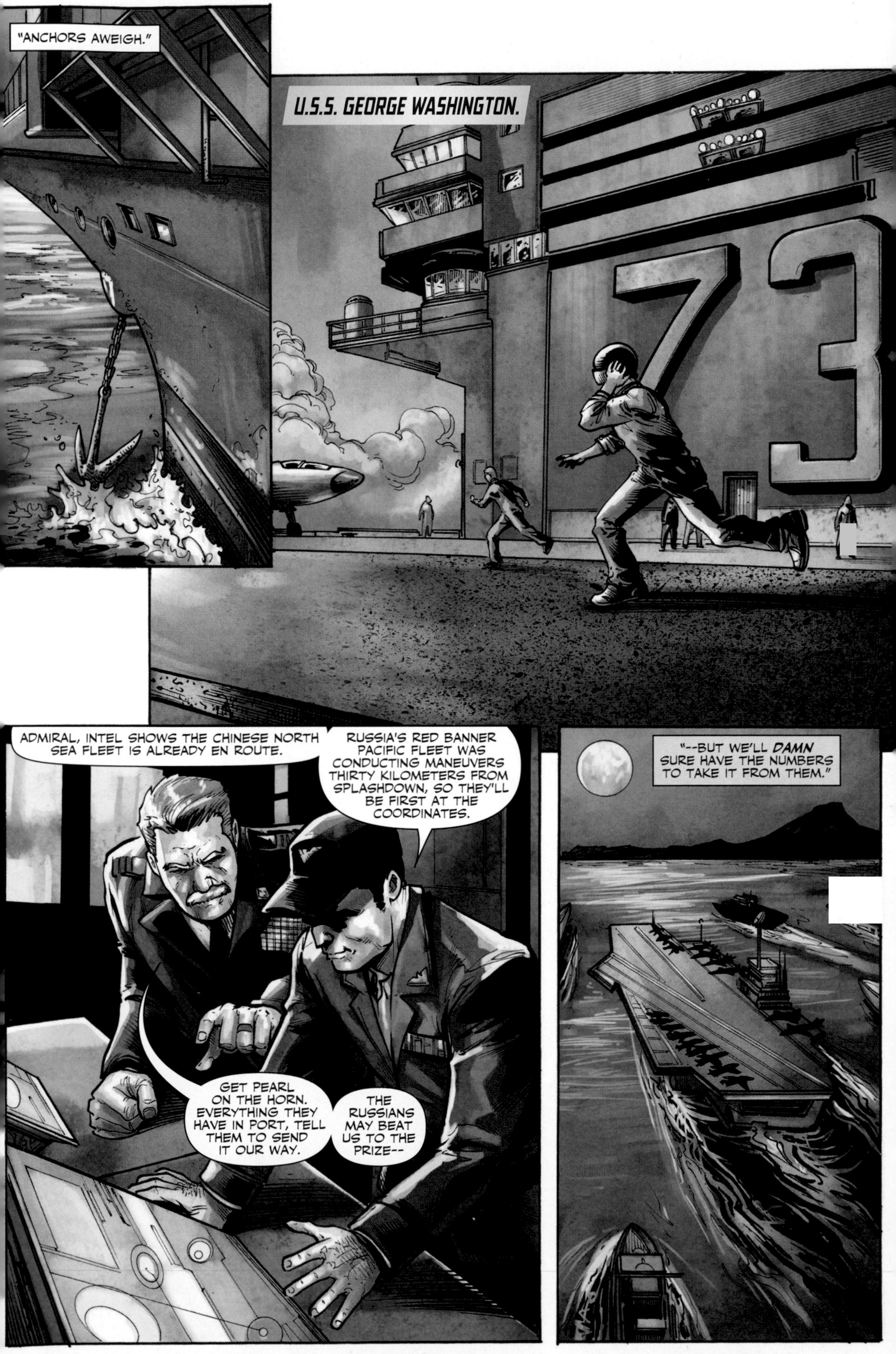
"ANCHORS AWEIGH."
U.S.S. GEORGE WASHINGTON.
73
ADMIRAL, INTEL SHOWS THE CHINESE NORTH SEA FLEET IS ALREADY EN ROUTE.
RUSSIA'S RED BANNER PACIFIC FLEET WAS CONDUCTING MANEUVERS THIRTY KILOMETERS FROM SPLASHDOWN, SO THEY'LL BE FIRST AT THE COORDINATES.
GET PEARL ON THE HORN. EVERYTHING THEY HAVE IN PORT, TELL THEM TO SEND IT OUR WAY.
THE RUSSIANS MAY BEAT US TO THE PRIZE--
"--BUT WE'LL *DAMN* SURE HAVE THE NUMBERS TO TAKE IT FROM THEM."

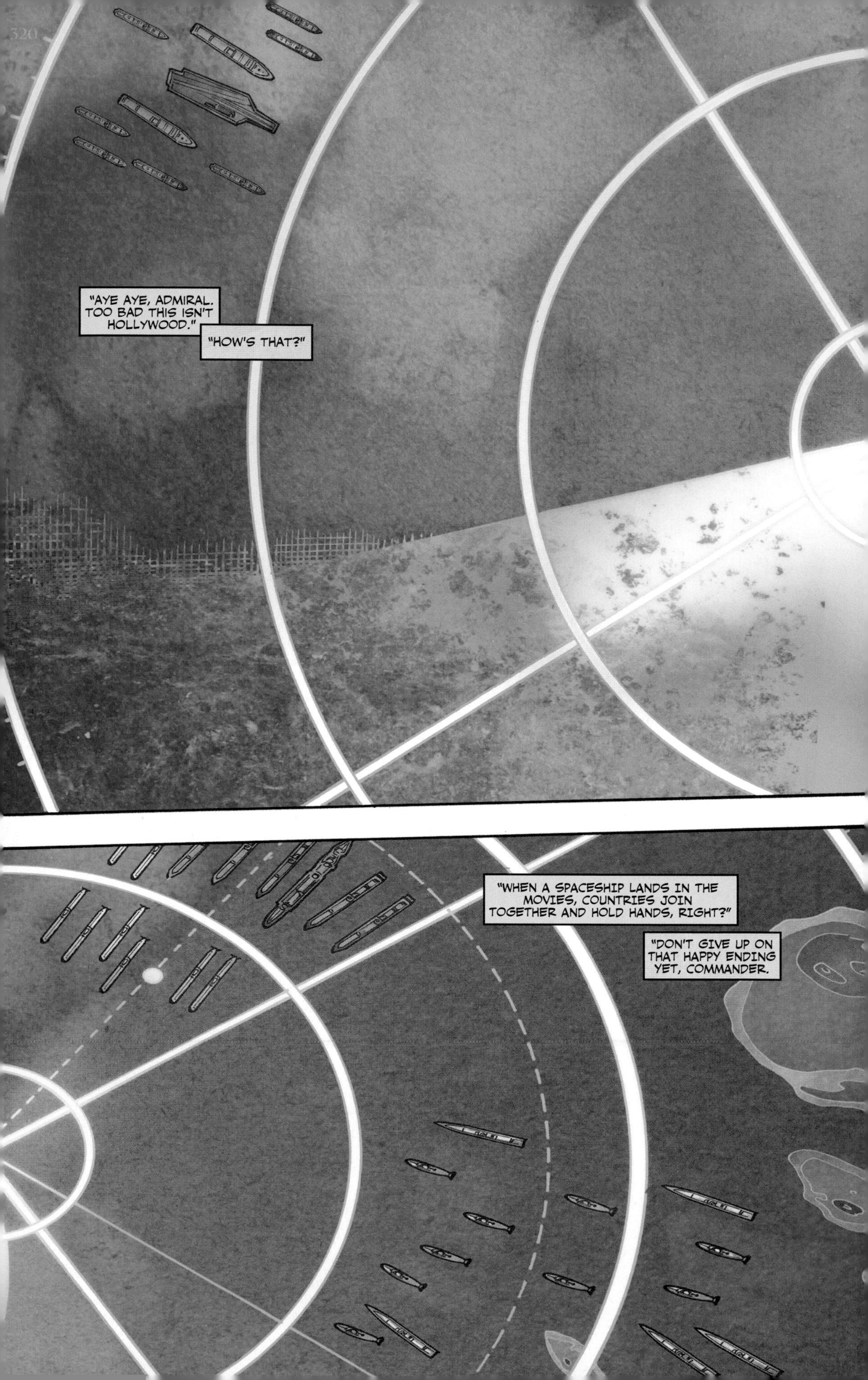
"AYE AYE, ADMIRAL. TOO BAD THIS ISN'T HOLLYWOOD."
"HOW'S THAT?"
"WHEN A SPACESHIP LANDS IN THE MOVIES, COUNTRIES JOIN TOGETHER AND HOLD HANDS, RIGHT?"
"DON'T GIVE UP ON THAT HAPPY ENDING YET, COMMANDER.

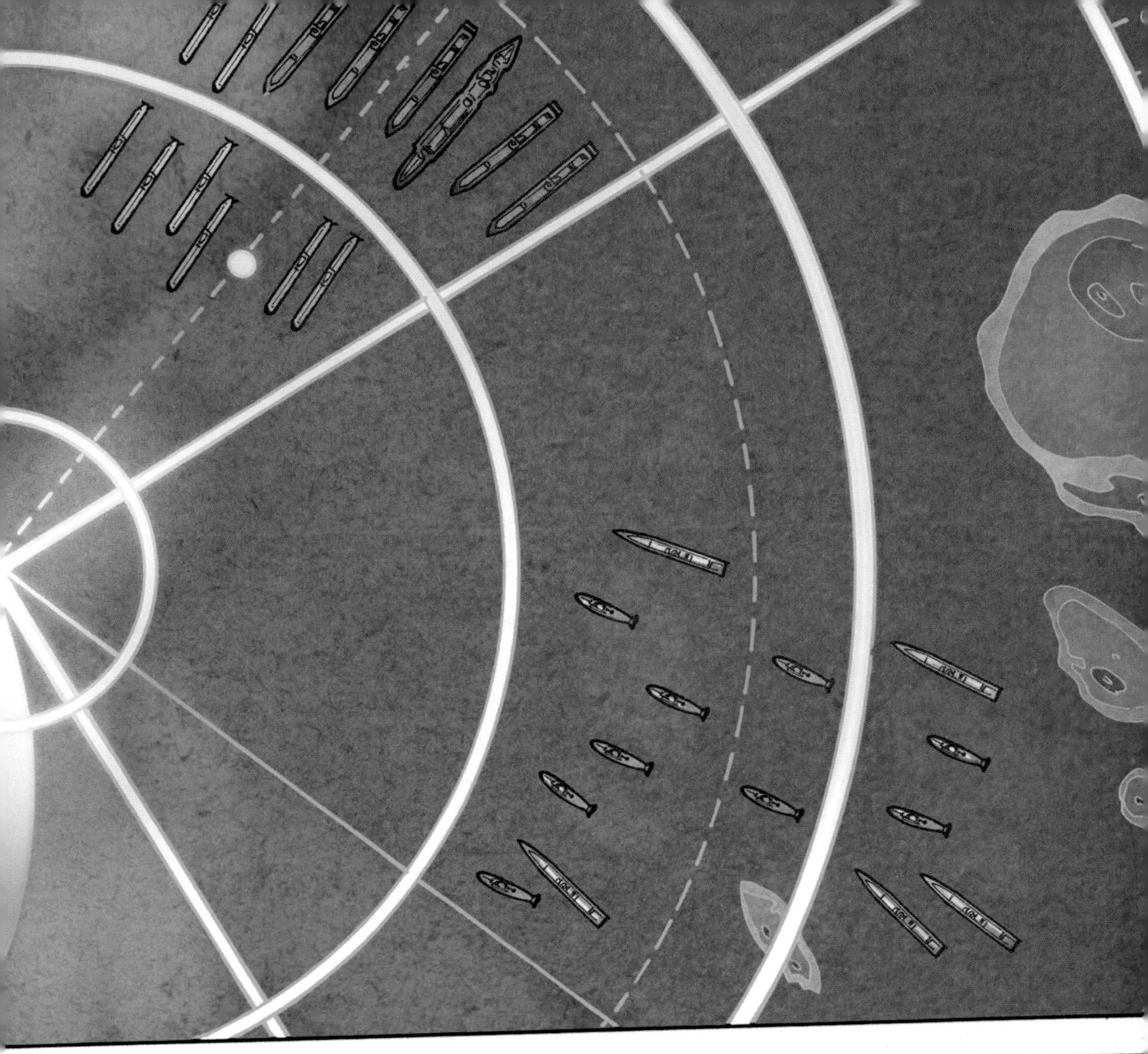

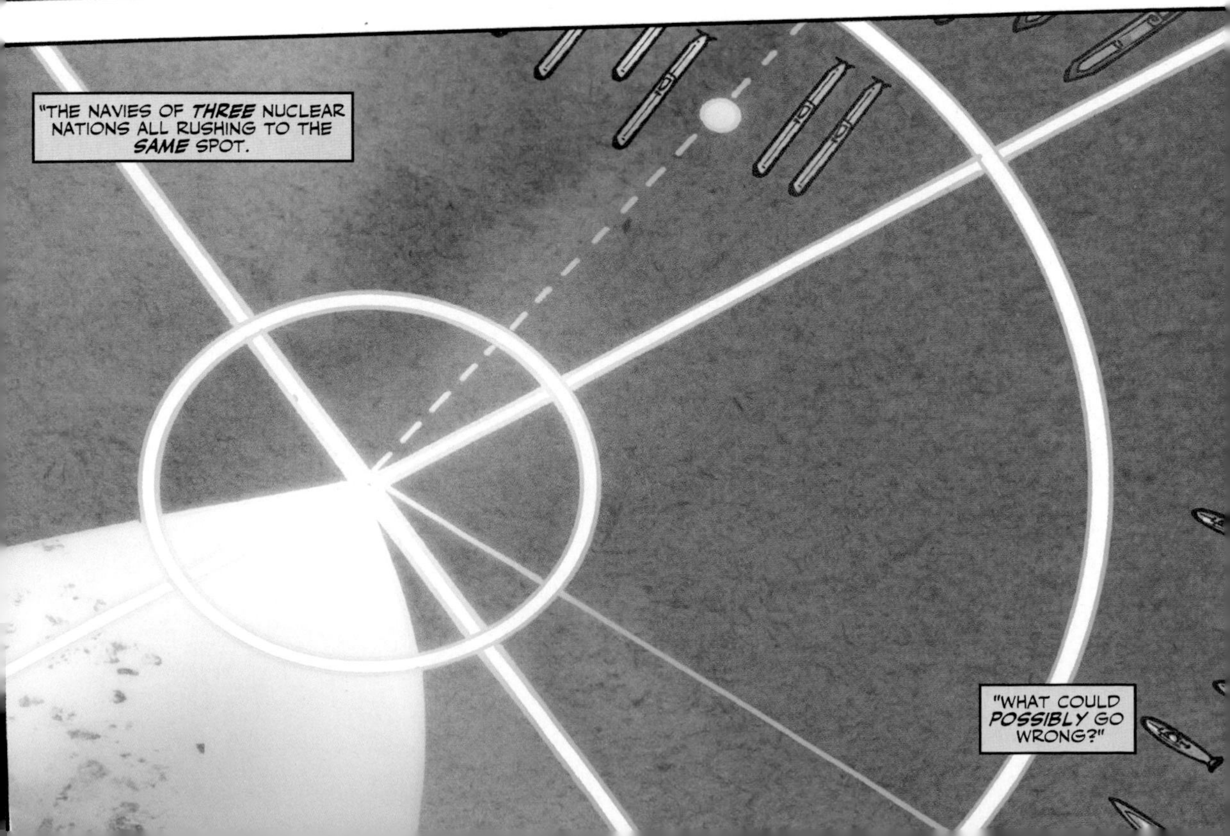
"THE NAVIES OF THREE NUCLEAR NATIONS ALL RUSHING TO THE SAME SPOT.
"WHAT COULD POSSIBLY GO WRONG?"

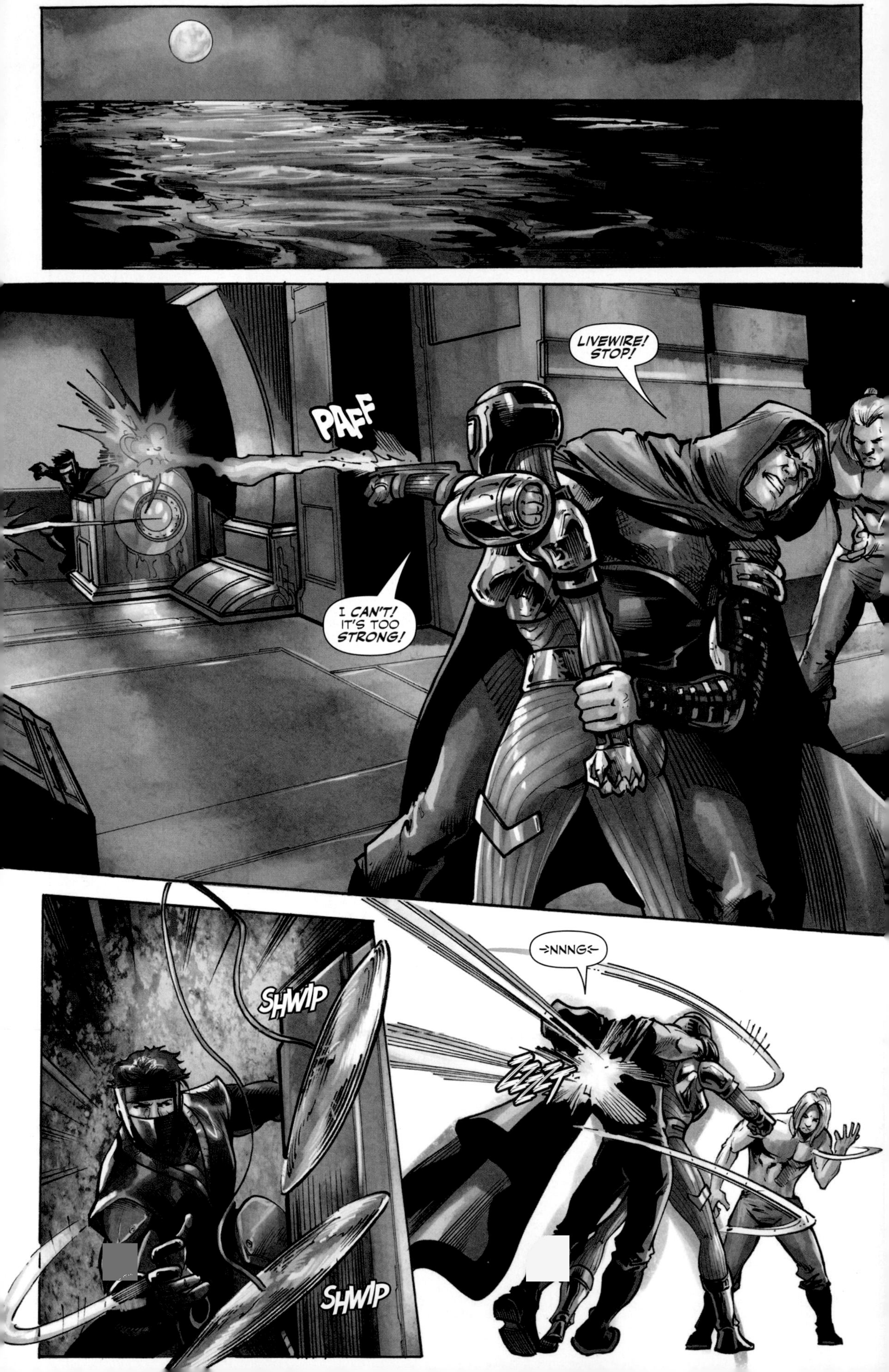
LIVEWIRE! STOP!
PAFF
I CAN'T! IT'S TOO STRONG!
SHWIP
SHWIP
NNNG

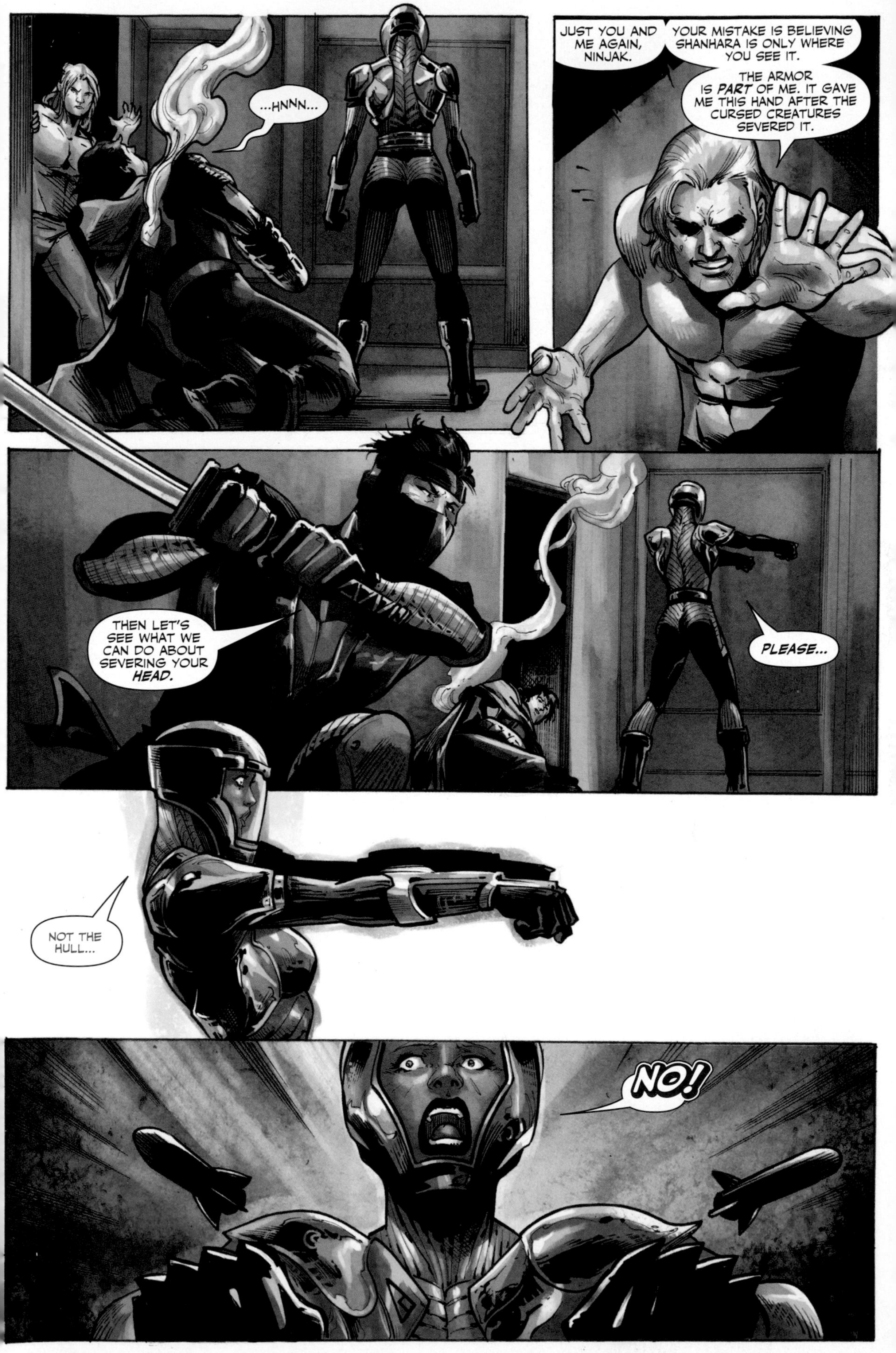
...HNNN...
JUST YOU AND ME AGAIN, NINJAK.
YOUR MISTAKE IS BELIEVING SHANHARA IS ONLY WHERE YOU SEE IT.
THE ARMOR IS PART OF ME. IT GAVE ME THIS HAND AFTER THE CURSED CREATURES SEVERED IT.
THEN LET'S SEE WHAT WE CAN DO ABOUT SEVERING YOUR HEAD.
PLEASE...
NOT THE HULL...
NO!

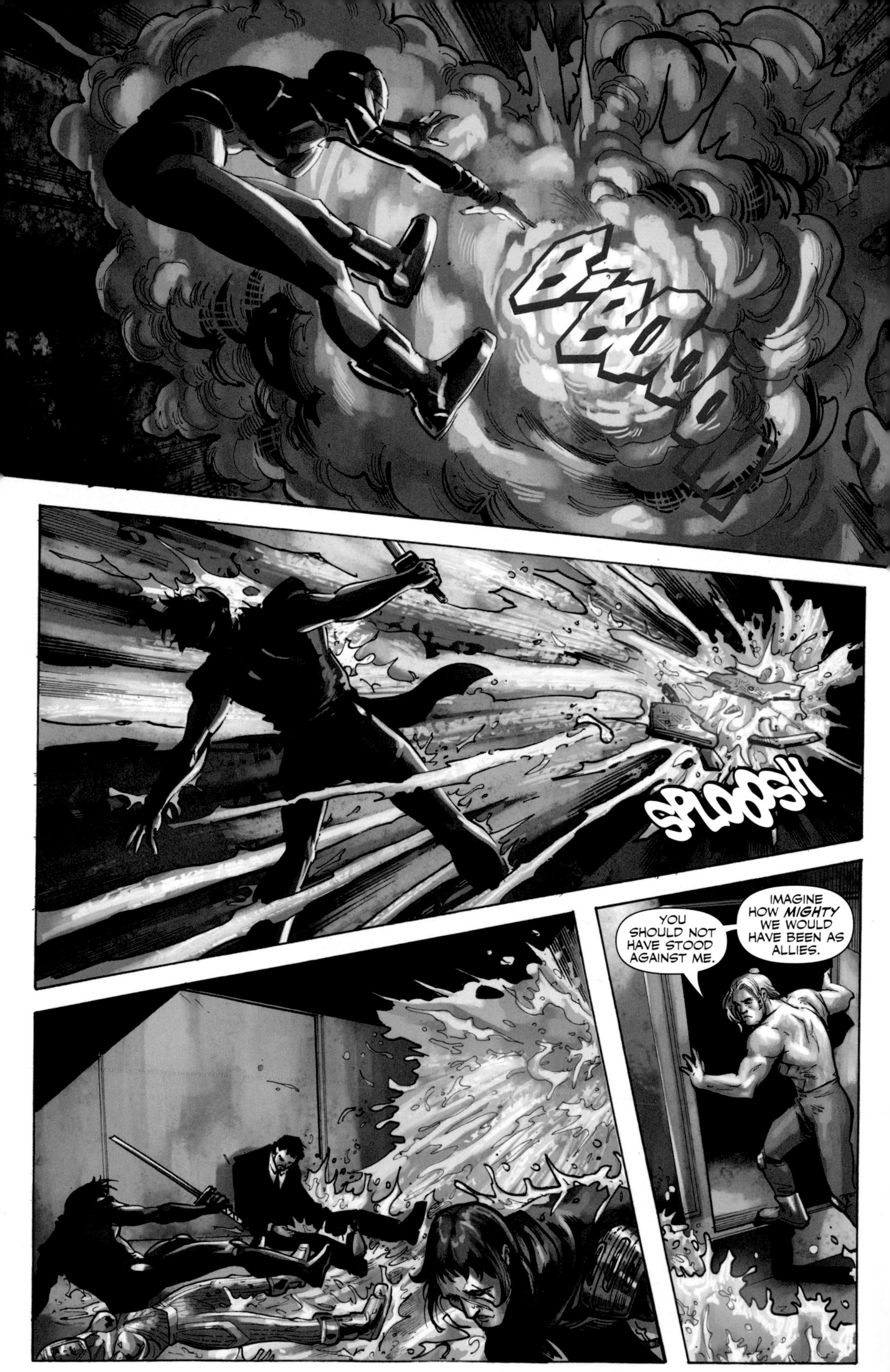
BLOOOM
SPLOOSH
YOU SHOULD NOT HAVE STOOD AGAINST ME.
IMAGINE HOW *MIGHTY* WE WOULD HAVE BEEN AS ALLIES.

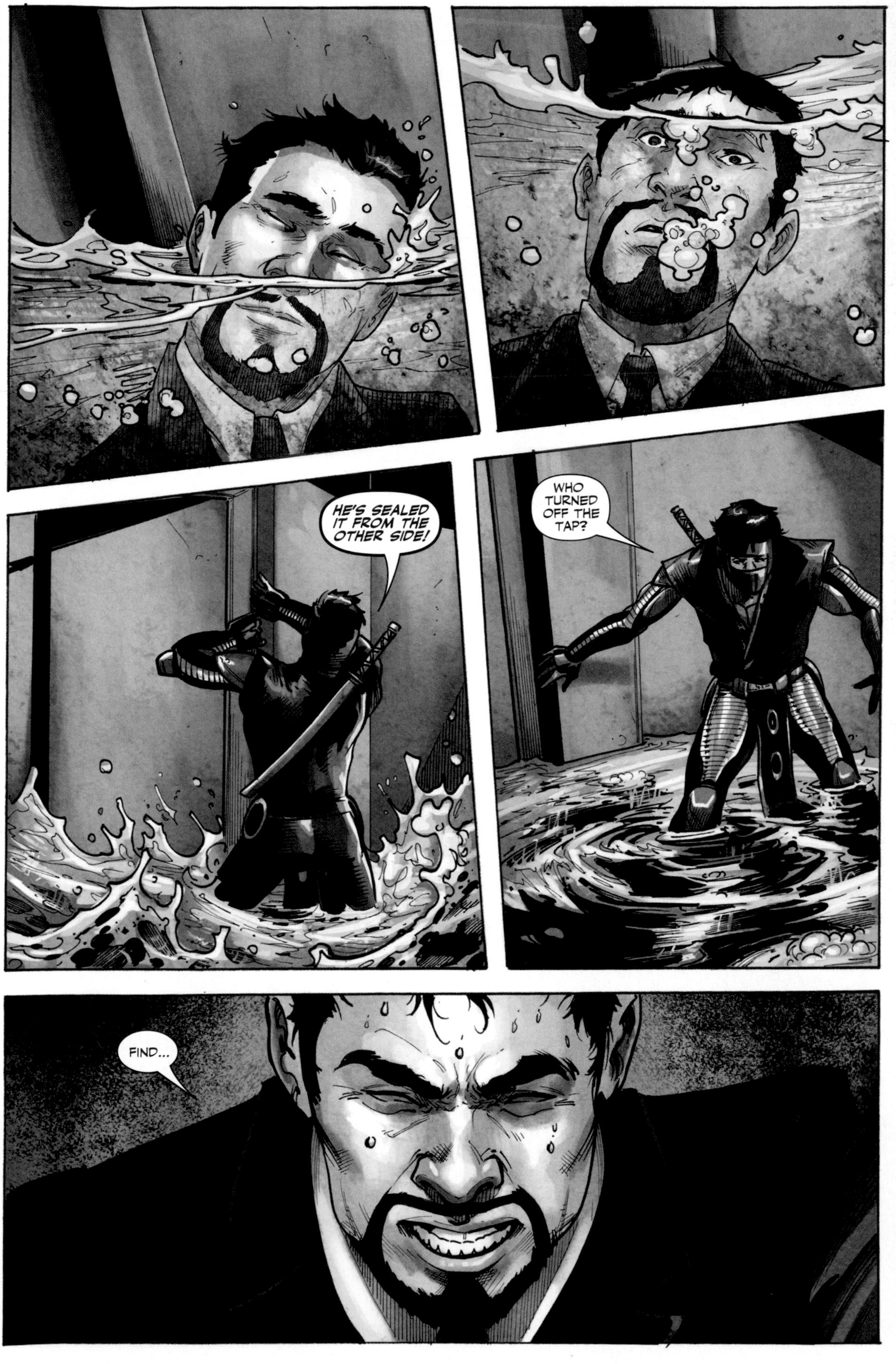
HE'S SEALED IT FROM THE OTHER SIDE!
WHO TURNED OFF THE TAP?
FIND...

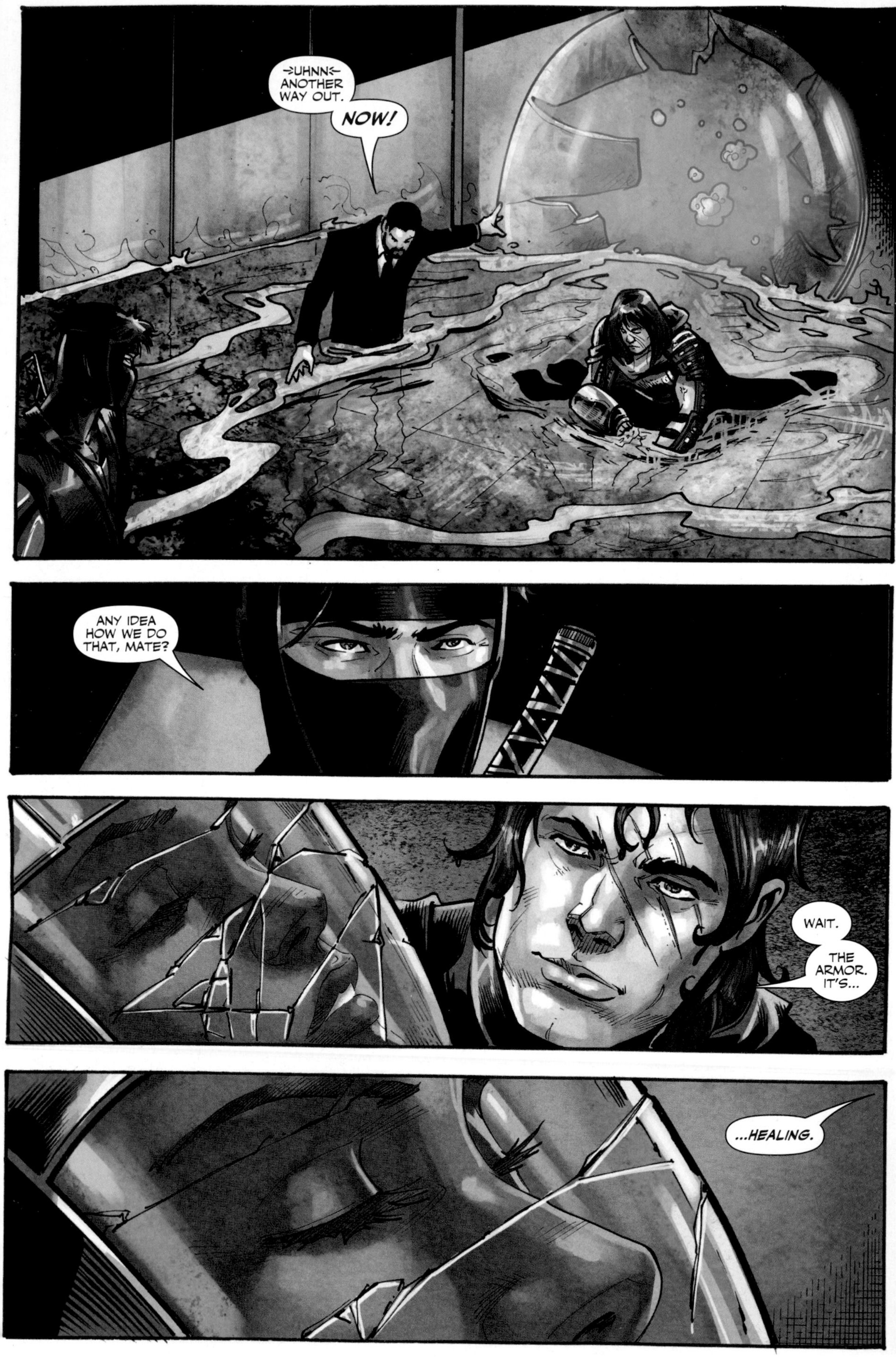

-UHNN- ANOTHER WAY OUT.
NOW!
ANY IDEA HOW WE DO THAT, MATE?
WAIT.
THE ARMOR. IT'S...
...HEALING.

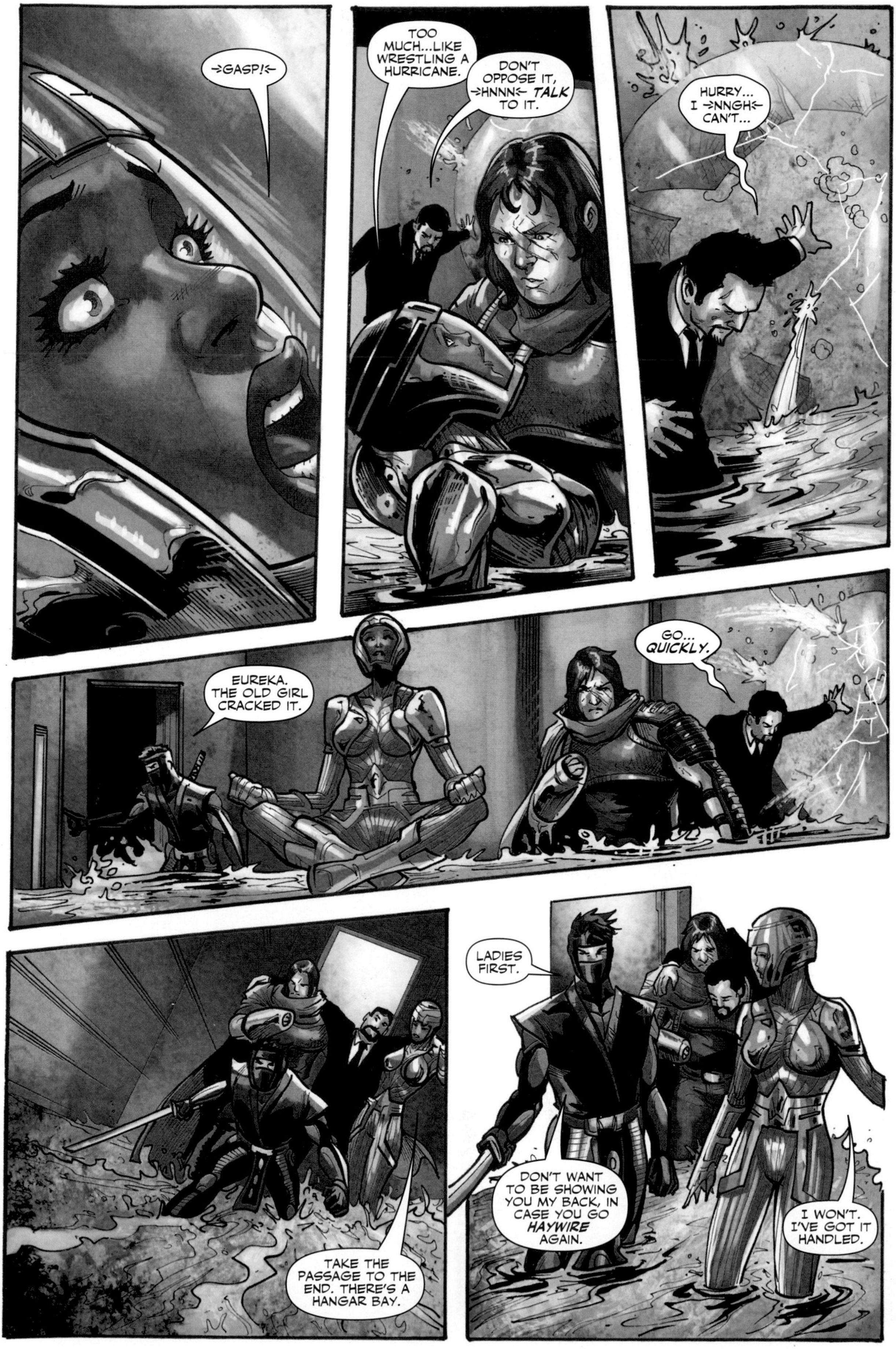

>GASP!<
TOO MUCH...LIKE WRESTLING A HURRICANE.
DON'T OPPOSE IT, >HNNN< TALK TO IT.
HURRY... I >NNGH< CAN'T...
EUREKA. THE OLD GIRL CRACKED IT.
GO... QUICKLY.
TAKE THE PASSAGE TO THE END. THERE'S A HANGAR BAY.
LADIES FIRST.
DON'T WANT TO BE SHOWING YOU MY BACK, IN CASE YOU GO HAYWIRE AGAIN.
I WON'T. I'VE GOT IT HANDLED.

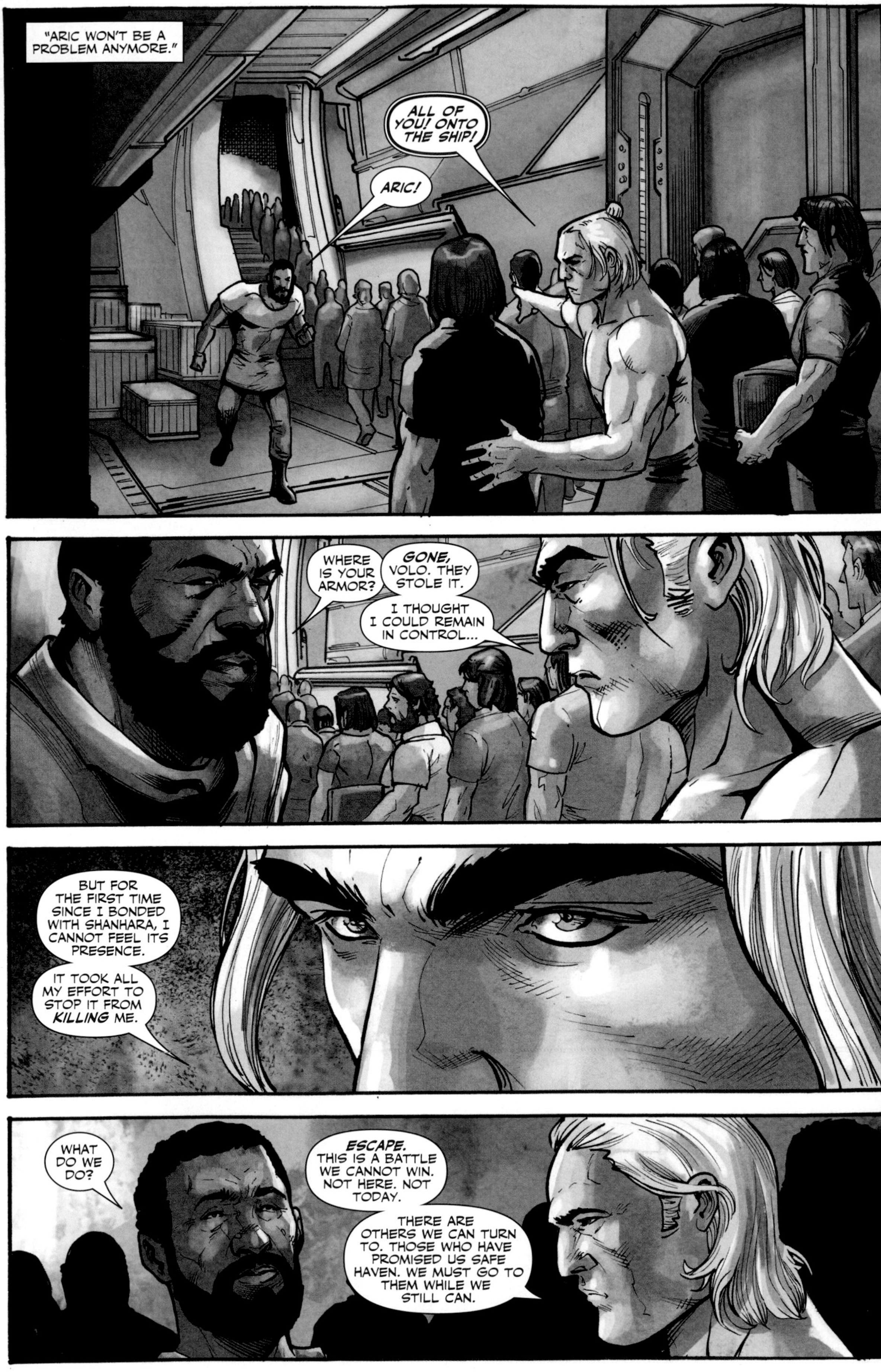
"ARIC WON'T BE A PROBLEM ANYMORE."
ALL OF YOU! ONTO THE SHIP!
ARIC!
WHERE IS YOUR ARMOR?
GONE, VOLO. THEY STOLE IT.
I THOUGHT I COULD REMAIN IN CONTROL...
BUT FOR THE FIRST TIME SINCE I BONDED WITH SHANHARA, I CANNOT FEEL ITS PRESENCE.
IT TOOK ALL MY EFFORT TO STOP IT FROM KILLING ME.
WHAT DO WE DO?
ESCAPE. THIS IS A BATTLE WE CANNOT WIN. NOT HERE. NOT TODAY.
THERE ARE OTHERS WE CAN TURN TO. THOSE WHO HAVE PROMISED US SAFE HAVEN. WE MUST GO TO THEM WHILE WE STILL CAN.

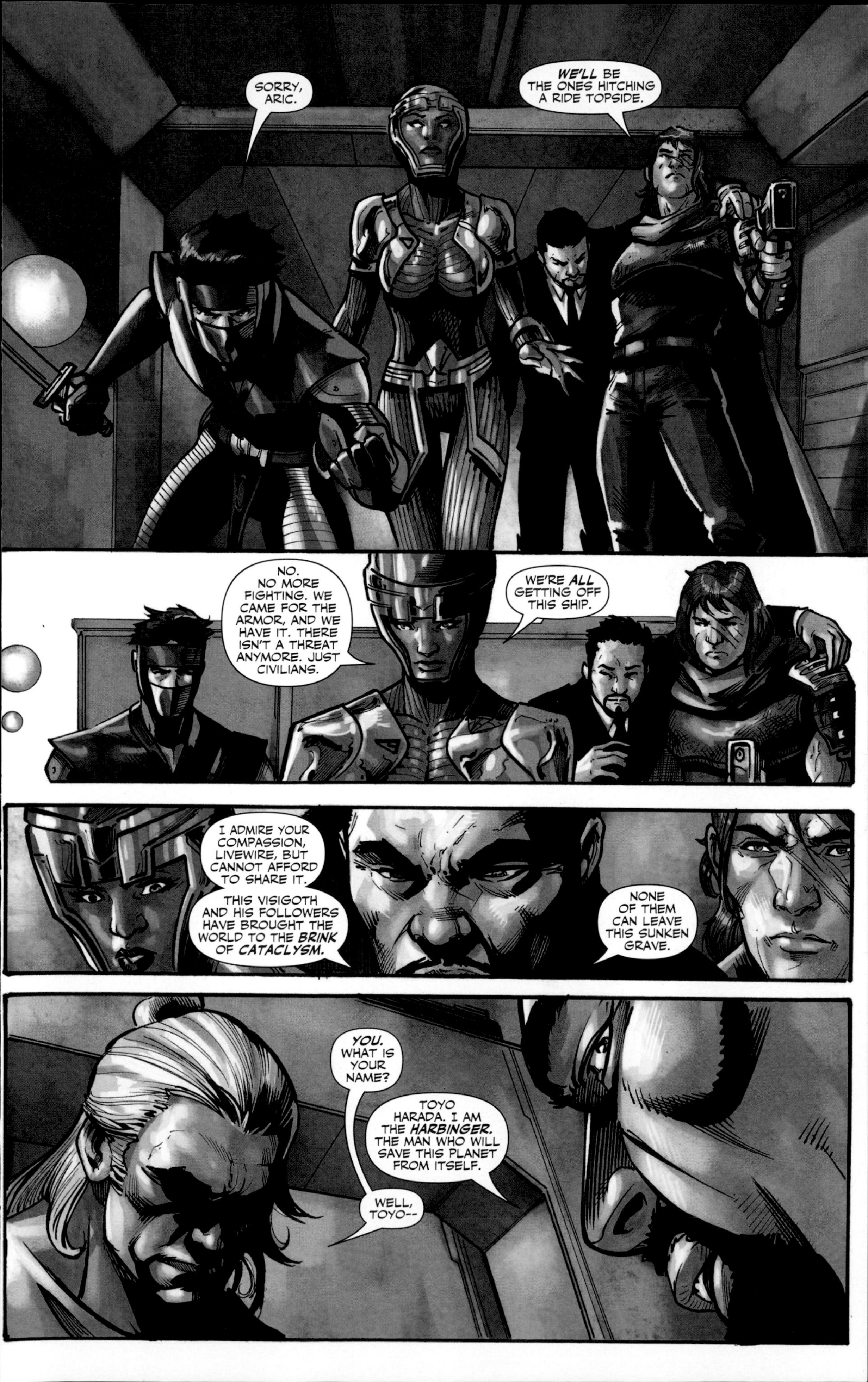
SORRY, ARIC.
WE'LL BE THE ONES HITCHING A RIDE TOPSIDE.
NO. NO MORE FIGHTING. WE CAME FOR THE ARMOR, AND WE HAVE IT. THERE ISN'T A THREAT ANYMORE. JUST CIVILIANS.
WE'RE ALL GETTING OFF THIS SHIP.
I ADMIRE YOUR COMPASSION, LIVEWIRE, BUT CANNOT AFFORD TO SHARE IT.
THIS VISIGOTH AND HIS FOLLOWERS HAVE BROUGHT THE WORLD TO THE BRINK OF CATACLYSM.
NONE OF THEM CAN LEAVE THIS SUNKEN GRAVE.
YOU. WHAT IS YOUR NAME?
TOYO HARADA. I AM THE HARBINGER. THE MAN WHO WILL SAVE THIS PLANET FROM ITSELF.
WELL, TOYO--

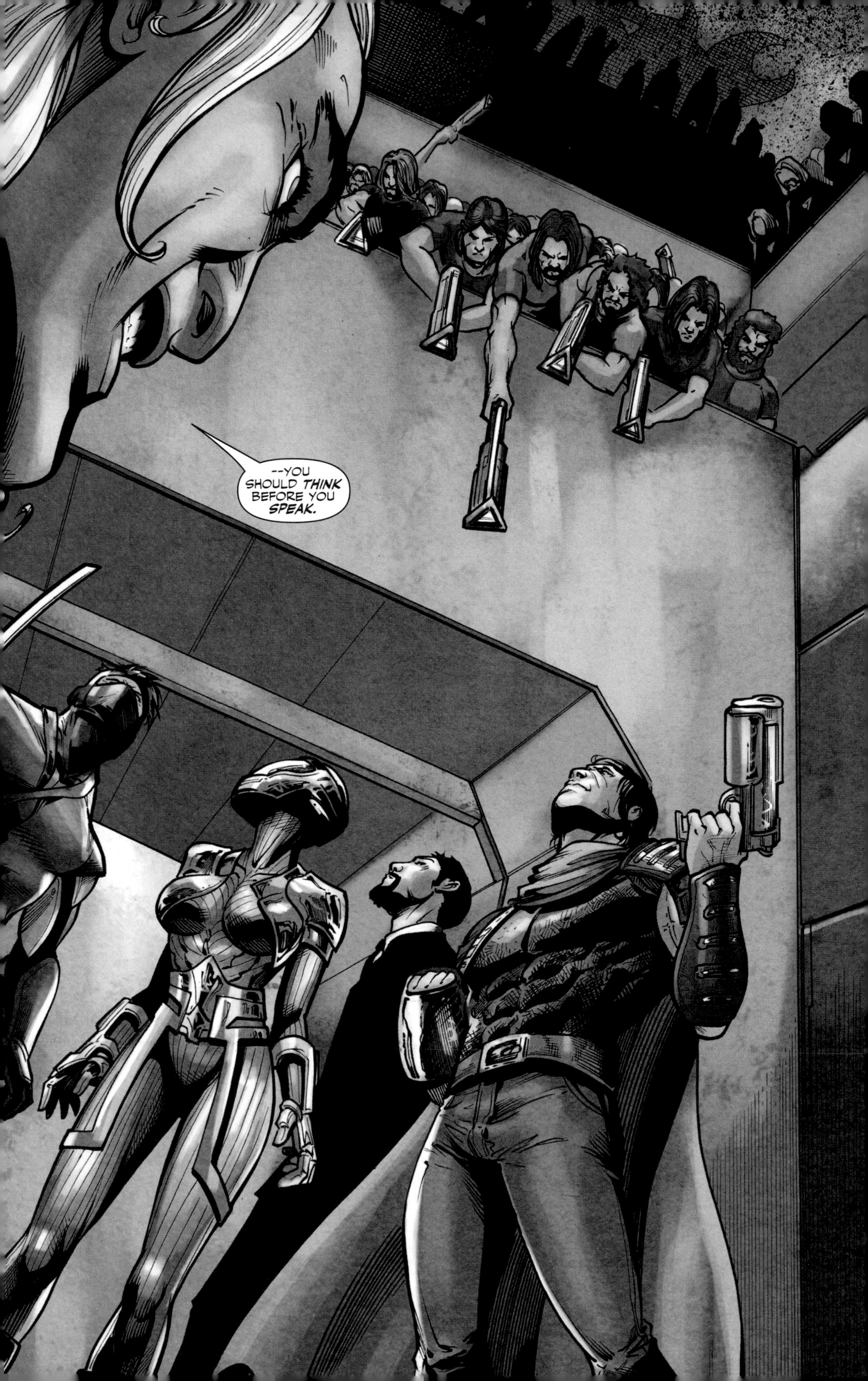
--YOU SHOULD *THINK* BEFORE YOU *SPEAK.*

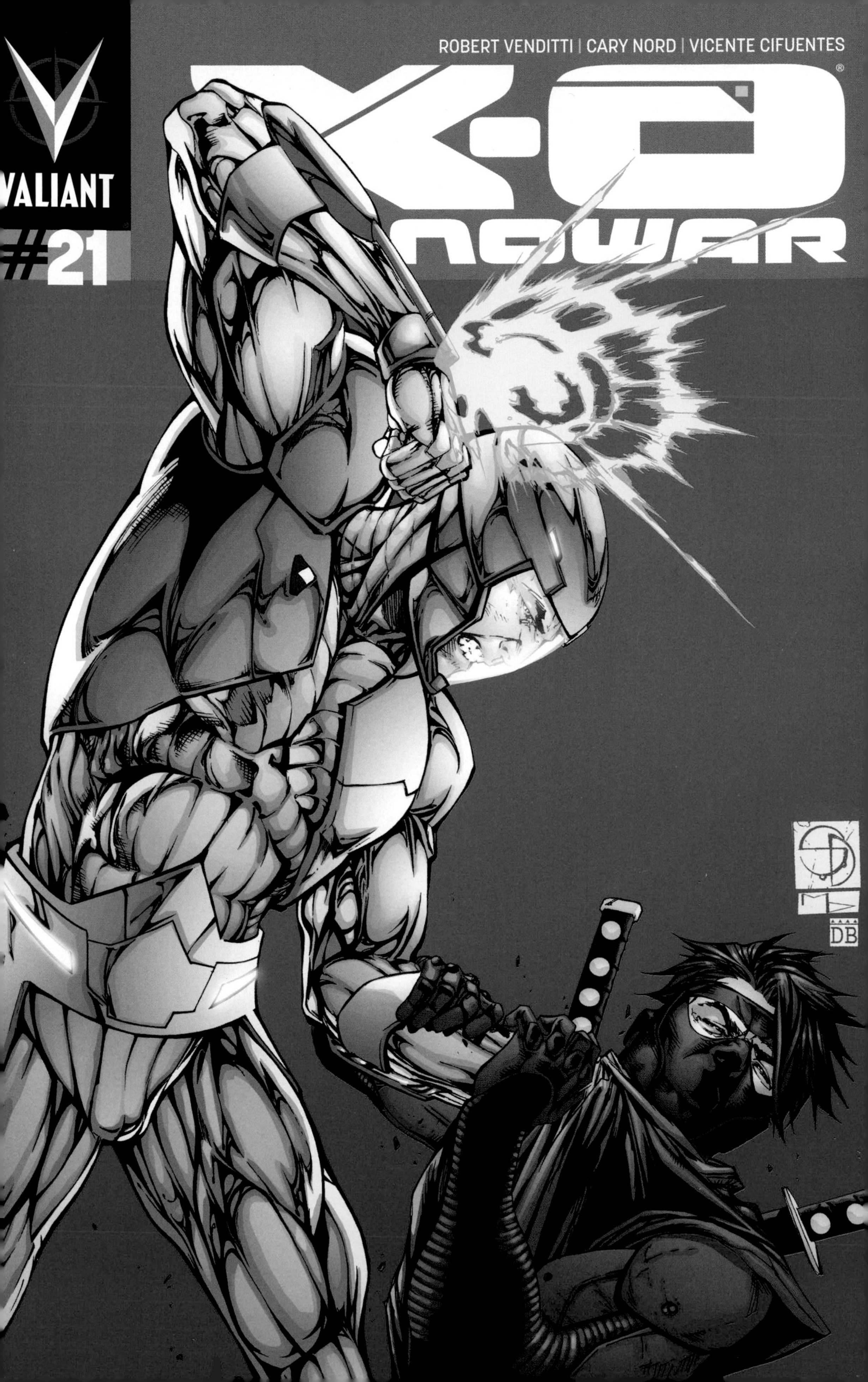
ROBERT VENDITTI | CARY NORD | VICENTE CIFUENTES
VALIANT
#21

PREVIOUSLY IN...

UNITY

Trapped at the bottom of the sea and stripped of his armor, Aric faces the combined might of Unity with the fate of his people hanging in the balance...

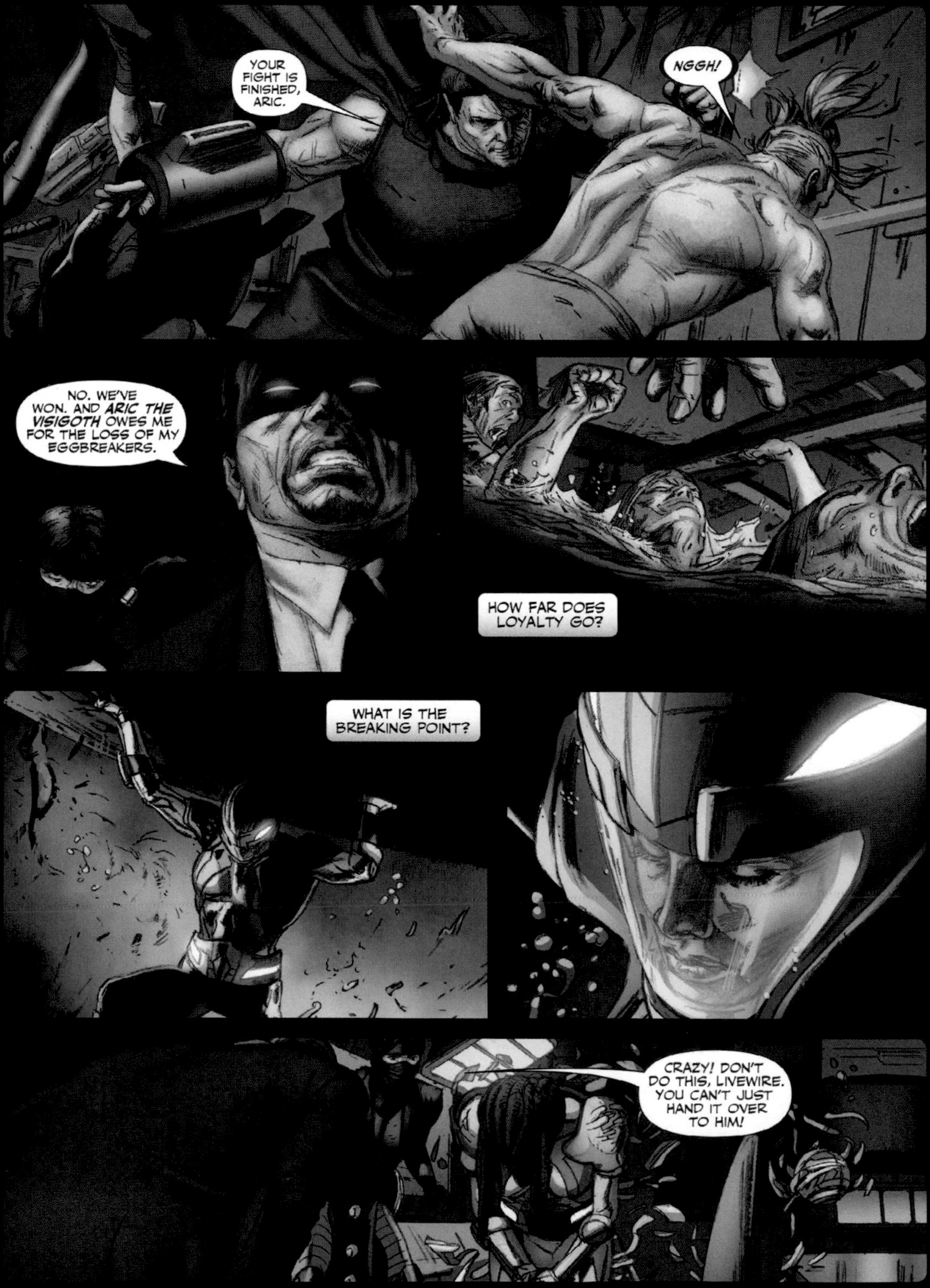
YOUR FIGHT IS FINISHED, ARIC.
NGGH!
NO. WE'VE WON. AND ARIC THE VISIGOTH OWES ME FOR THE LOSS OF MY EGGBREAKERS.
HOW FAR DOES LOYALTY GO?
WHAT IS THE BREAKING POINT?
CRAZY! DON'T DO THIS, LIVEWIRE. YOU CAN'T JUST HAND IT OVER TO HIM!

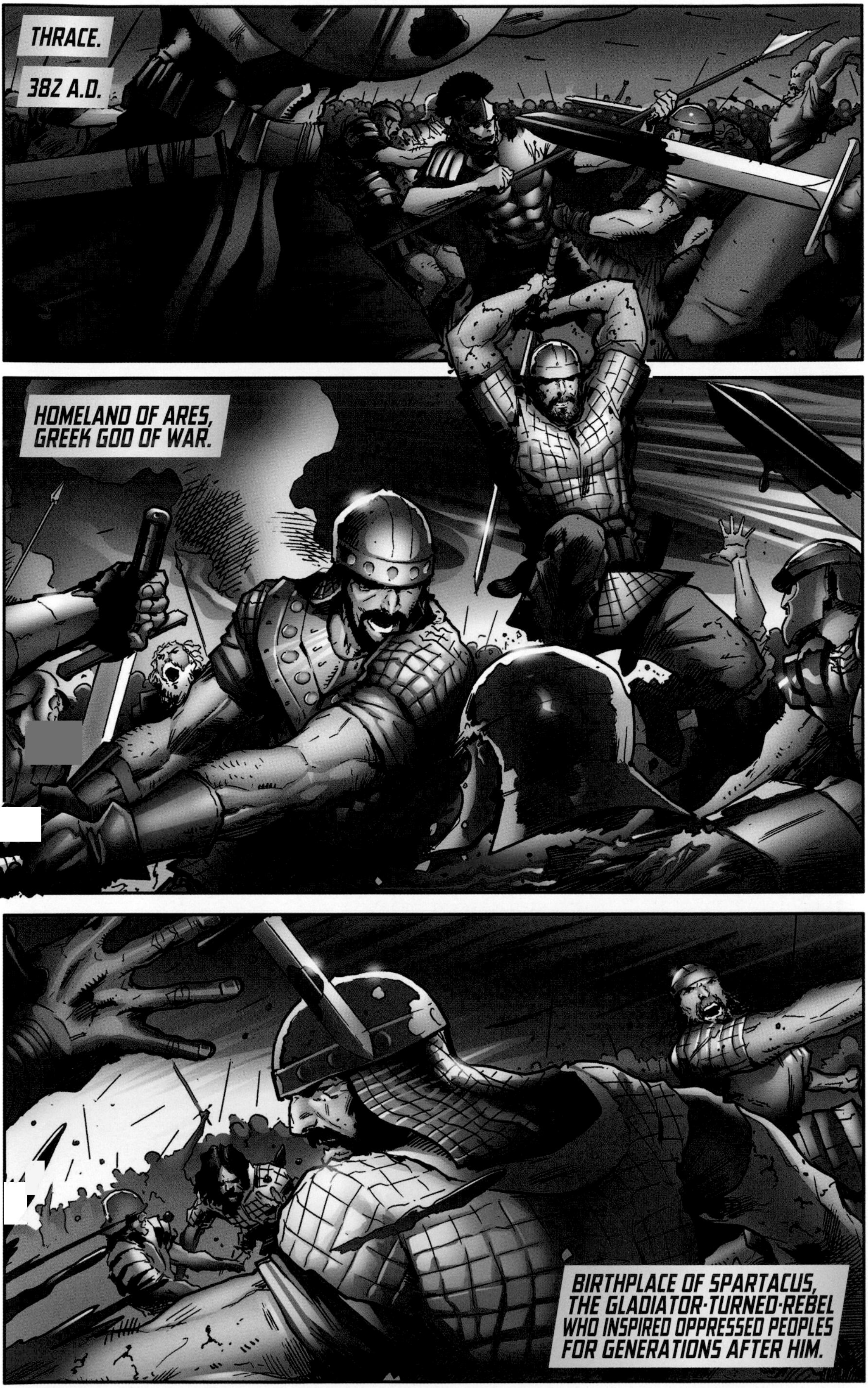
THRACE.
382 A.D.
HOMELAND OF ARES, GREEK GOD OF WAR.
BIRTHPLACE OF SPARTACUS, THE GLADIATOR-TURNED-REBEL WHO INSPIRED OPPRESSED PEOPLES FOR GENERATIONS AFTER HIM.

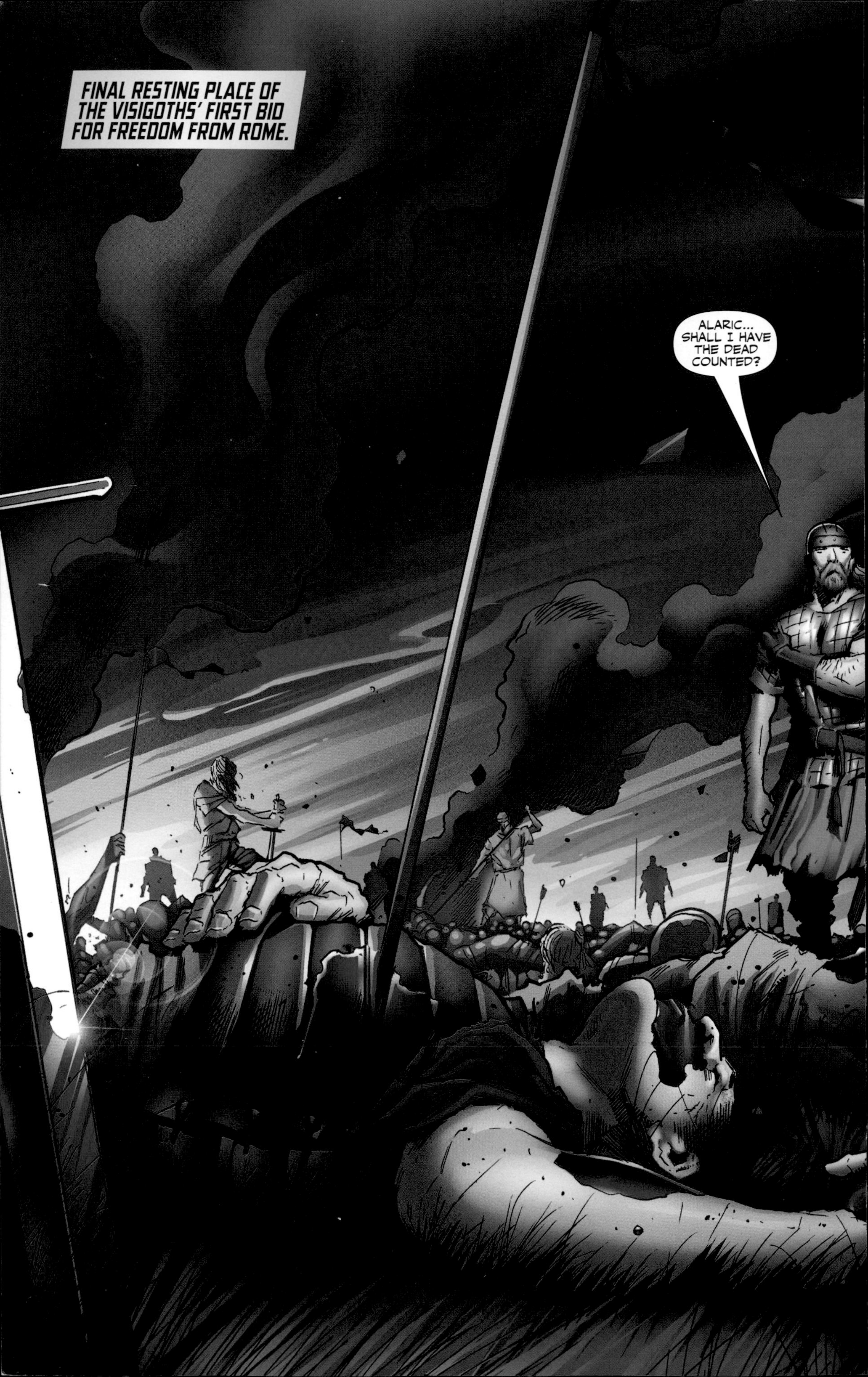
FINAL RESTING PLACE OF THE VISIGOTHS' FIRST BID FOR FREEDOM FROM ROME.
ALARIC... SHALL I HAVE THE DEAD COUNTED?

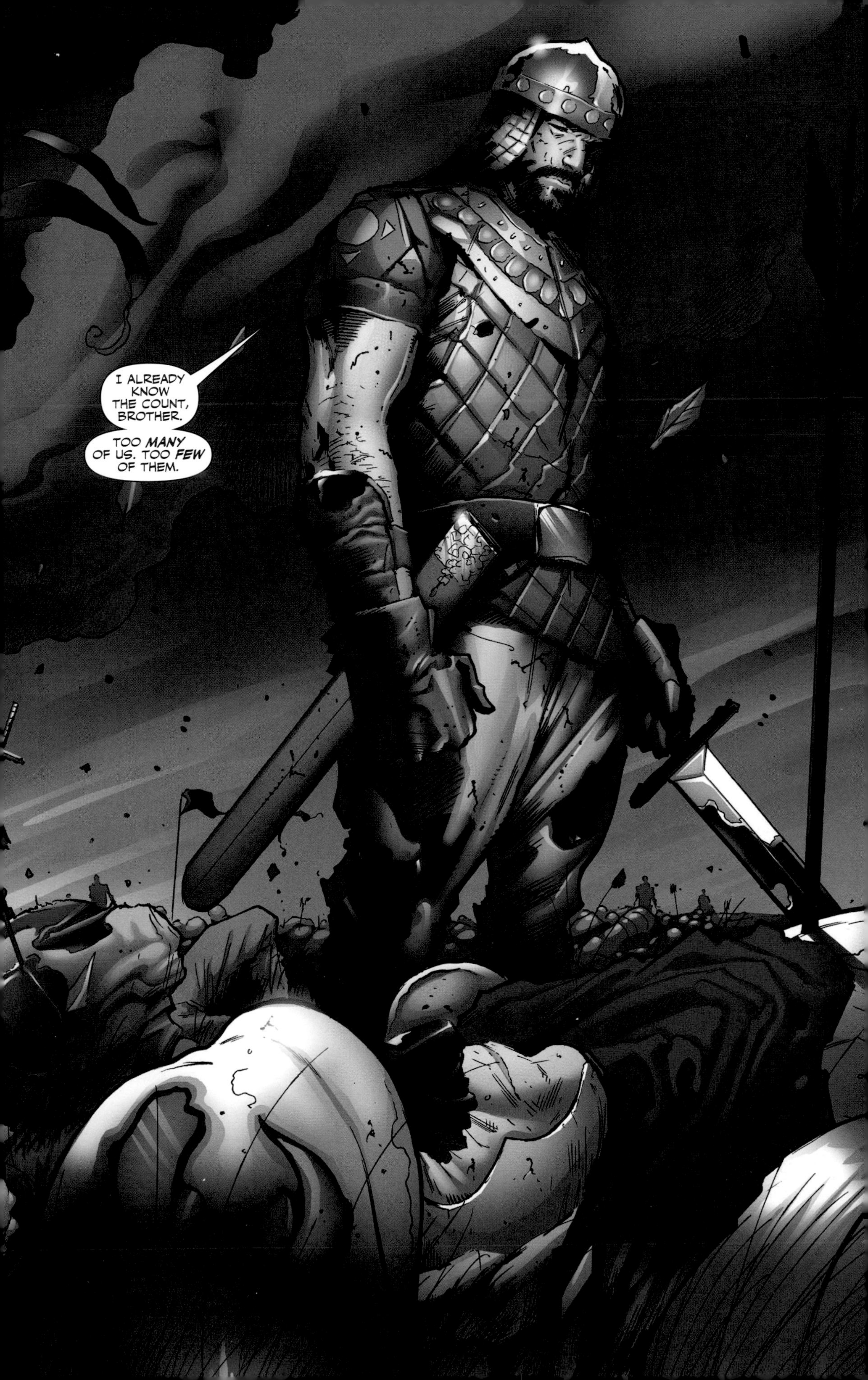
I ALREADY KNOW THE COUNT, BROTHER.
TOO MANY OF US. TOO FEW OF THEM.

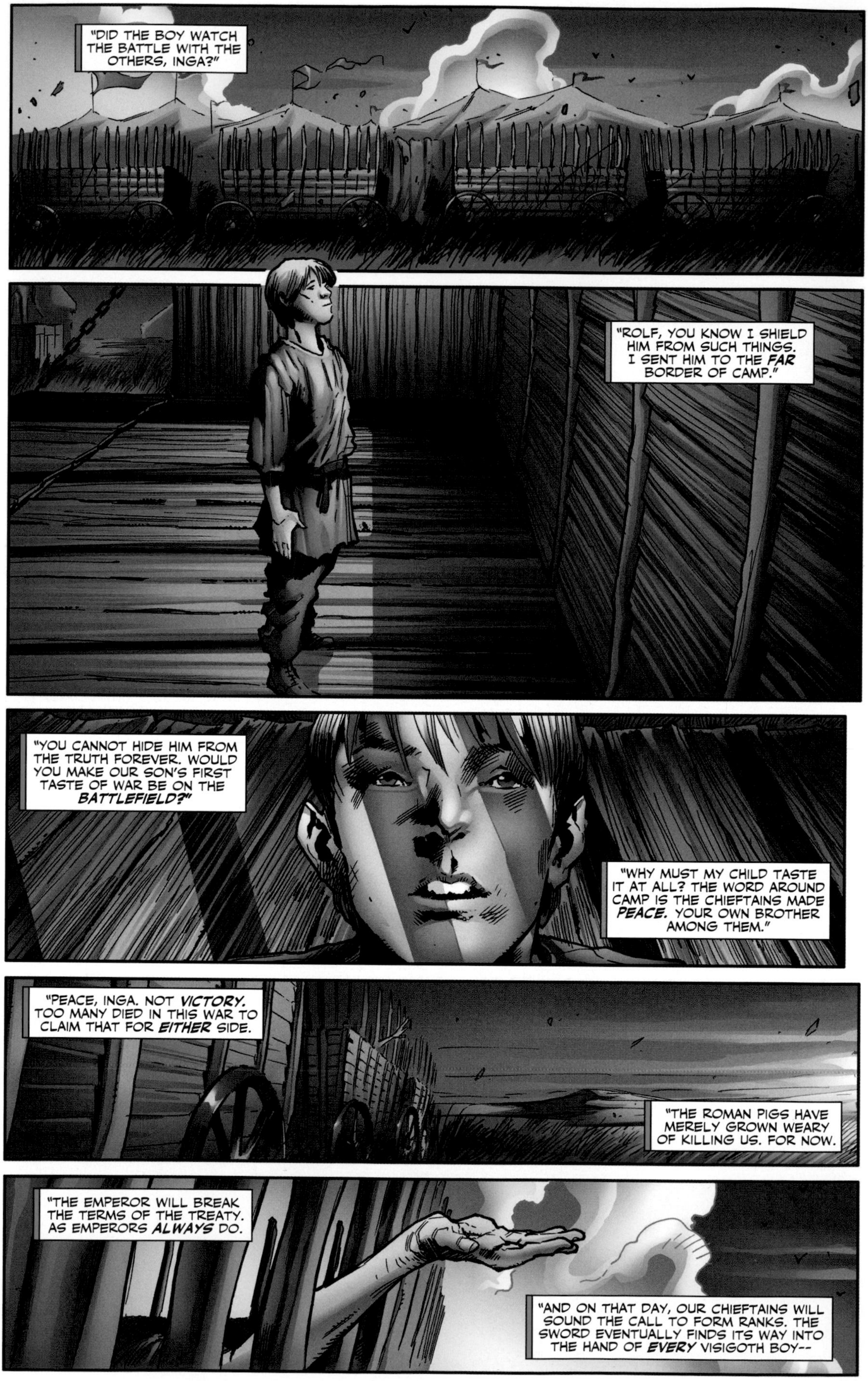
"DID THE BOY WATCH THE BATTLE WITH THE OTHERS, INGA?"
"ROLF, YOU KNOW I SHIELD HIM FROM SUCH THINGS. I SENT HIM TO THE FAR BORDER OF CAMP."
"YOU CANNOT HIDE HIM FROM THE TRUTH FOREVER. WOULD YOU MAKE OUR SON'S FIRST TASTE OF WAR BE ON THE BATTLEFIELD?"
"WHY MUST MY CHILD TASTE IT AT ALL? THE WORD AROUND CAMP IS THE CHIEFTAINS MADE PEACE. YOUR OWN BROTHER AMONG THEM."
"PEACE, INGA. NOT VICTORY. TOO MANY DIED IN THIS WAR TO CLAIM THAT FOR EITHER SIDE.
"THE ROMAN PIGS HAVE MERELY GROWN WEARY OF KILLING US. FOR NOW.
"THE EMPEROR WILL BREAK THE TERMS OF THE TREATY. AS EMPERORS ALWAYS DO.
"AND ON THAT DAY, OUR CHIEFTAINS WILL SOUND THE CALL TO FORM RANKS. THE SWORD EVENTUALLY FINDS ITS WAY INTO THE HAND OF EVERY VISIGOTH BOY--

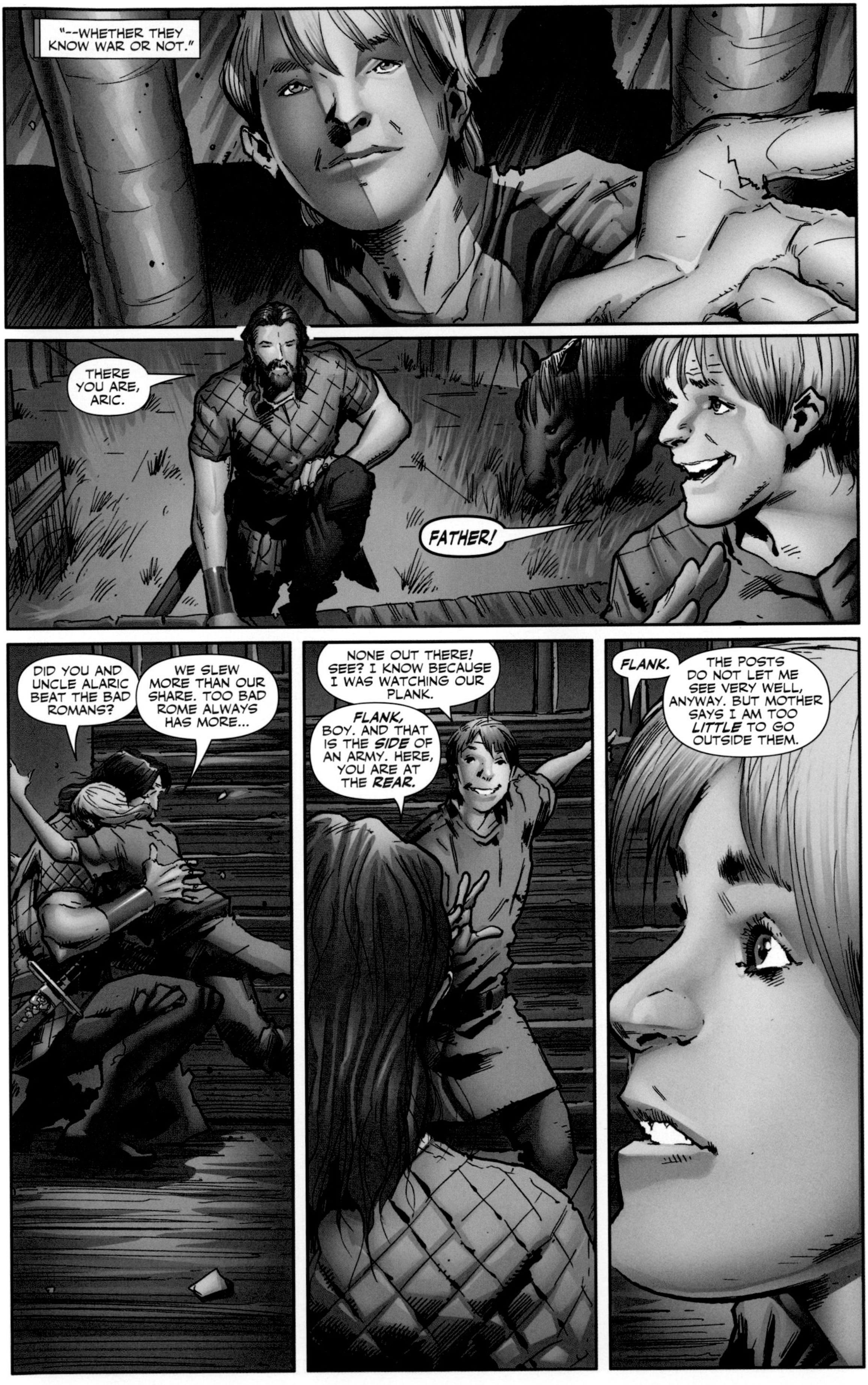
"--WHETHER THEY KNOW WAR OR NOT."
THERE YOU ARE, ARIC.
FATHER!
DID YOU AND UNCLE ALARIC BEAT THE BAD ROMANS?
WE SLEW MORE THAN OUR SHARE. TOO BAD ROME ALWAYS HAS MORE...
NONE OUT THERE! SEE? I KNOW BECAUSE I WAS WATCHING OUR PLANK.
FLANK, BOY. AND THAT IS THE SIDE OF AN ARMY. HERE, YOU ARE AT THE REAR.
FLANK.
THE POSTS DO NOT LET ME SEE VERY WELL, ANYWAY. BUT MOTHER SAYS I AM TOO LITTLE TO GO OUTSIDE THEM.

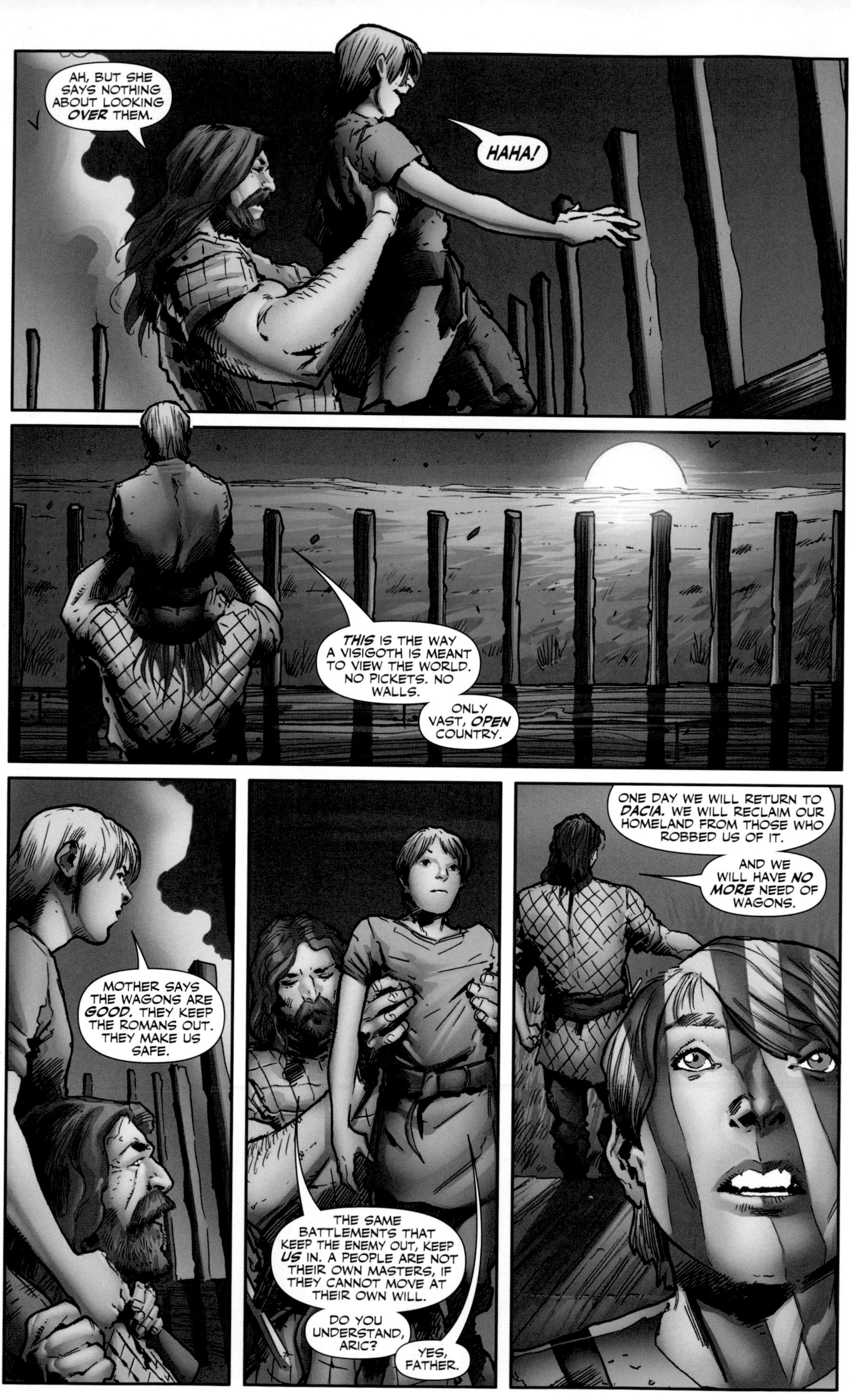
AH, BUT SHE SAYS NOTHING ABOUT LOOKING *OVER* THEM.
HAHA!
THIS IS THE WAY A VISIGOTH IS MEANT TO VIEW THE WORLD. NO PICKETS. NO WALLS.
ONLY VAST, *OPEN* COUNTRY.
MOTHER SAYS THE WAGONS ARE *GOOD.* THEY KEEP THE ROMANS OUT. THEY MAKE US SAFE.
THE SAME BATTLEMENTS THAT KEEP THE ENEMY OUT, KEEP *US* IN. A PEOPLE ARE NOT THEIR OWN MASTERS, IF THEY CANNOT MOVE AT THEIR OWN WILL.
DO YOU UNDERSTAND, ARIC?
YES, FATHER.
ONE DAY WE WILL RETURN TO *DACIA.* WE WILL RECLAIM OUR HOMELAND FROM THOSE WHO ROBBED US OF IT.
AND WE WILL HAVE *NO MORE* NEED OF WAGONS.

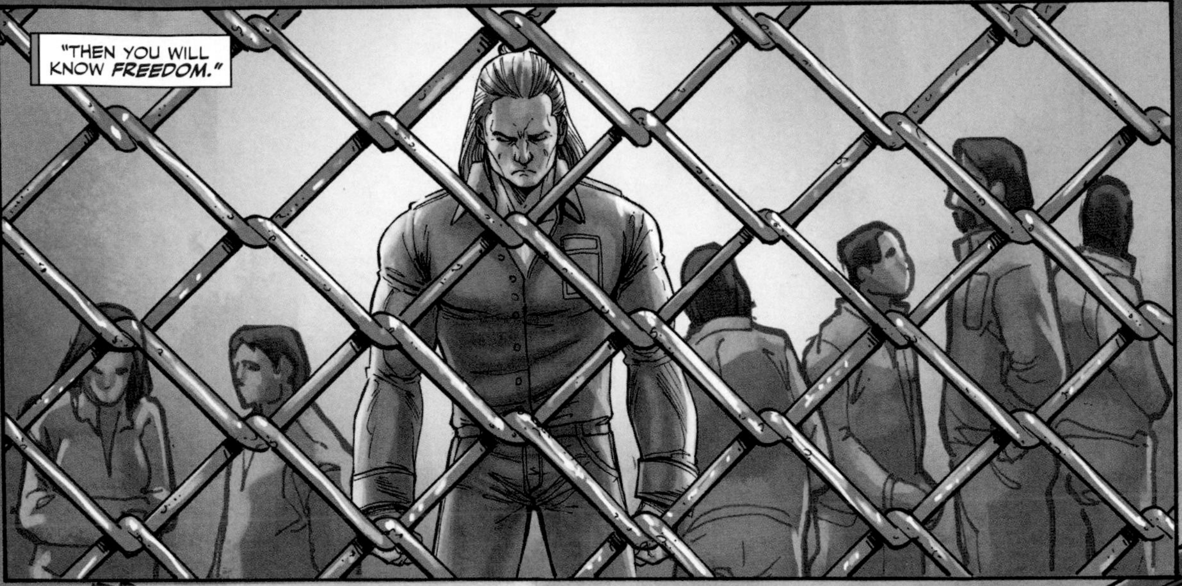
"THEN YOU WILL KNOW FREEDOM."

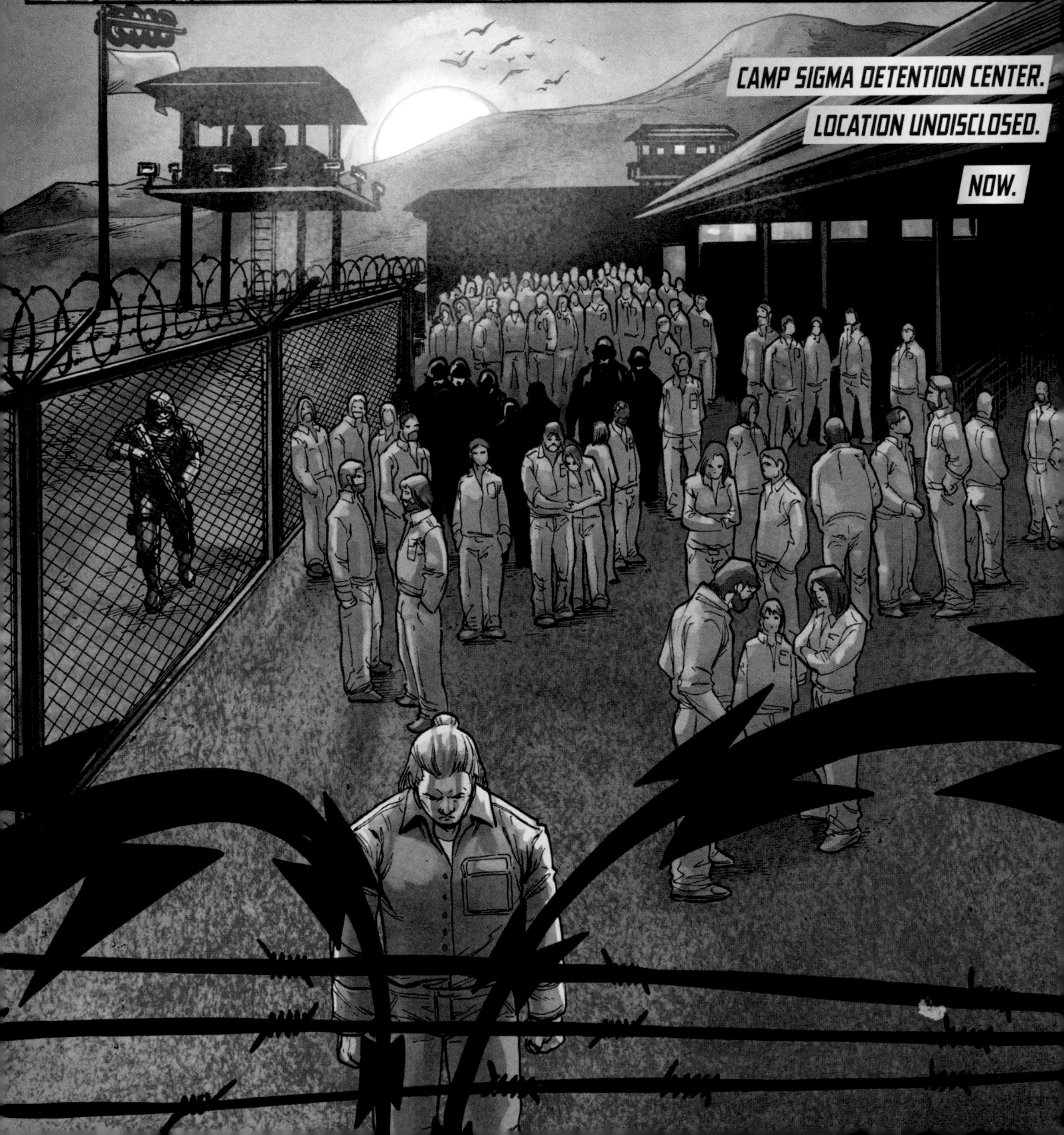
CAMP SIGMA DETENTION CENTER.
LOCATION UNDISCLOSED.
NOW.

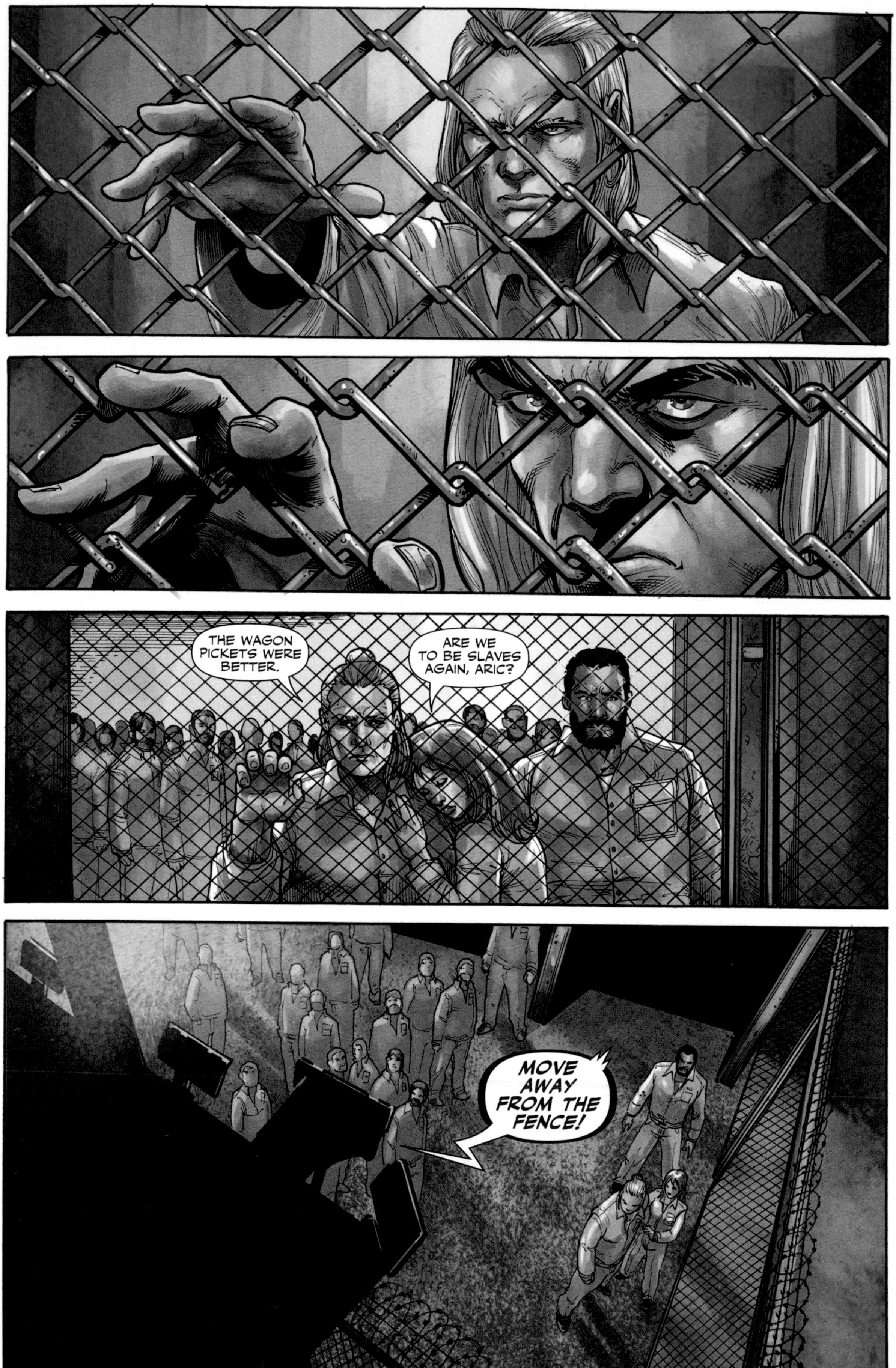
THE WAGON PICKETS WERE BETTER.
ARE WE TO BE SLAVES AGAIN, ARIC?
MOVE AWAY FROM THE FENCE!

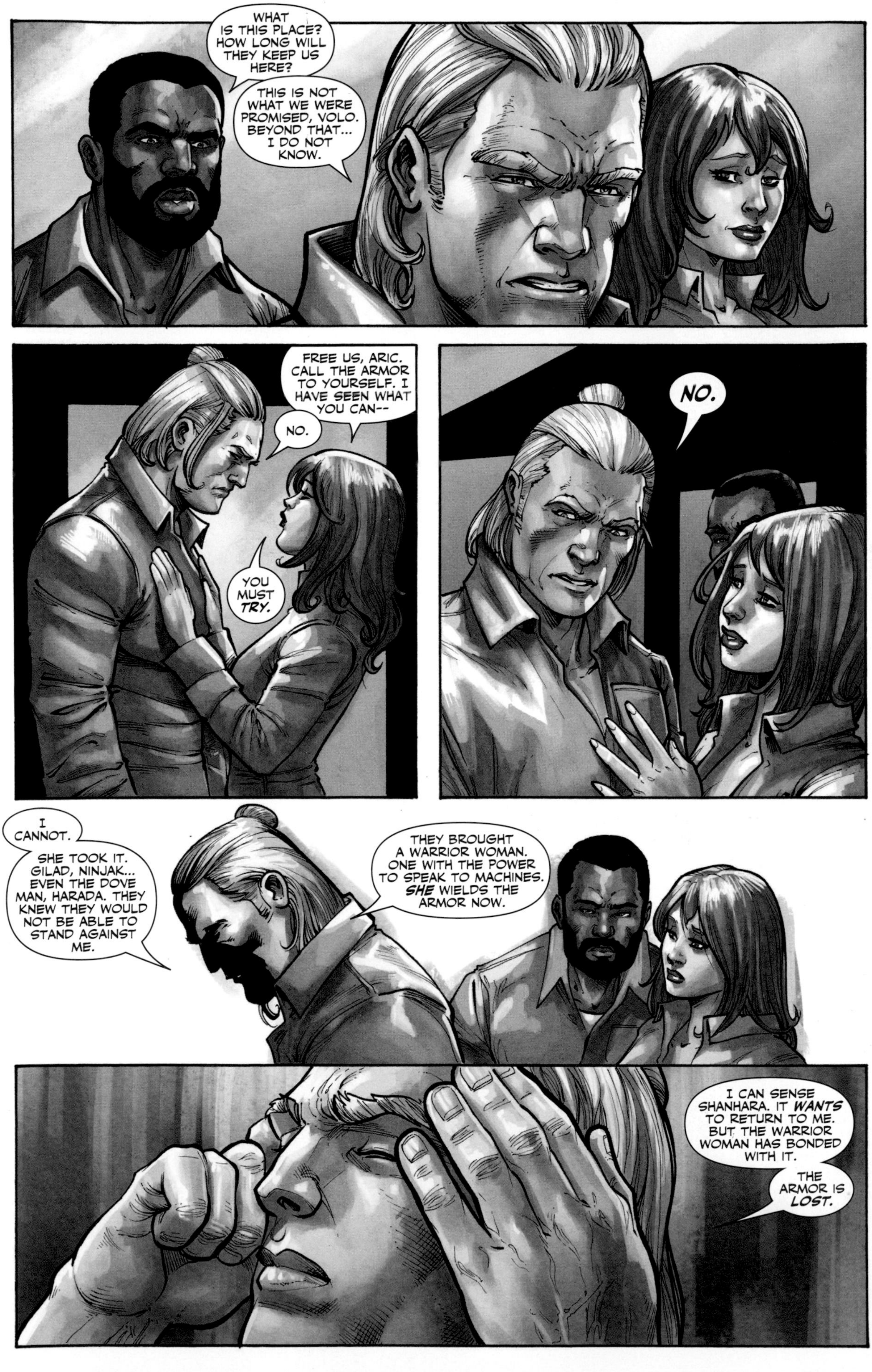
WHAT IS THIS PLACE? HOW LONG WILL THEY KEEP US HERE?
THIS IS NOT WHAT WE WERE PROMISED, VOLO. BEYOND THAT... I DO NOT KNOW.
FREE US, ARIC. CALL THE ARMOR TO YOURSELF. I HAVE SEEN WHAT YOU CAN--
NO.
YOU MUST *TRY.*
NO.
I CANNOT.
SHE TOOK IT. GILAD, NINJAK... EVEN THE DOVE MAN, HARADA. THEY KNEW THEY WOULD NOT BE ABLE TO STAND AGAINST ME.
THEY BROUGHT A WARRIOR WOMAN. ONE WITH THE POWER TO SPEAK TO MACHINES. *SHE* WIELDS THE ARMOR NOW.
I CAN SENSE SHANHARA. IT *WANTS* TO RETURN TO ME. BUT THE WARRIOR WOMAN HAS BONDED WITH IT.
THE ARMOR IS *LOST.*

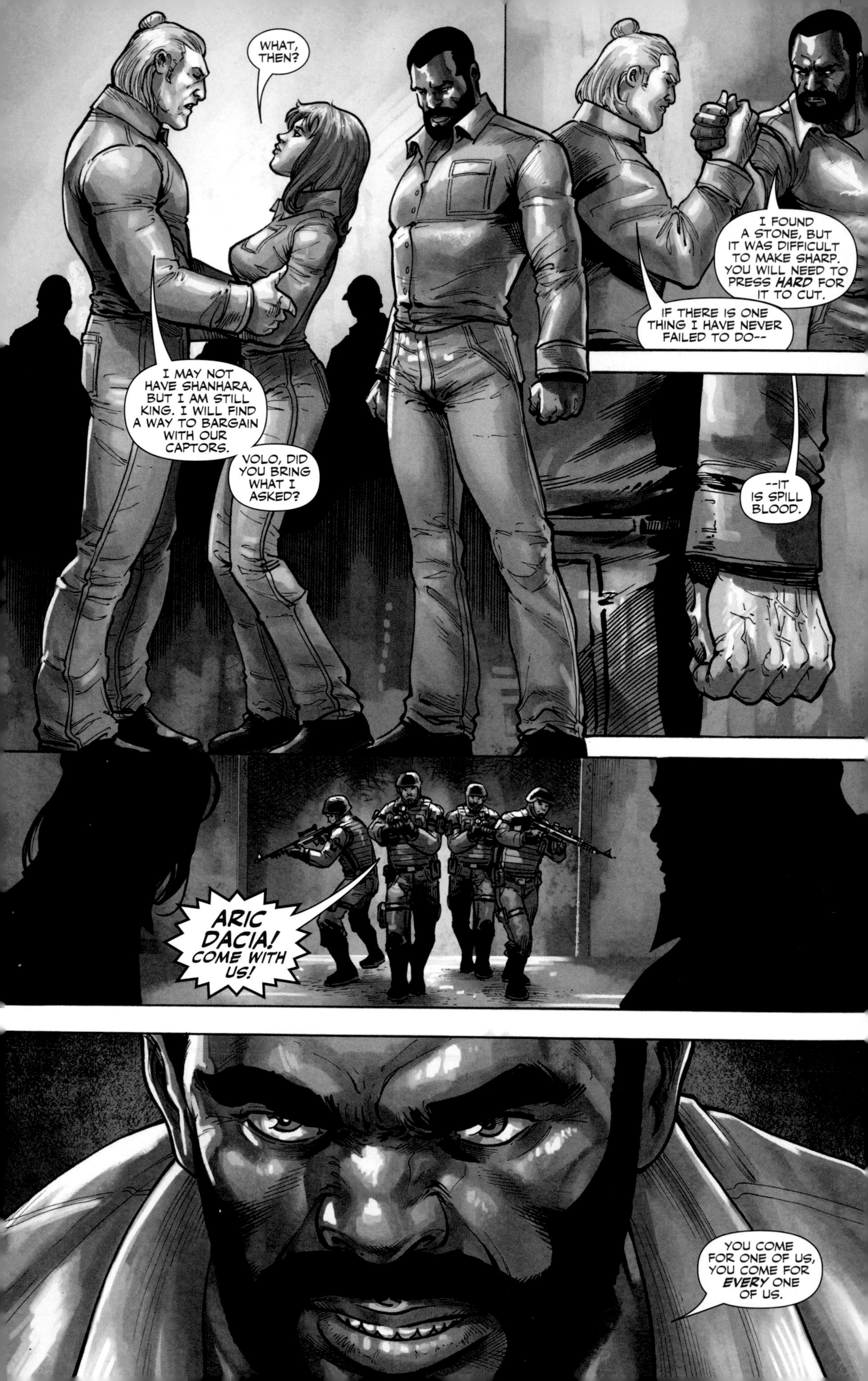
WHAT, THEN?
I MAY NOT HAVE SHANHARA, BUT I AM STILL KING. I WILL FIND A WAY TO BARGAIN WITH OUR CAPTORS.
VOLO, DID YOU BRING WHAT I ASKED?
I FOUND A STONE, BUT IT WAS DIFFICULT TO MAKE SHARP. YOU WILL NEED TO PRESS HARD FOR IT TO CUT.
IF THERE IS ONE THING I HAVE NEVER FAILED TO DO--
--IT IS SPILL BLOOD.
ARIC DACIA! COME WITH US!
YOU COME FOR ONE OF US, YOU COME FOR EVERY ONE OF US.

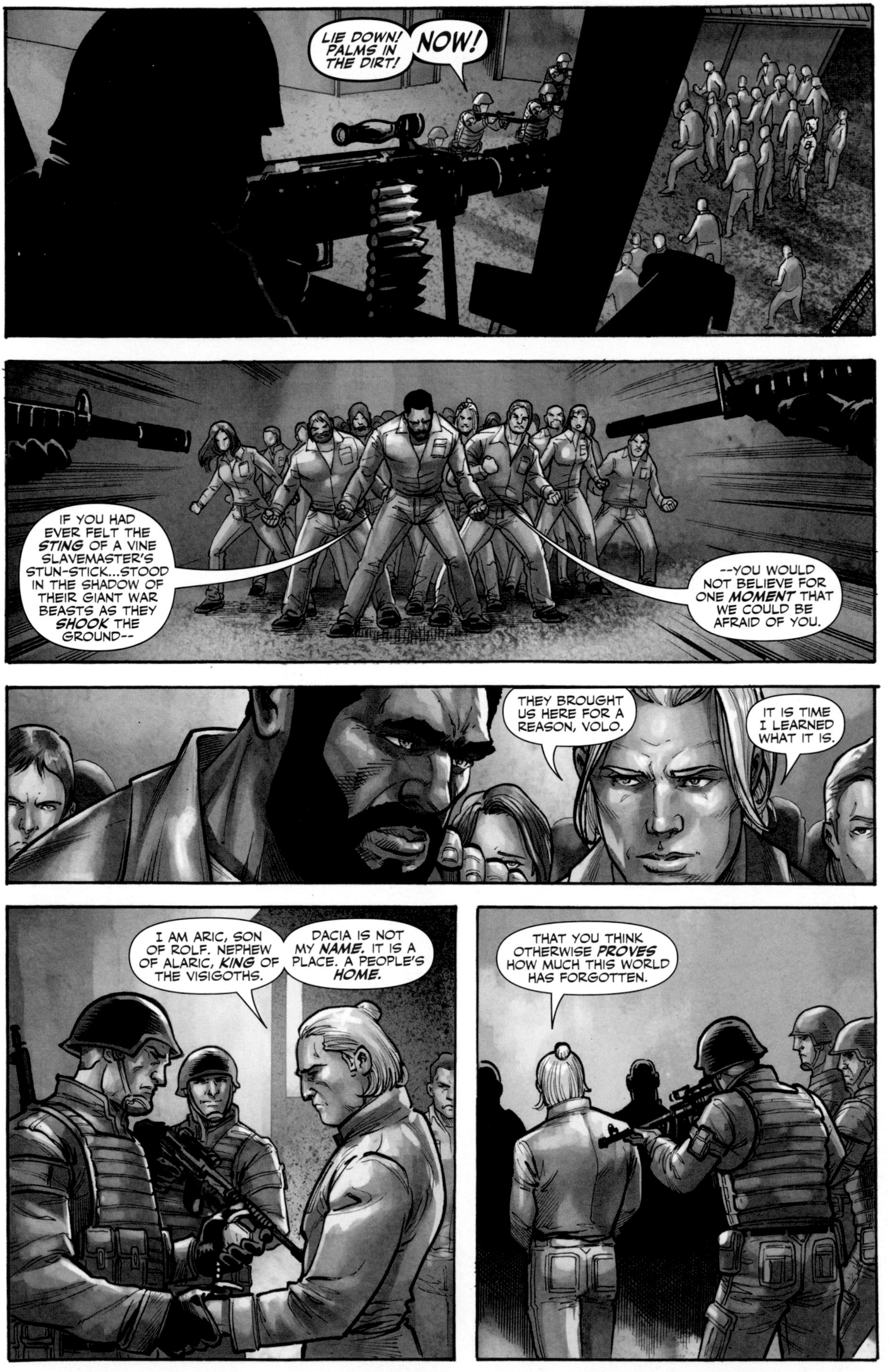
LIE DOWN! PALMS IN THE DIRT!
NOW!
IF YOU HAD EVER FELT THE STING OF A VINE SLAVEMASTER'S STUN-STICK...STOOD IN THE SHADOW OF THEIR GIANT WAR BEASTS AS THEY SHOOK THE GROUND--
--YOU WOULD NOT BELIEVE FOR ONE MOMENT THAT WE COULD BE AFRAID OF YOU.
THEY BROUGHT US HERE FOR A REASON, VOLO.
IT IS TIME I LEARNED WHAT IT IS.
I AM ARIC, SON OF ROLF. NEPHEW OF ALARIC, KING OF THE VISIGOTHS.
DACIA IS NOT MY NAME. IT IS A PLACE. A PEOPLE'S HOME.
THAT YOU THINK OTHERWISE PROVES HOW MUCH THIS WORLD HAS FORGOTTEN.

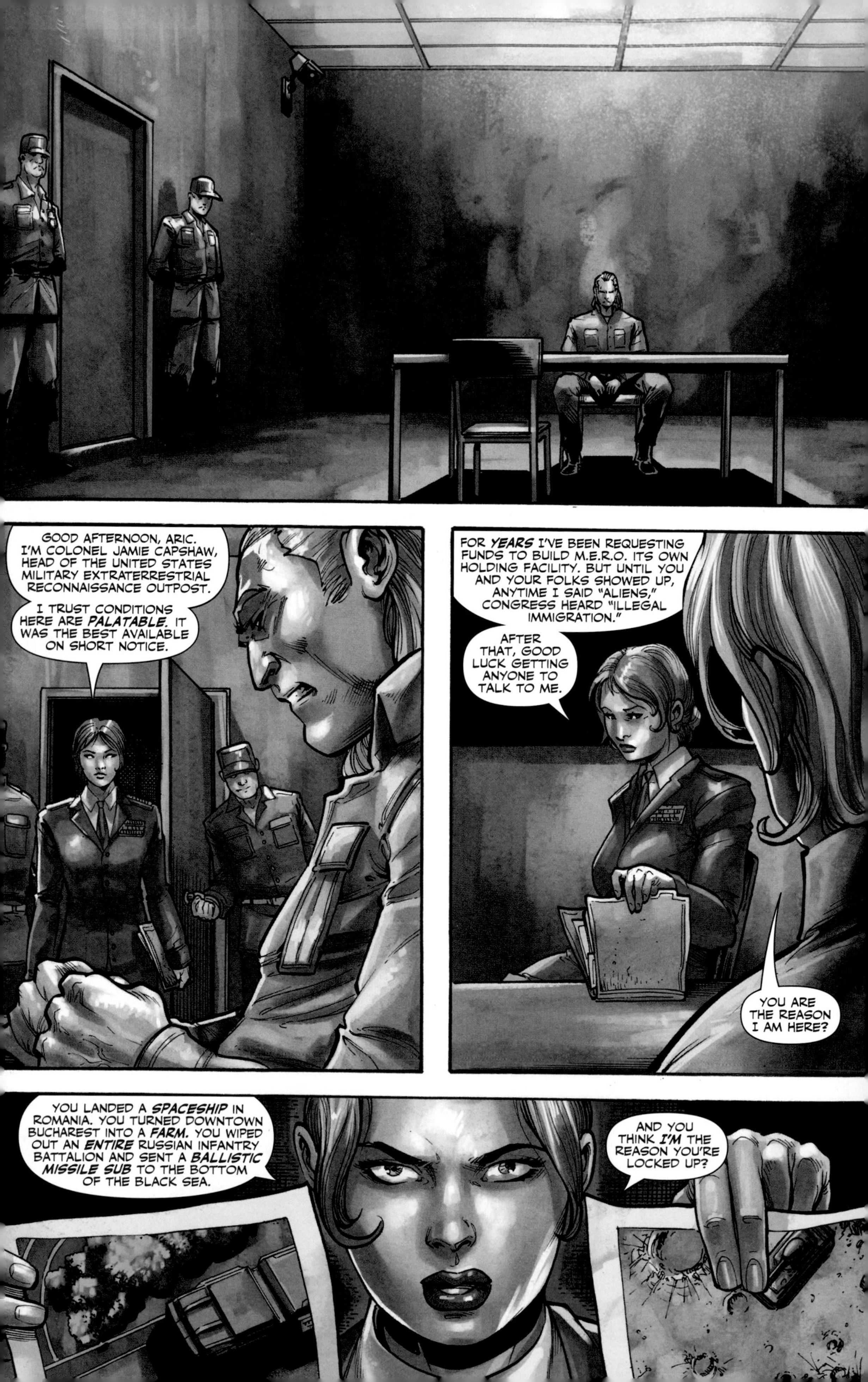
GOOD AFTERNOON, ARIC. I'M COLONEL JAMIE CAPSHAW, HEAD OF THE UNITED STATES MILITARY EXTRATERRESTRIAL RECONNAISSANCE OUTPOST.
I TRUST CONDITIONS HERE ARE PALATABLE. IT WAS THE BEST AVAILABLE ON SHORT NOTICE.
FOR YEARS I'VE BEEN REQUESTING FUNDS TO BUILD M.E.R.O. ITS OWN HOLDING FACILITY. BUT UNTIL YOU AND YOUR FOLKS SHOWED UP, ANYTIME I SAID "ALIENS," CONGRESS HEARD "ILLEGAL IMMIGRATION."
AFTER THAT, GOOD LUCK GETTING ANYONE TO TALK TO ME.
YOU ARE THE REASON I AM HERE?
YOU LANDED A SPACESHIP IN ROMANIA. YOU TURNED DOWNTOWN BUCHAREST INTO A FARM. YOU WIPED OUT AN ENTIRE RUSSIAN INFANTRY BATTALION AND SENT A BALLISTIC MISSILE SUB TO THE BOTTOM OF THE BLACK SEA.
AND YOU THINK I'M THE REASON YOU'RE LOCKED UP?

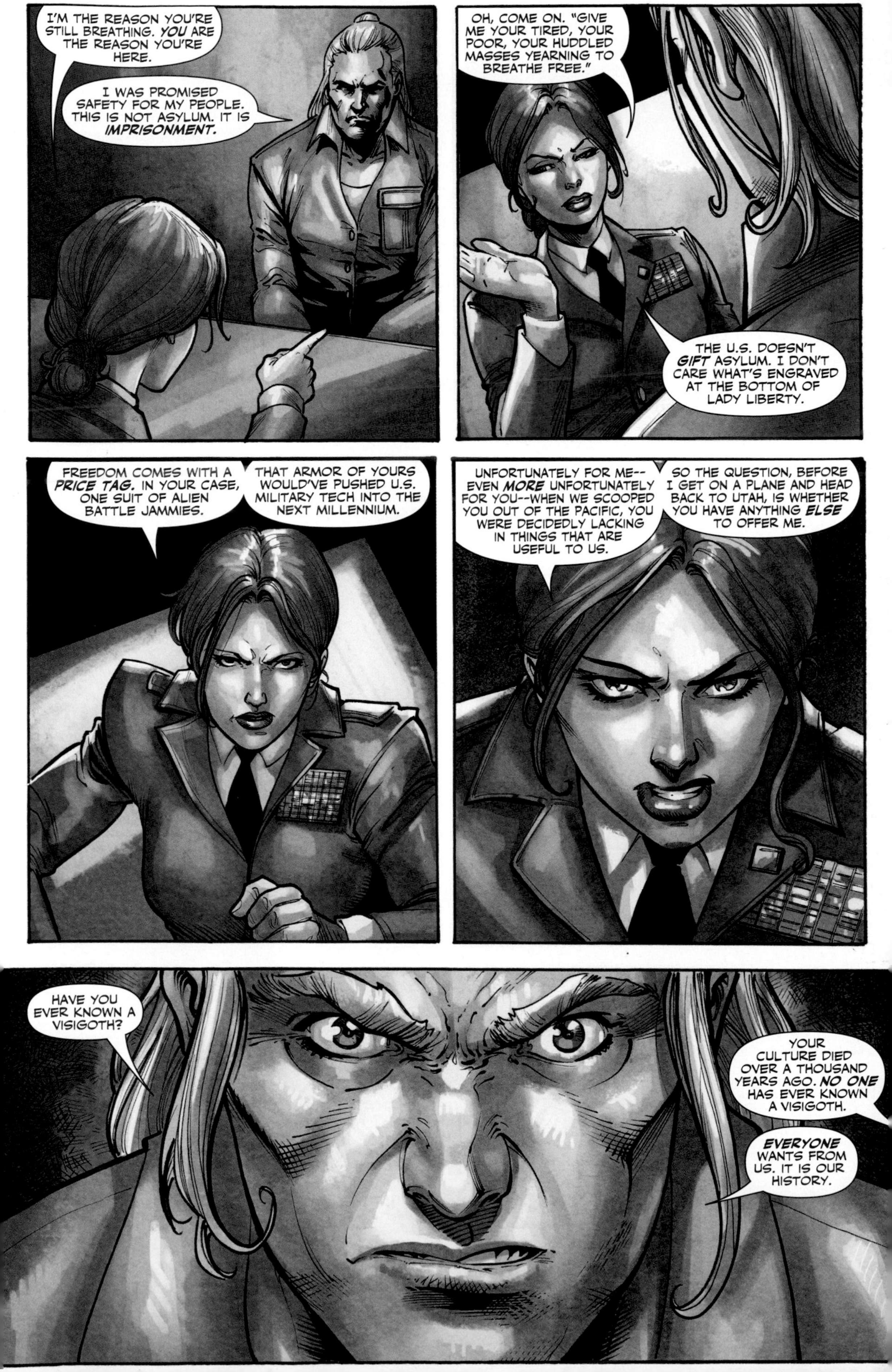

I'M THE REASON YOU'RE STILL BREATHING. *YOU* ARE THE REASON YOU'RE HERE.
I WAS PROMISED SAFETY FOR MY PEOPLE. THIS IS NOT ASYLUM. IT IS *IMPRISONMENT.*
OH, COME ON. "GIVE ME YOUR TIRED, YOUR POOR, YOUR HUDDLED MASSES YEARNING TO BREATHE FREE."
THE U.S. DOESN'T *GIFT* ASYLUM. I DON'T CARE WHAT'S ENGRAVED AT THE BOTTOM OF LADY LIBERTY.
FREEDOM COMES WITH A *PRICE TAG.* IN YOUR CASE, ONE SUIT OF ALIEN BATTLE JAMMIES.
THAT ARMOR OF YOURS WOULD'VE PUSHED U.S. MILITARY TECH INTO THE NEXT MILLENNIUM.
UNFORTUNATELY FOR ME-- EVEN *MORE* UNFORTUNATELY FOR YOU--WHEN WE SCOOPED YOU OUT OF THE PACIFIC, YOU WERE DECIDEDLY LACKING IN THINGS THAT ARE USEFUL TO US.
SO THE QUESTION, BEFORE I GET ON A PLANE AND HEAD BACK TO UTAH, IS WHETHER YOU HAVE ANYTHING *ELSE* TO OFFER ME.
HAVE YOU EVER KNOWN A VISIGOTH?
YOUR CULTURE DIED OVER A THOUSAND YEARS AGO. *NO ONE* HAS EVER KNOWN A VISIGOTH.
EVERYONE WANTS FROM US. IT IS OUR HISTORY.

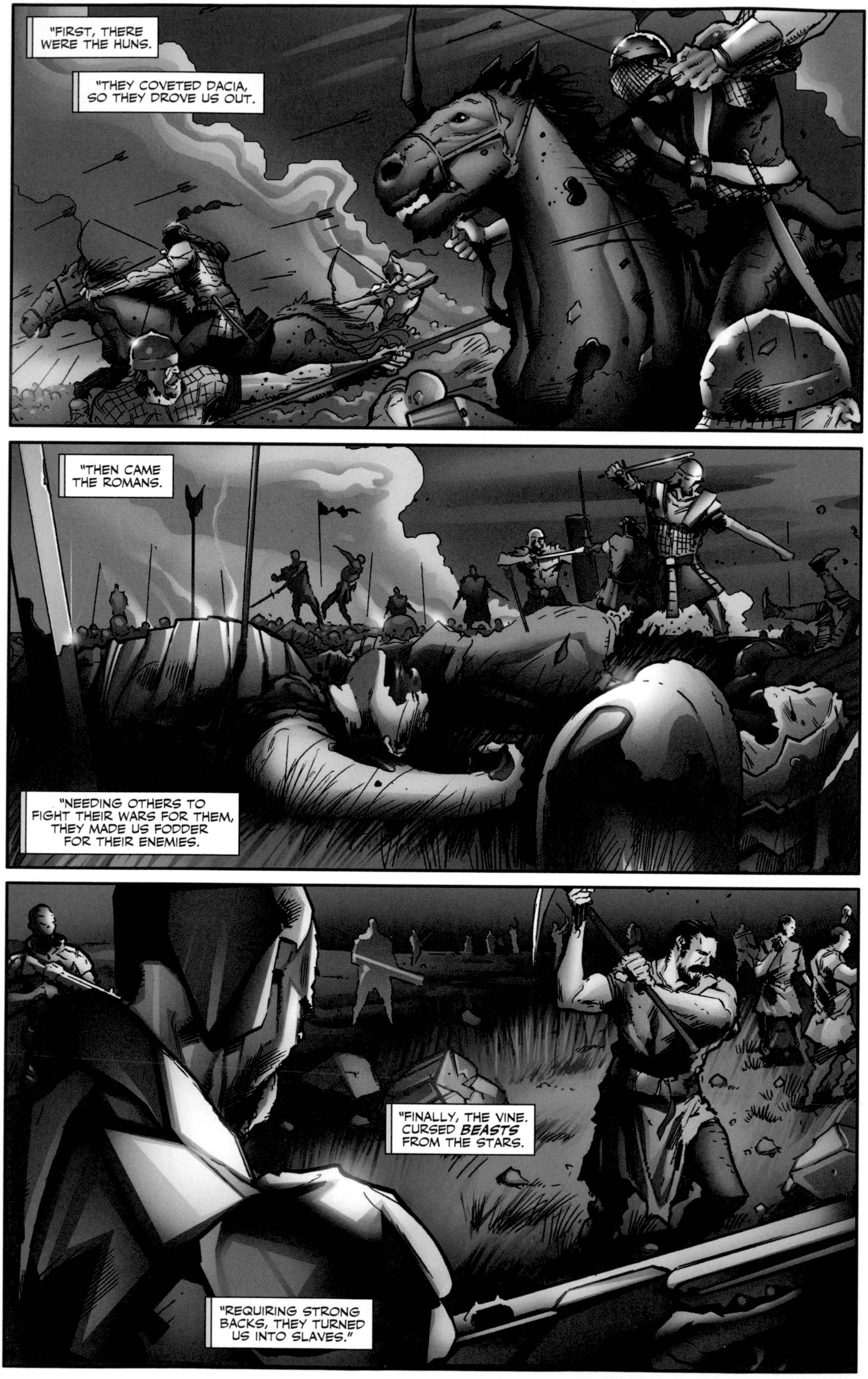
"FIRST, THERE WERE THE HUNS.
"THEY COVETED DACIA, SO THEY DROVE US OUT.
"THEN CAME THE ROMANS.
"NEEDING OTHERS TO FIGHT THEIR WARS FOR THEM, THEY MADE US FODDER FOR THEIR ENEMIES.
"FINALLY, THE VINE. CURSED BEASTS FROM THE STARS.
"REQUIRING STRONG BACKS, THEY TURNED US INTO SLAVES."

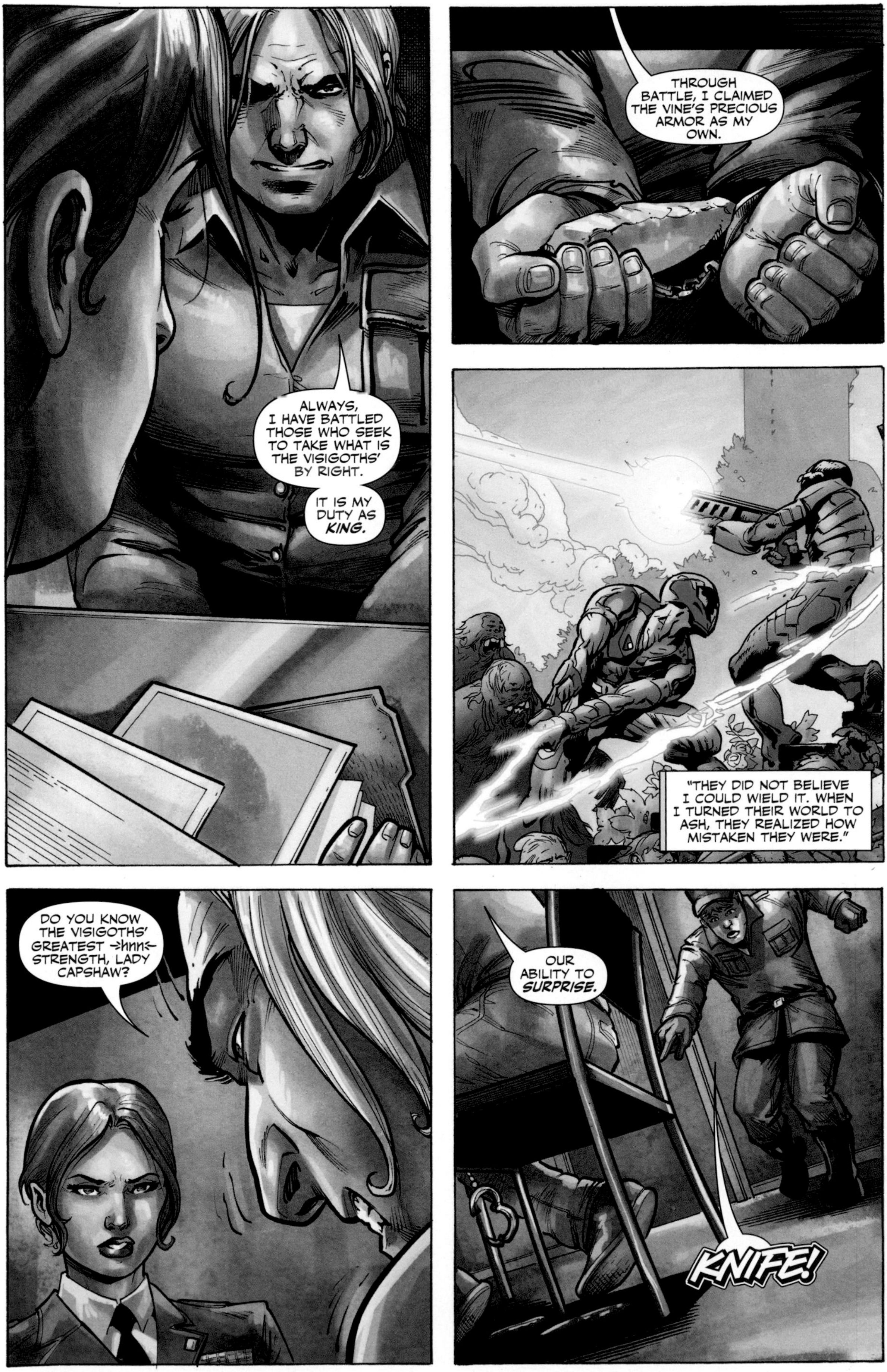
ALWAYS, I HAVE BATTLED THOSE WHO SEEK TO TAKE WHAT IS THE VISIGOTHS' BY RIGHT.
IT IS MY DUTY AS *KING.*
THROUGH BATTLE, I CLAIMED THE VINE'S PRECIOUS ARMOR AS MY OWN.
"THEY DID NOT BELIEVE I COULD WIELD IT. WHEN I TURNED THEIR WORLD TO ASH, THEY REALIZED HOW MISTAKEN THEY WERE."
DO YOU KNOW THE VISIGOTHS' GREATEST -hnn- STRENGTH, LADY CAPSHAW?
OUR ABILITY TO *SURPRISE.*
KNIFE!

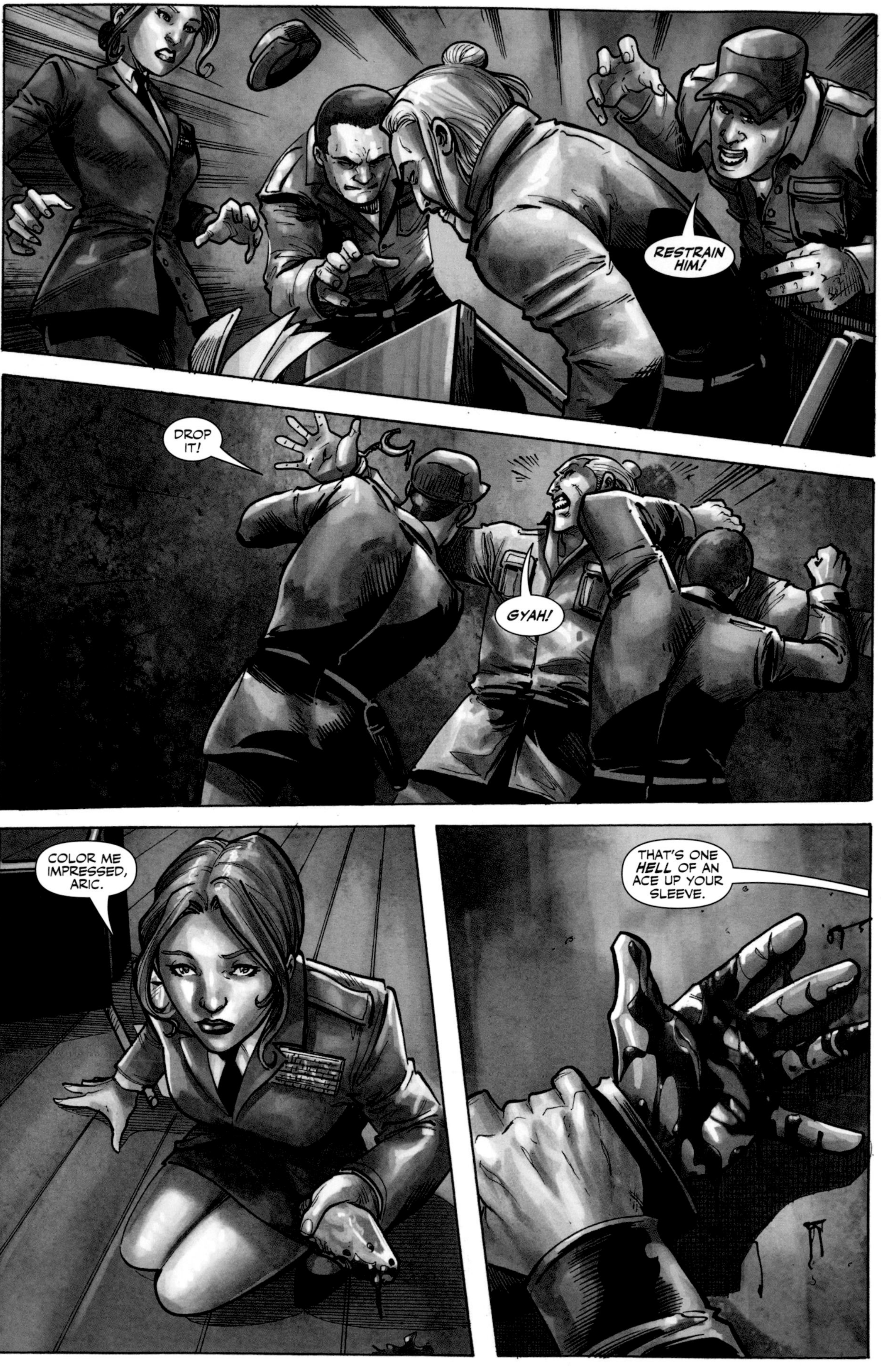
RESTRAIN HIM!
DROP IT!
GYAH!
COLOR ME IMPRESSED, ARIC.
THAT'S ONE HELL OF AN ACE UP YOUR SLEEVE.

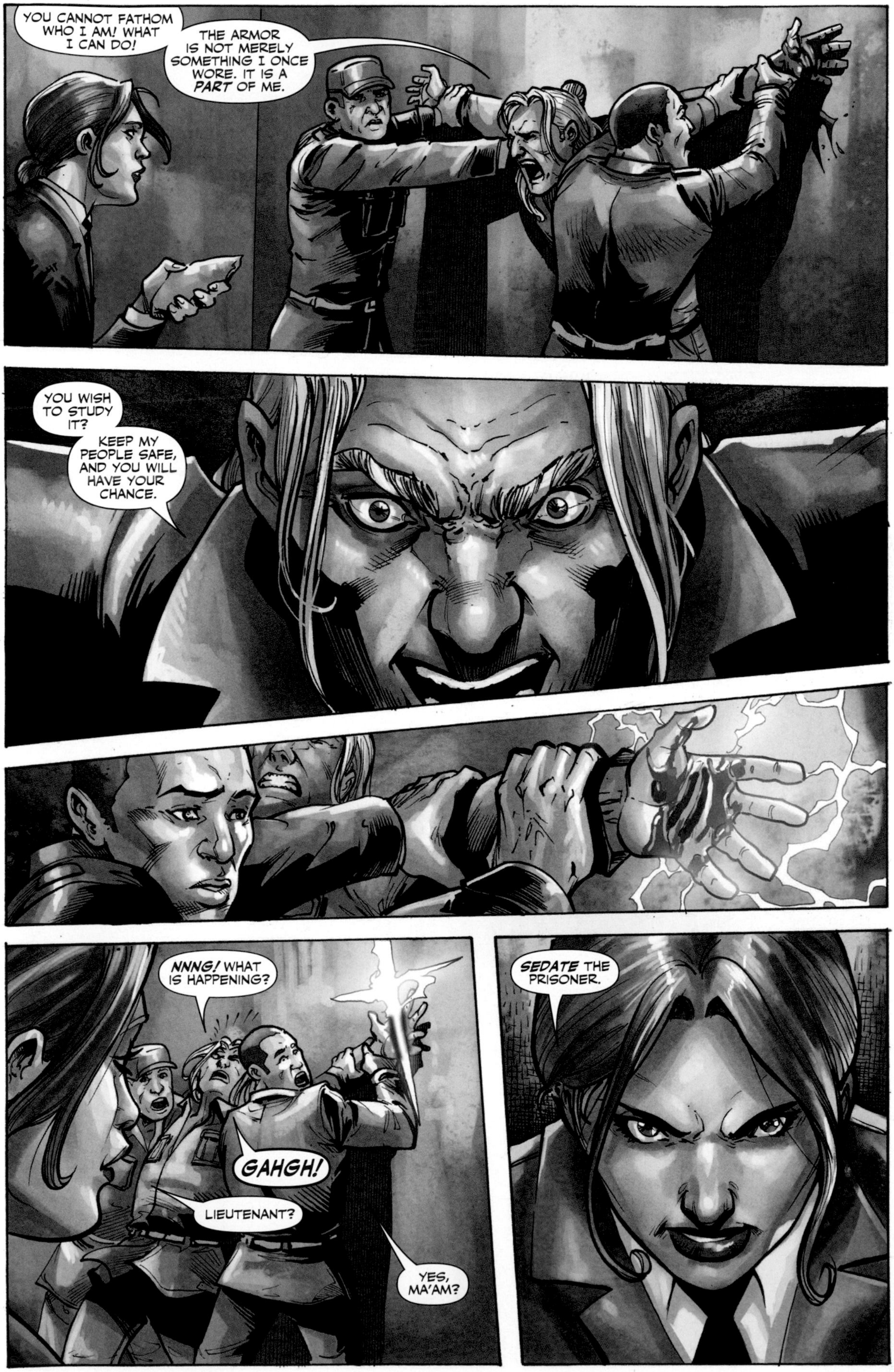
YOU CANNOT FATHOM WHO I AM! WHAT I CAN DO!
THE ARMOR IS NOT MERELY SOMETHING I ONCE WORE. IT IS A *PART* OF ME.
YOU WISH TO STUDY IT?
KEEP MY PEOPLE SAFE, AND YOU WILL HAVE YOUR CHANCE.
NNNG! WHAT IS HAPPENING?
GAHGH!
LIEUTENANT?
YES, MA'AM?
SEDATE THE PRISONER.

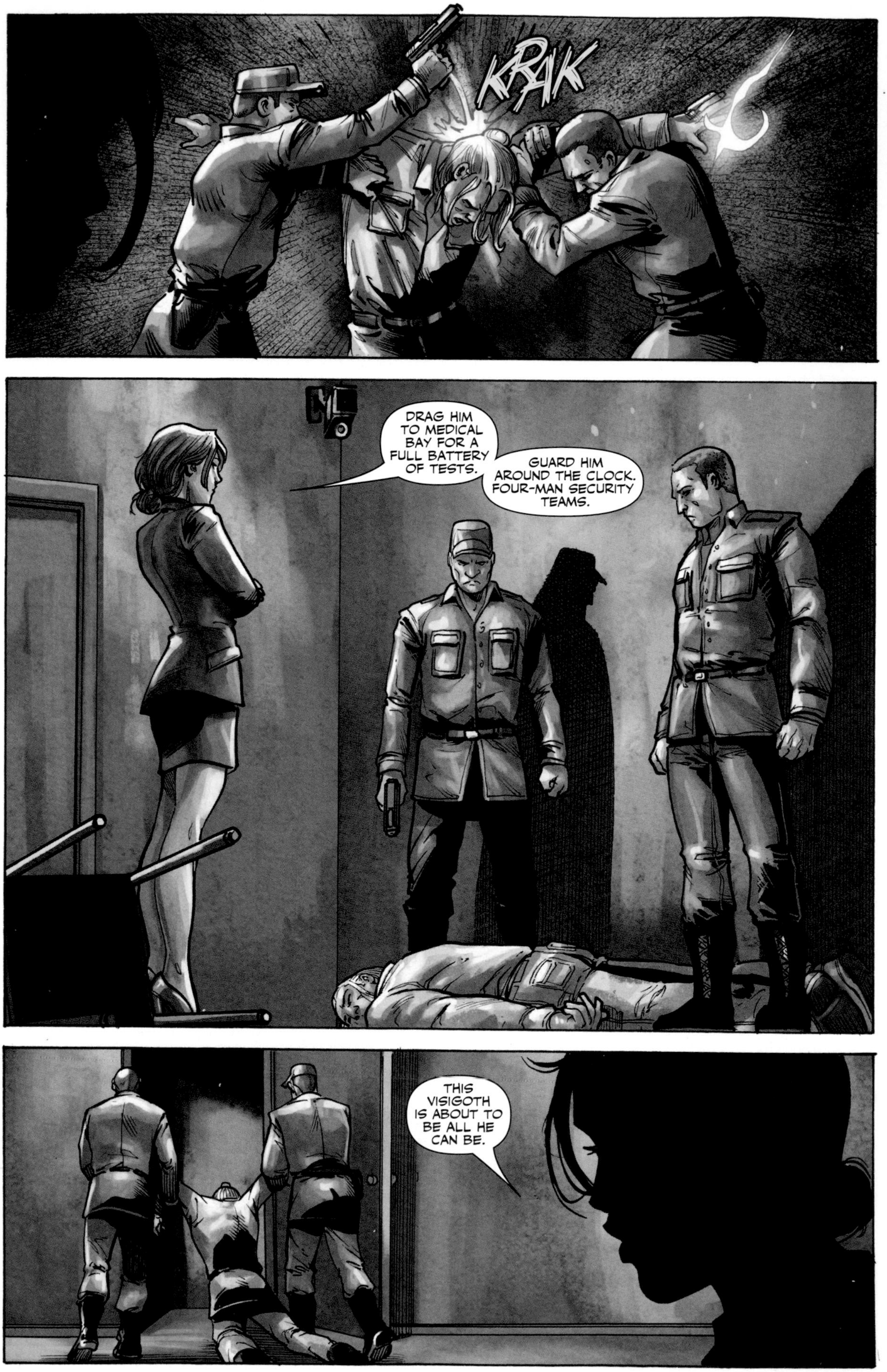
KRAK
DRAG HIM TO MEDICAL BAY FOR A FULL BATTERY OF TESTS.
GUARD HIM AROUND THE CLOCK. FOUR-MAN SECURITY TEAMS.
THIS VISIGOTH IS ABOUT TO BE ALL HE CAN BE.

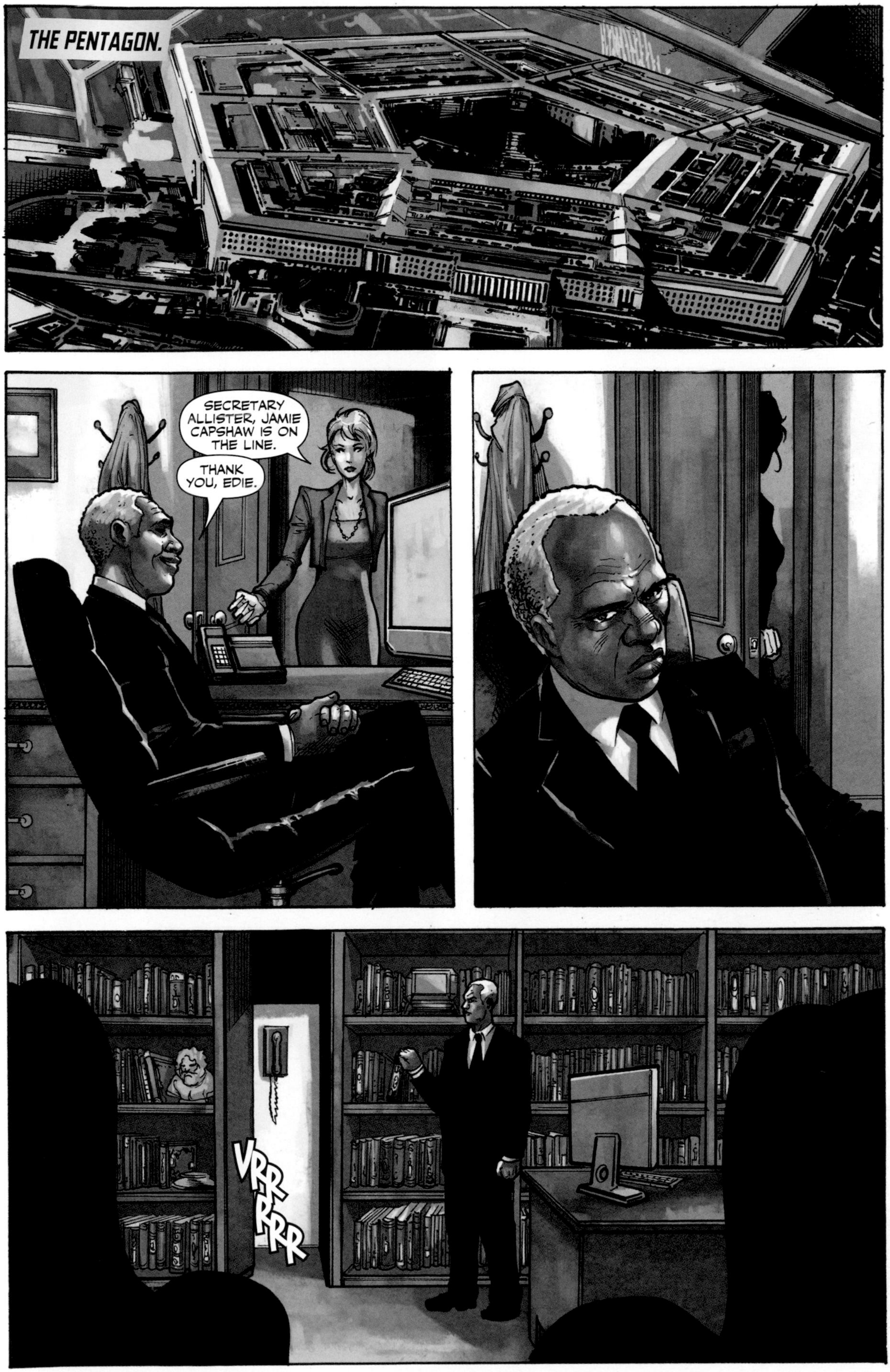
THE PENTAGON.
SECRETARY ALLISTER, JAMIE CAPSHAW IS ON THE LINE.
THANK YOU, EDIE.
VRRRRRR

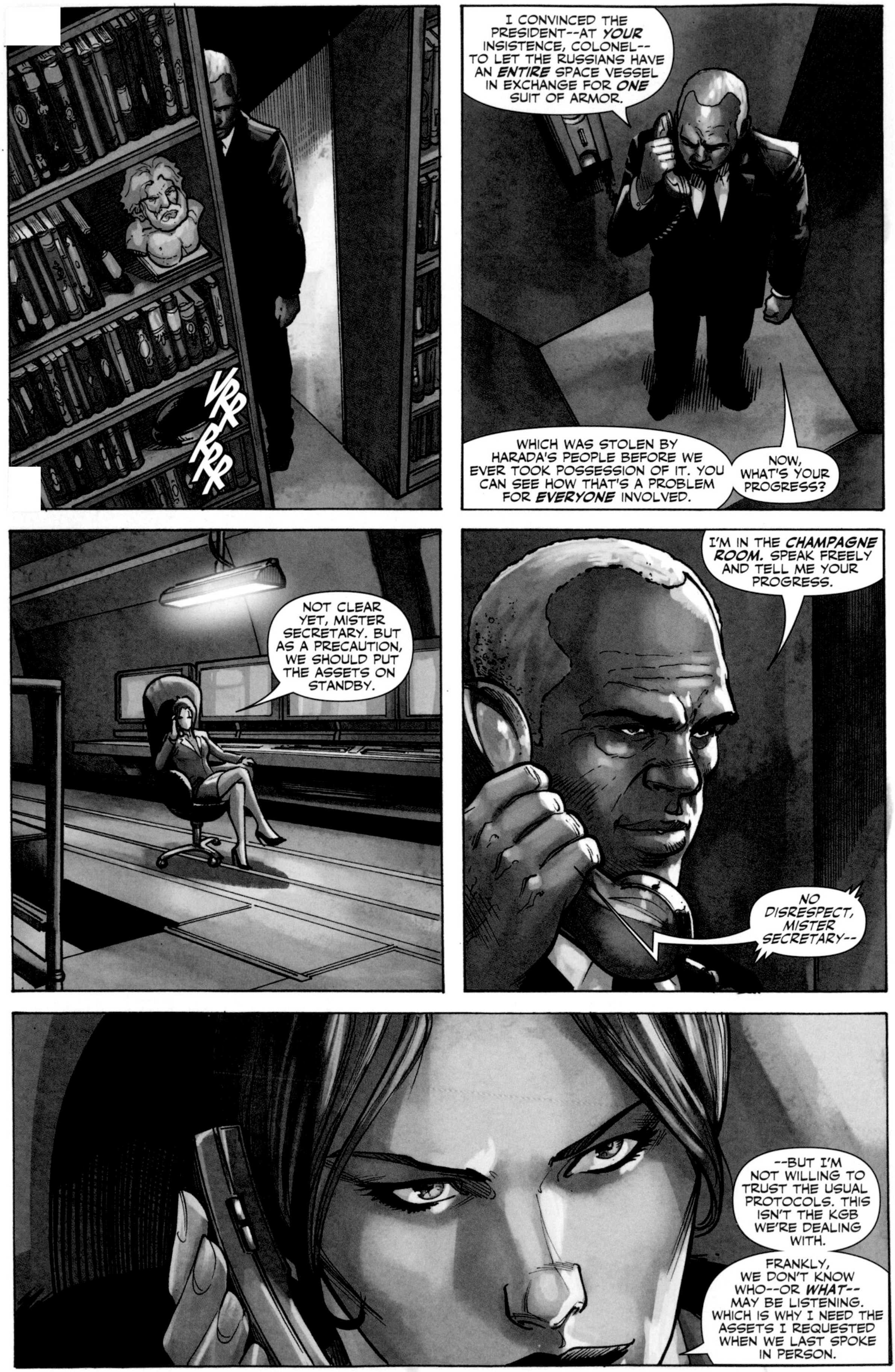
VRRRRRR
I CONVINCED THE PRESIDENT--AT *YOUR* INSISTENCE, COLONEL--TO LET THE RUSSIANS HAVE AN *ENTIRE* SPACE VESSEL IN EXCHANGE FOR *ONE* SUIT OF ARMOR.
WHICH WAS STOLEN BY HARADA'S PEOPLE BEFORE WE EVER TOOK POSSESSION OF IT. YOU CAN SEE HOW THAT'S A PROBLEM FOR *EVERYONE* INVOLVED.
NOW, WHAT'S YOUR PROGRESS?
NOT CLEAR YET, MISTER SECRETARY. BUT AS A PRECAUTION, WE SHOULD PUT THE ASSETS ON STANDBY.
I'M IN THE *CHAMPAGNE ROOM.* SPEAK FREELY AND TELL ME YOUR PROGRESS.
NO DISRESPECT, MISTER SECRETARY--
--BUT I'M NOT WILLING TO TRUST THE USUAL PROTOCOLS. THIS ISN'T THE KGB WE'RE DEALING WITH.
FRANKLY, WE DON'T KNOW WHO--OR *WHAT*--MAY BE LISTENING. WHICH IS WHY I NEED THE ASSETS I REQUESTED WHEN WE LAST SPOKE IN PERSON.

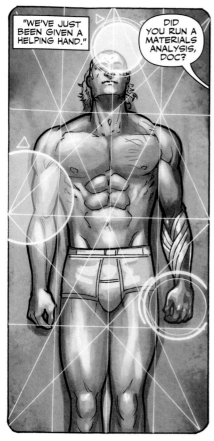

"WE'VE JUST BEEN GIVEN A HELPING HAND."

DID YOU RUN A MATERIALS ANALYSIS, DOC?

I CONDUCTED AN *EVERYTHING* ANALYSIS.

ALL I KNOW IS IT ISN'T FROM AROUND HERE. NOR DOES IT MATCH ANY OF THE VINE TECH WE RECOVERED FROM THE ATTACK IN MANHATTAN.

AND? WHAT'S THAT RUNNING ALL THE WAY UP HIS ARM?

WHAT ARE WE LOOKING AT? SOME KIND OF EXTRA-TERRESTRIAL PROSTHETIC?

AND ENOUGH WITH THE, "I DON'T KNOW." THE WORLD IS FULL OF PEOPLE WHO DON'T KNOW THINGS. THAT'S NOT WHAT I CONTRACTED YOU FOR.

YOU'RE ASKING ME TO USE *GRAY'S ANATOMY* TO DIAGNOSE THE *FICTIONAL.* IT CAN'T BE DONE.

HOW MUCH GAS ARE YOU PUMPING IN?

ENOUGH TO OVERDOSE A PLUS-SIZED ELEPHANT. I'VE UPPED IT THREE TIMES. SOMEHOW, HIS BODY KEEPS COMPENSATING.

VENT IT.

HE'LL WAKE UP--

DO IT.

A NORMAL PATIENT WOULD BE GROGGY, BUT MY GUESS IS HE'LL COME RIGHT OUT OF IT.

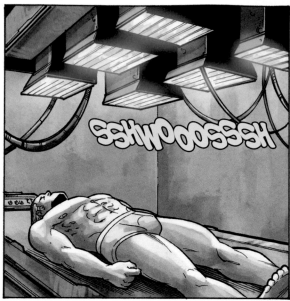

SSHWOOOSSSH

I SAT WITH YOU AS A KING ON BEHALF OF HIS PEOPLE. AND *THIS* IS HOW YOU TREAT ME?

MISTAKES WERE MADE ON BOTH SIDES, ARIC.

I'M PUTTING DOWN MY WEAPON. KILL ME IF YOU LIKE.

OR WE COULD TALK ABOUT WHAT AMERICA CAN DO FOR YOU...

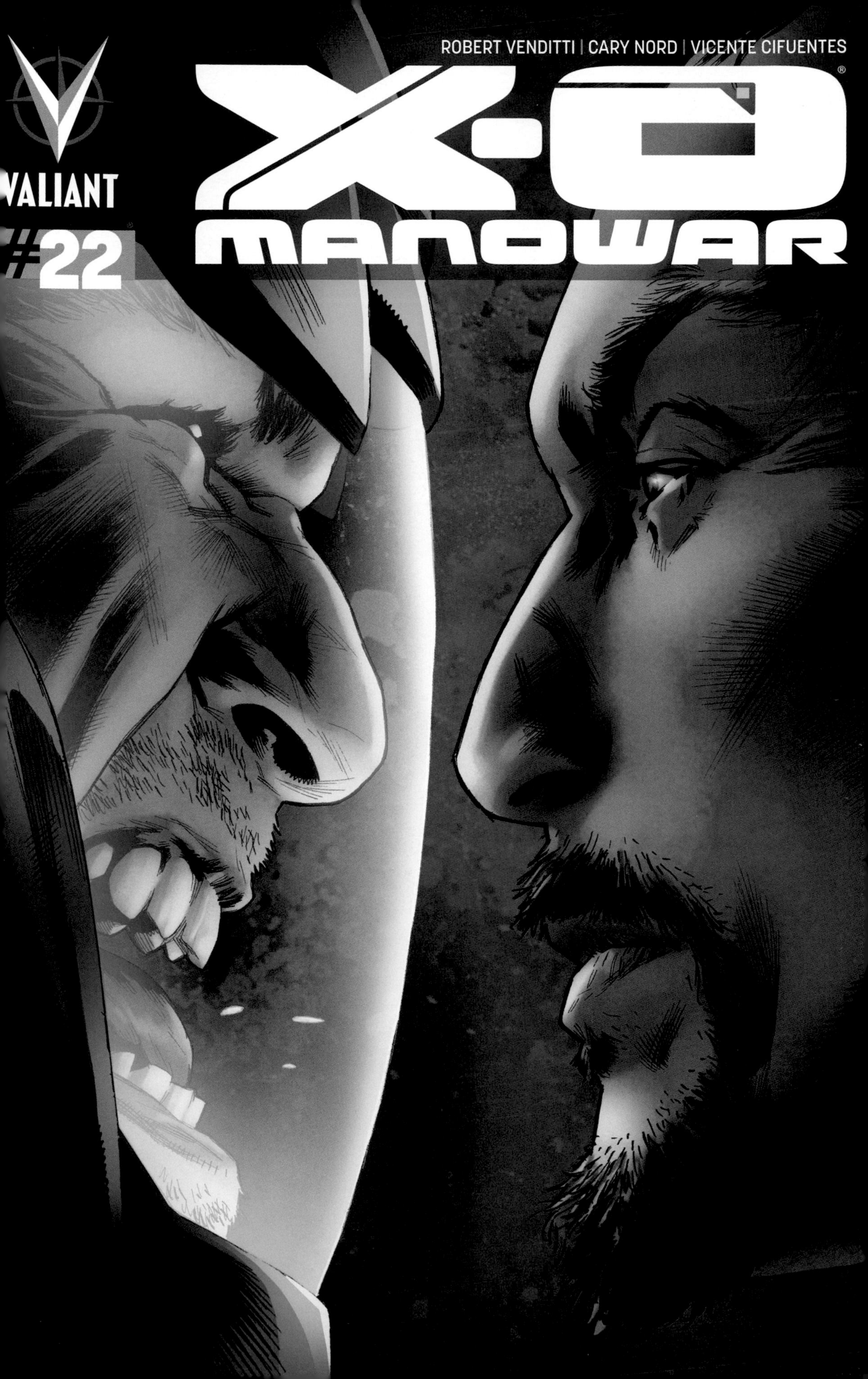
ROBERT VENDITTI | CARY NORD | VICENTE CIFUENTES
X-O MANOWAR
VALIANT
#22

PREVIOUSLY IN...

UNITY

Having ended Aric's occupation of Romania and negotiated the stand-down of the Russian and Chinese militaries, the members of Unity must decide the final fate of the X-O Manowar armor and contend with the emerging threat from one of their own...

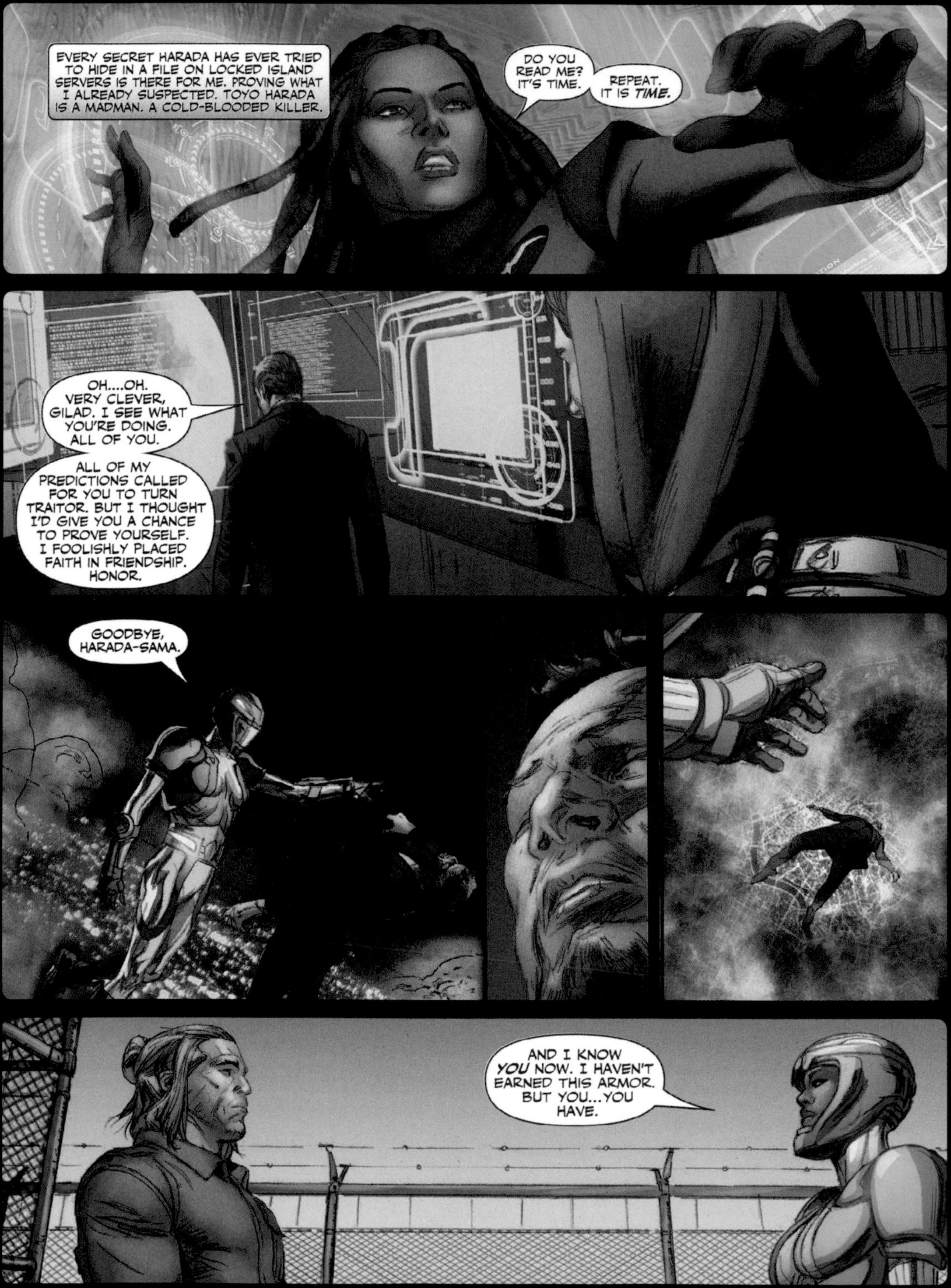

EVERY SECRET HARADA HAS EVER TRIED TO HIDE IN A FILE ON LOCKED ISLAND SERVERS IS THERE FOR ME. PROVING WHAT I ALREADY SUSPECTED. TOYO HARADA IS A MADMAN. A COLD-BLOODED KILLER.
DO YOU READ ME? IT'S TIME.
REPEAT. IT IS *TIME.*
OH....OH. VERY CLEVER, GILAD. I SEE WHAT YOU'RE DOING. ALL OF YOU.
ALL OF MY PREDICTIONS CALLED FOR YOU TO TURN TRAITOR. BUT I THOUGHT I'D GIVE YOU A CHANCE TO PROVE YOURSELF. I FOOLISHLY PLACED FAITH IN FRIENDSHIP. HONOR.
GOODBYE, HARADA-SAMA.
AND I KNOW *YOU* NOW. I HAVEN'T EARNED THIS ARMOR. BUT YOU...YOU HAVE.

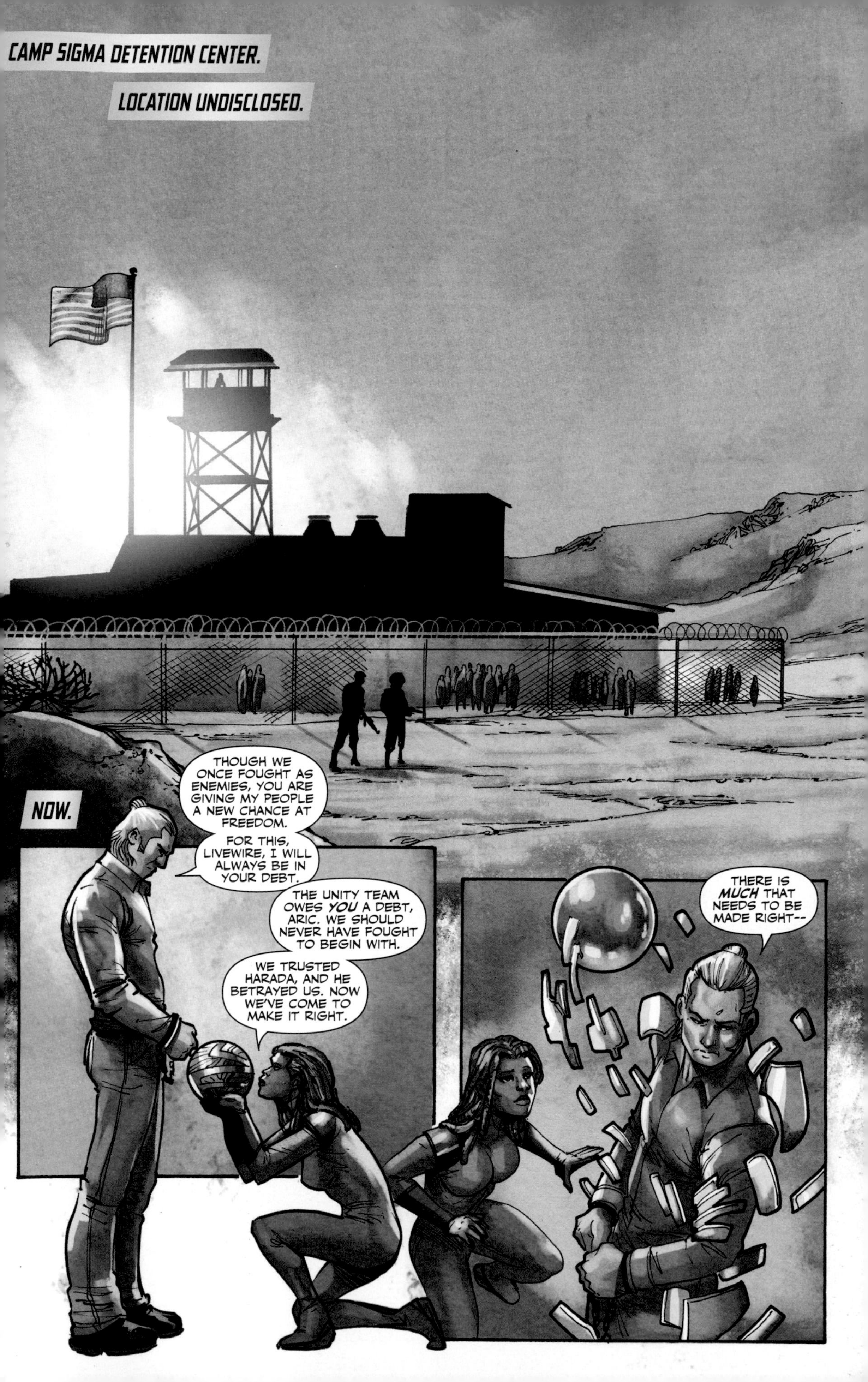
CAMP SIGMA DETENTION CENTER.
LOCATION UNDISCLOSED.
NOW.
THOUGH WE ONCE FOUGHT AS ENEMIES, YOU ARE GIVING MY PEOPLE A NEW CHANCE AT FREEDOM.
FOR THIS, LIVEWIRE, I WILL ALWAYS BE IN YOUR DEBT.
THE UNITY TEAM OWES YOU A DEBT, ARIC. WE SHOULD NEVER HAVE FOUGHT TO BEGIN WITH.
WE TRUSTED HARADA, AND HE BETRAYED US. NOW WE'VE COME TO MAKE IT RIGHT.
THERE IS MUCH THAT NEEDS TO BE MADE RIGHT--

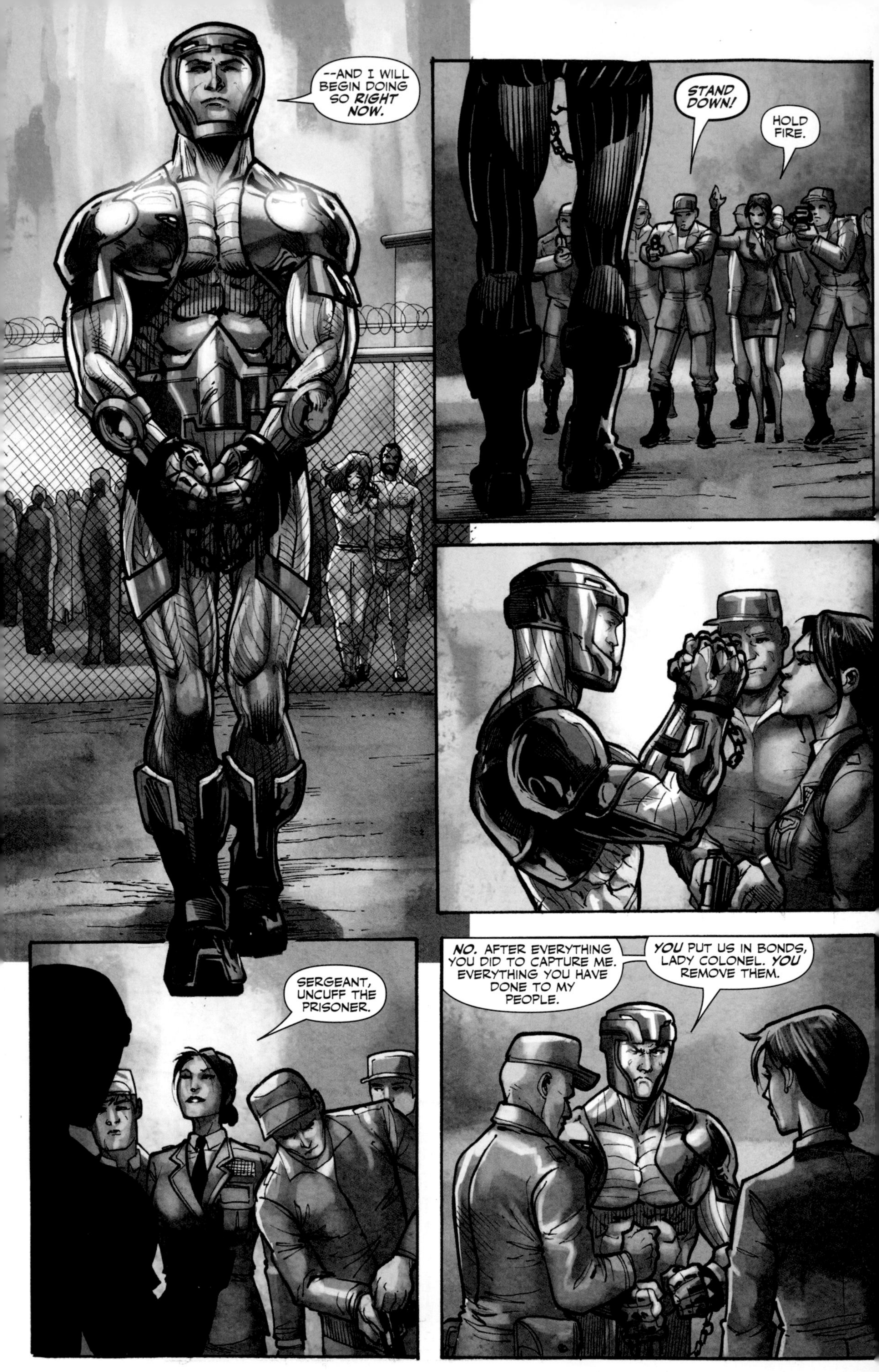
--AND I WILL BEGIN DOING SO RIGHT NOW.
STAND DOWN!
HOLD FIRE.
SERGEANT, UNCUFF THE PRISONER.
NO. AFTER EVERYTHING YOU DID TO CAPTURE ME. EVERYTHING YOU HAVE DONE TO MY PEOPLE.
YOU PUT US IN BONDS, LADY COLONEL. YOU REMOVE THEM.

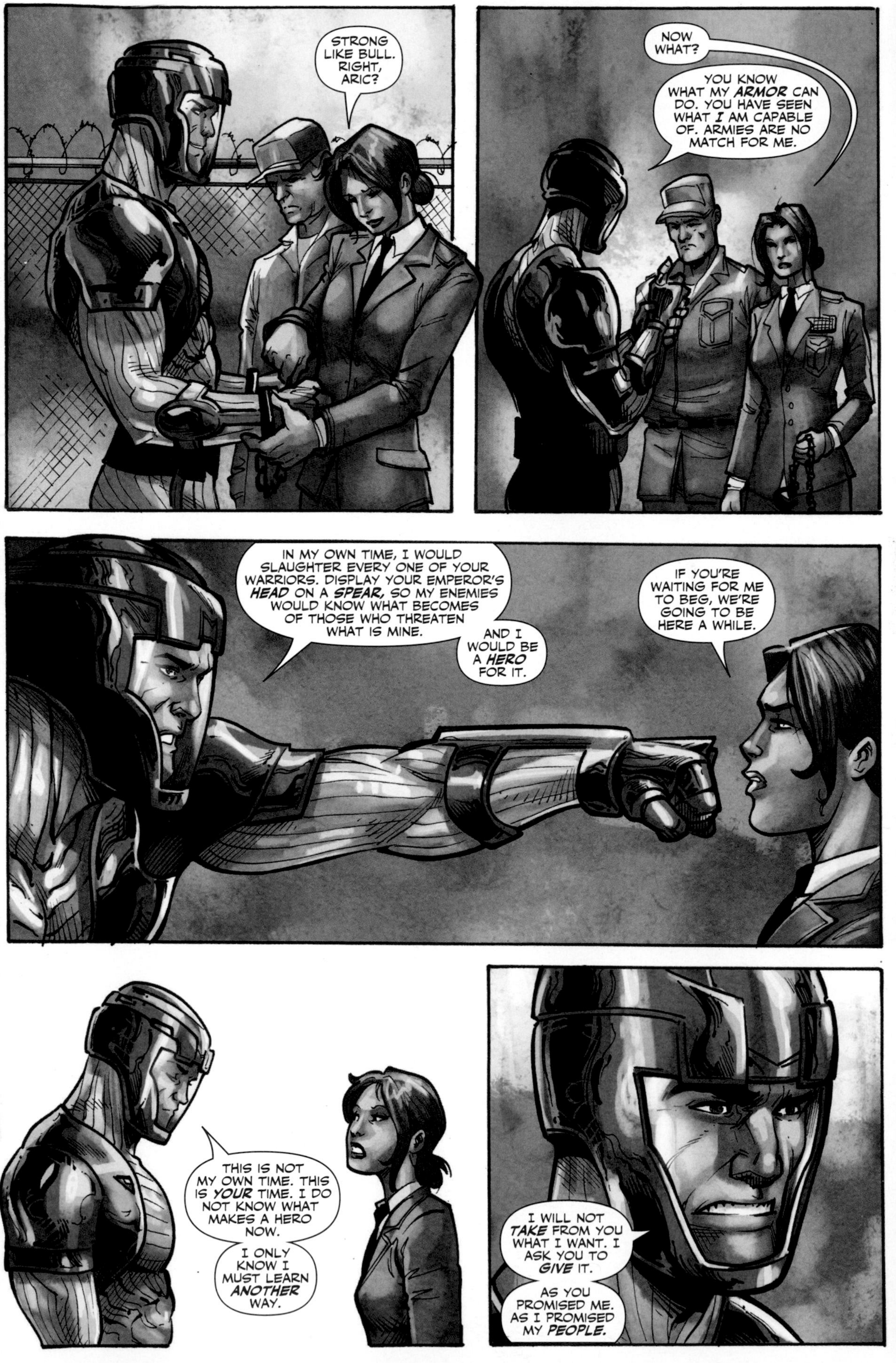
STRONG LIKE BULL. RIGHT, ARIC?
NOW WHAT?
YOU KNOW WHAT MY ARMOR CAN DO. YOU HAVE SEEN WHAT I AM CAPABLE OF. ARMIES ARE NO MATCH FOR ME.
IN MY OWN TIME, I WOULD SLAUGHTER EVERY ONE OF YOUR WARRIORS. DISPLAY YOUR EMPEROR'S HEAD ON A SPEAR, SO MY ENEMIES WOULD KNOW WHAT BECOMES OF THOSE WHO THREATEN WHAT IS MINE.
AND I WOULD BE A HERO FOR IT.
IF YOU'RE WAITING FOR ME TO BEG, WE'RE GOING TO BE HERE A WHILE.
THIS IS NOT MY OWN TIME. THIS IS YOUR TIME. I DO NOT KNOW WHAT MAKES A HERO NOW.
I ONLY KNOW I MUST LEARN ANOTHER WAY.
I WILL NOT TAKE FROM YOU WHAT I WANT. I ASK YOU TO GIVE IT.
AS YOU PROMISED ME. AS I PROMISED MY PEOPLE.

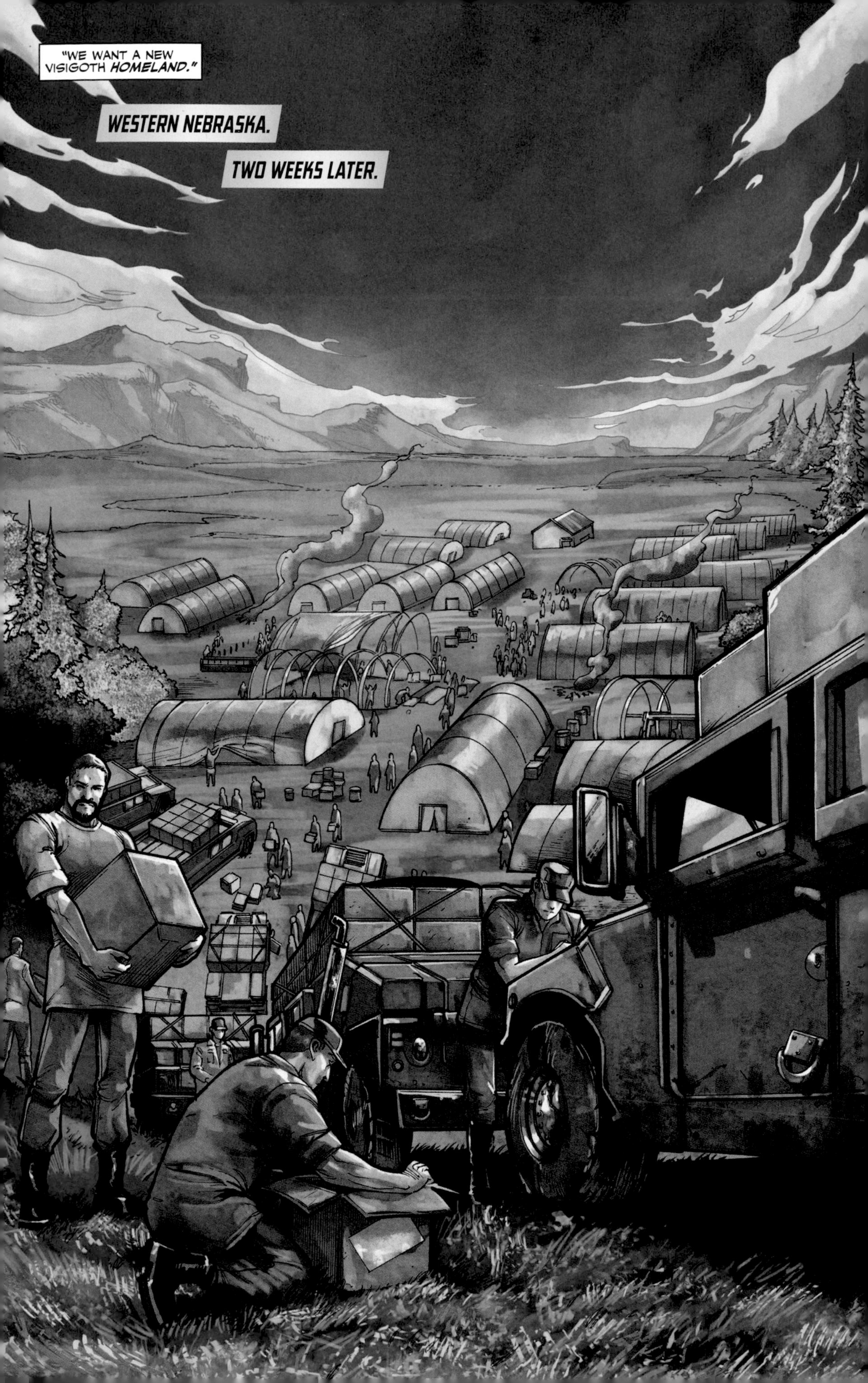
"WE WANT A NEW VISIGOTH *HOMELAND*."
WESTERN NEBRASKA.
TWO WEEKS LATER.

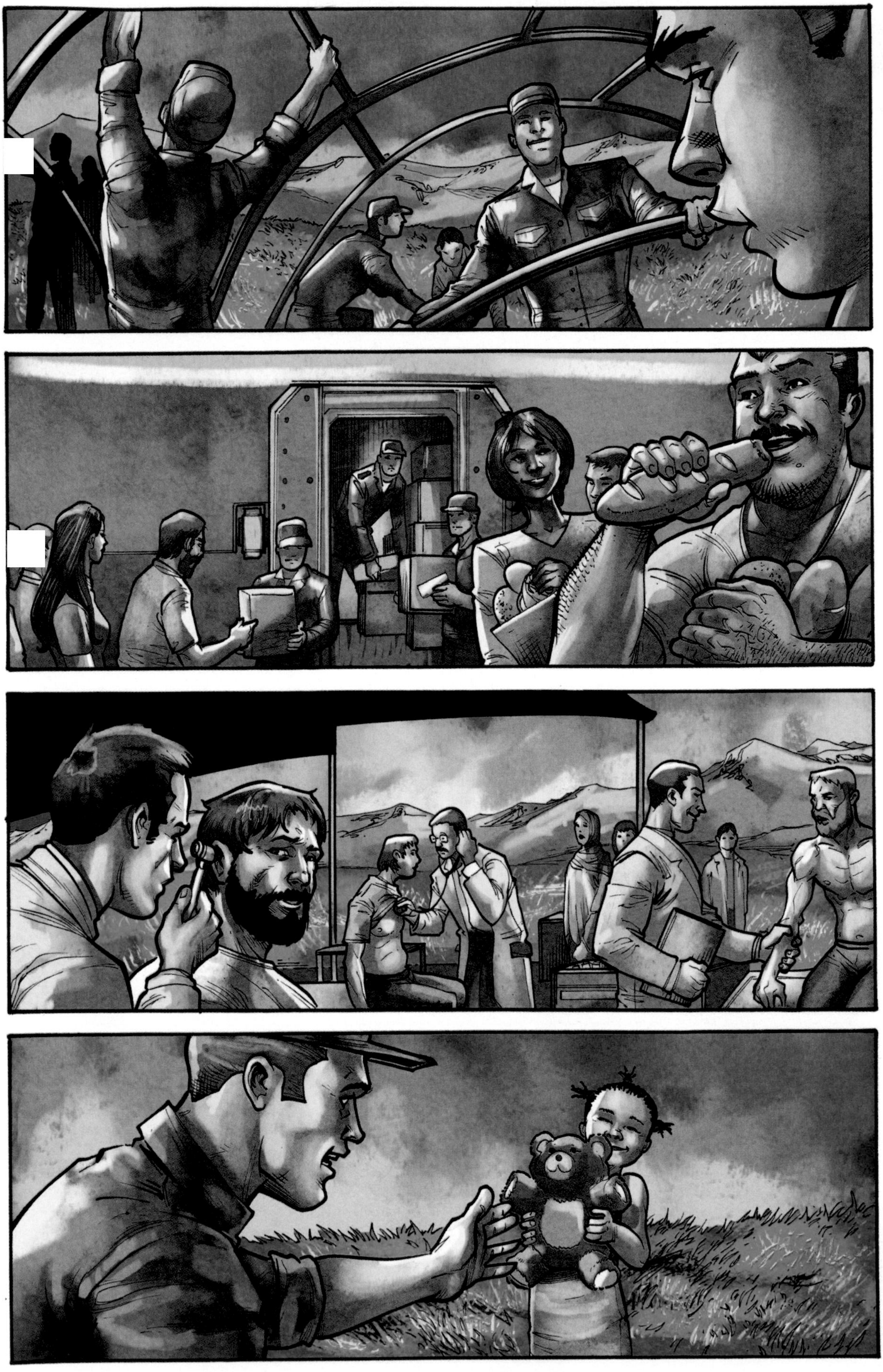

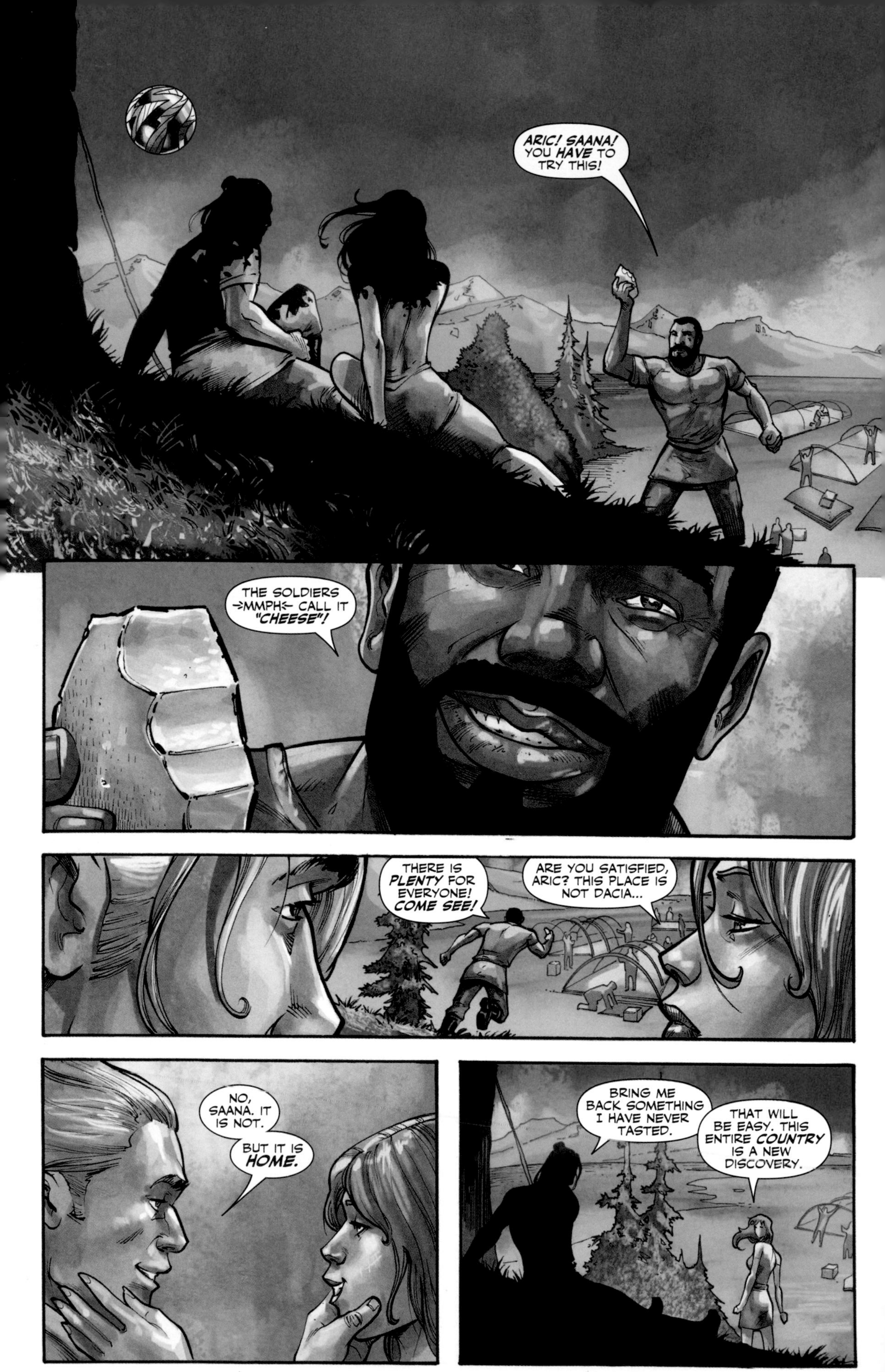
ARIC! SAANA! YOU HAVE TO TRY THIS!
THE SOLDIERS →MMPH← CALL IT "CHEESE"!
THERE IS PLENTY FOR EVERYONE! COME SEE!
ARE YOU SATISFIED, ARIC? THIS PLACE IS NOT DACIA...
NO, SAANA. IT IS NOT.
BUT IT IS HOME.
BRING ME BACK SOMETHING I HAVE NEVER TASTED.
THAT WILL BE EASY. THIS ENTIRE COUNTRY IS A NEW DISCOVERY.

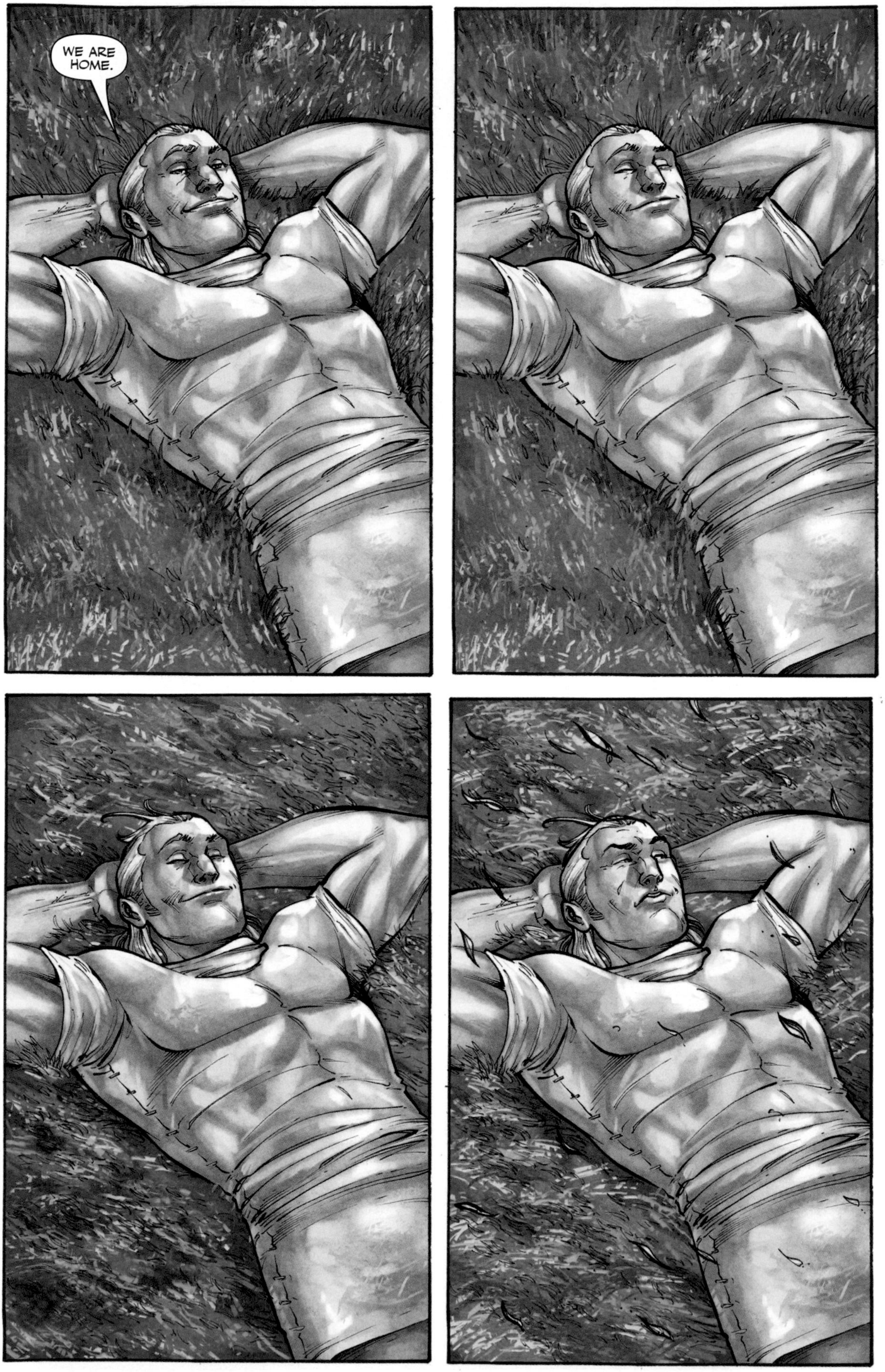
WE ARE HOME.

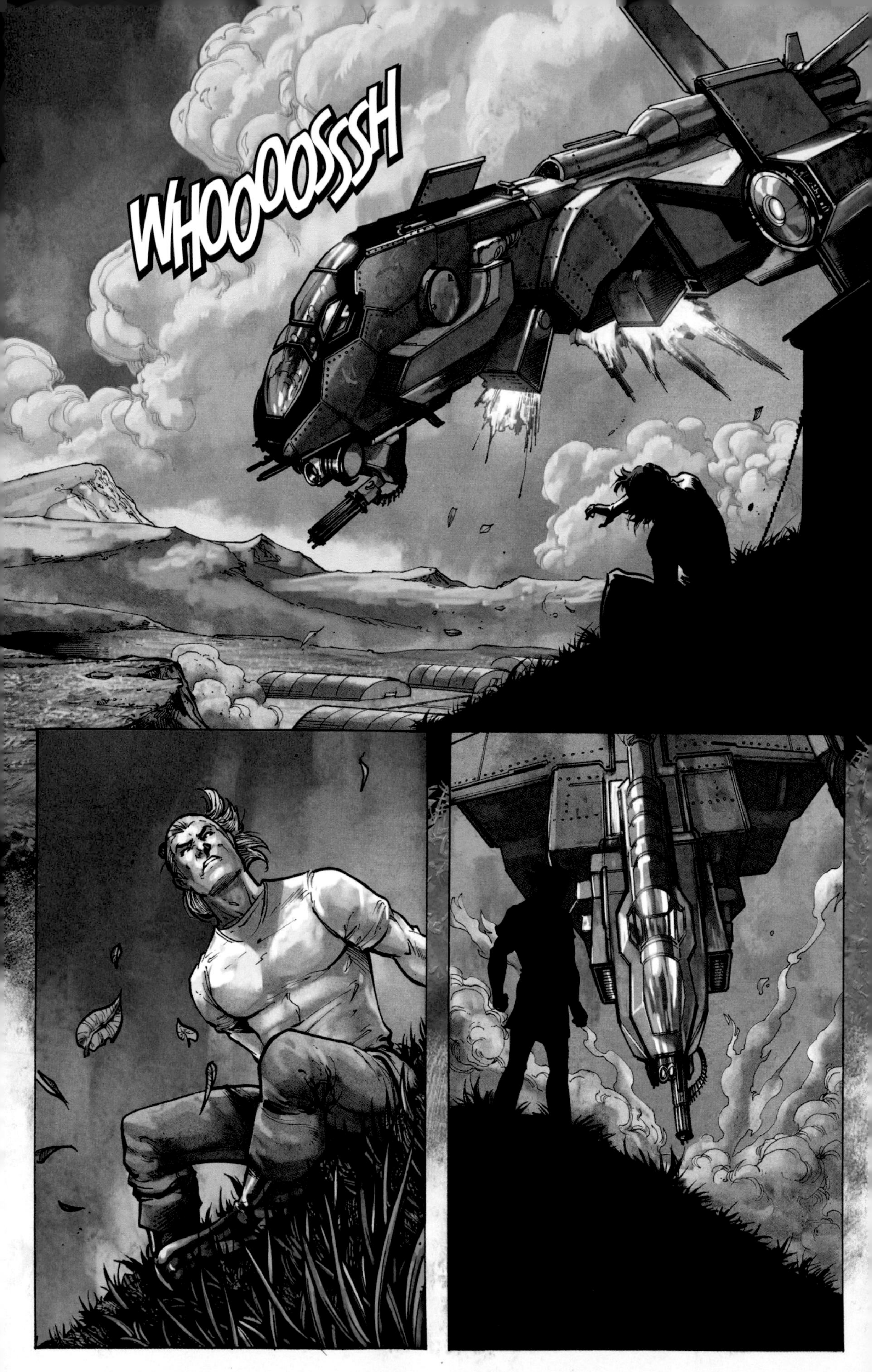
WHOOOOSSSH

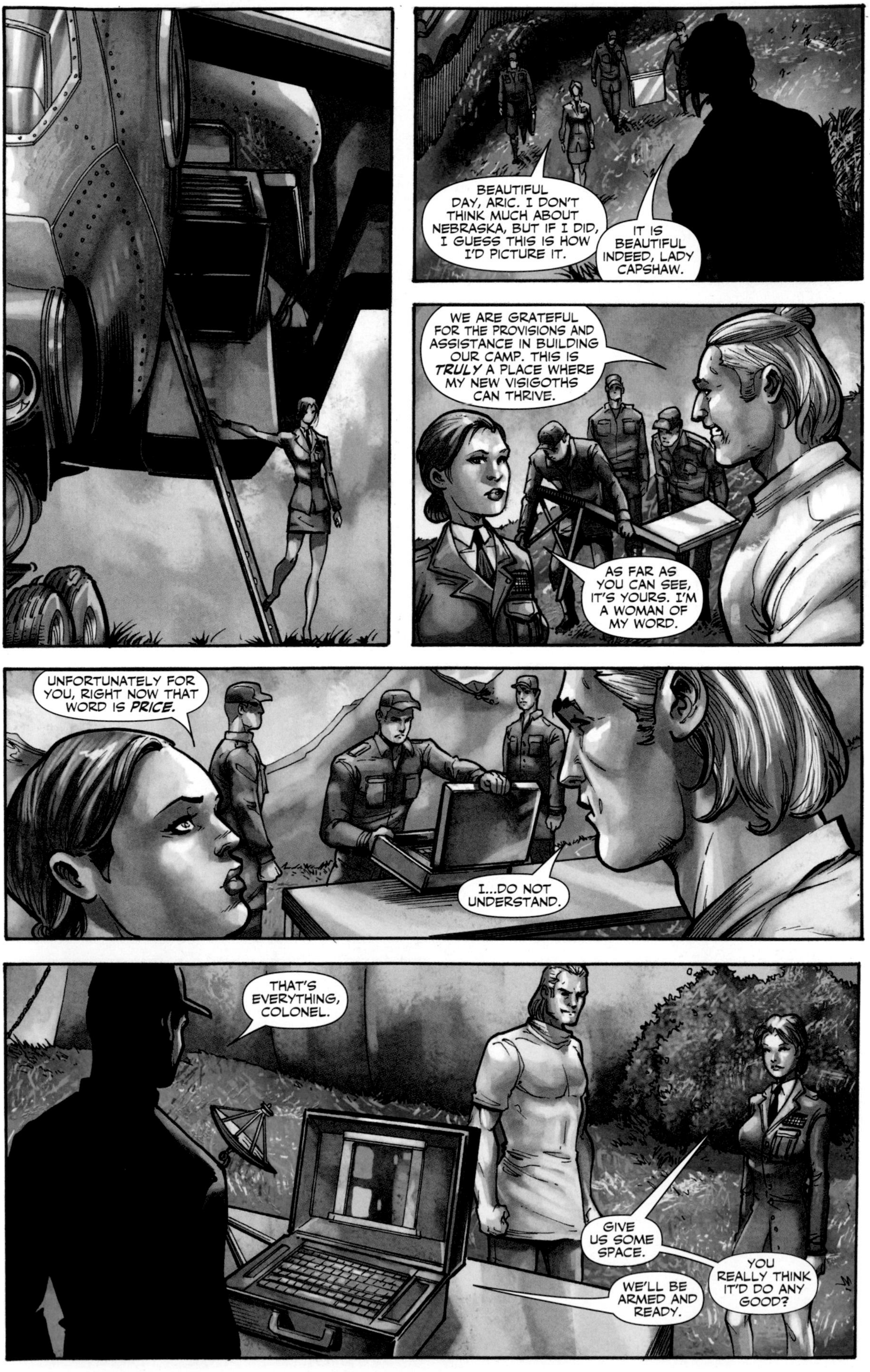
BEAUTIFUL DAY, ARIC. I DON'T THINK MUCH ABOUT NEBRASKA, BUT IF I DID, I GUESS THIS IS HOW I'D PICTURE IT.
IT IS BEAUTIFUL INDEED, LADY CAPSHAW.
WE ARE GRATEFUL FOR THE PROVISIONS AND ASSISTANCE IN BUILDING OUR CAMP. THIS IS *TRULY* A PLACE WHERE MY NEW VISIGOTHS CAN THRIVE.
AS FAR AS YOU CAN SEE, IT'S YOURS. I'M A WOMAN OF MY WORD.
UNFORTUNATELY FOR YOU, RIGHT NOW THAT WORD IS *PRICE.*
I...DO NOT UNDERSTAND.
THAT'S EVERYTHING, COLONEL.
GIVE US SOME SPACE.
WE'LL BE ARMED AND READY.
YOU REALLY THINK IT'D DO ANY GOOD?

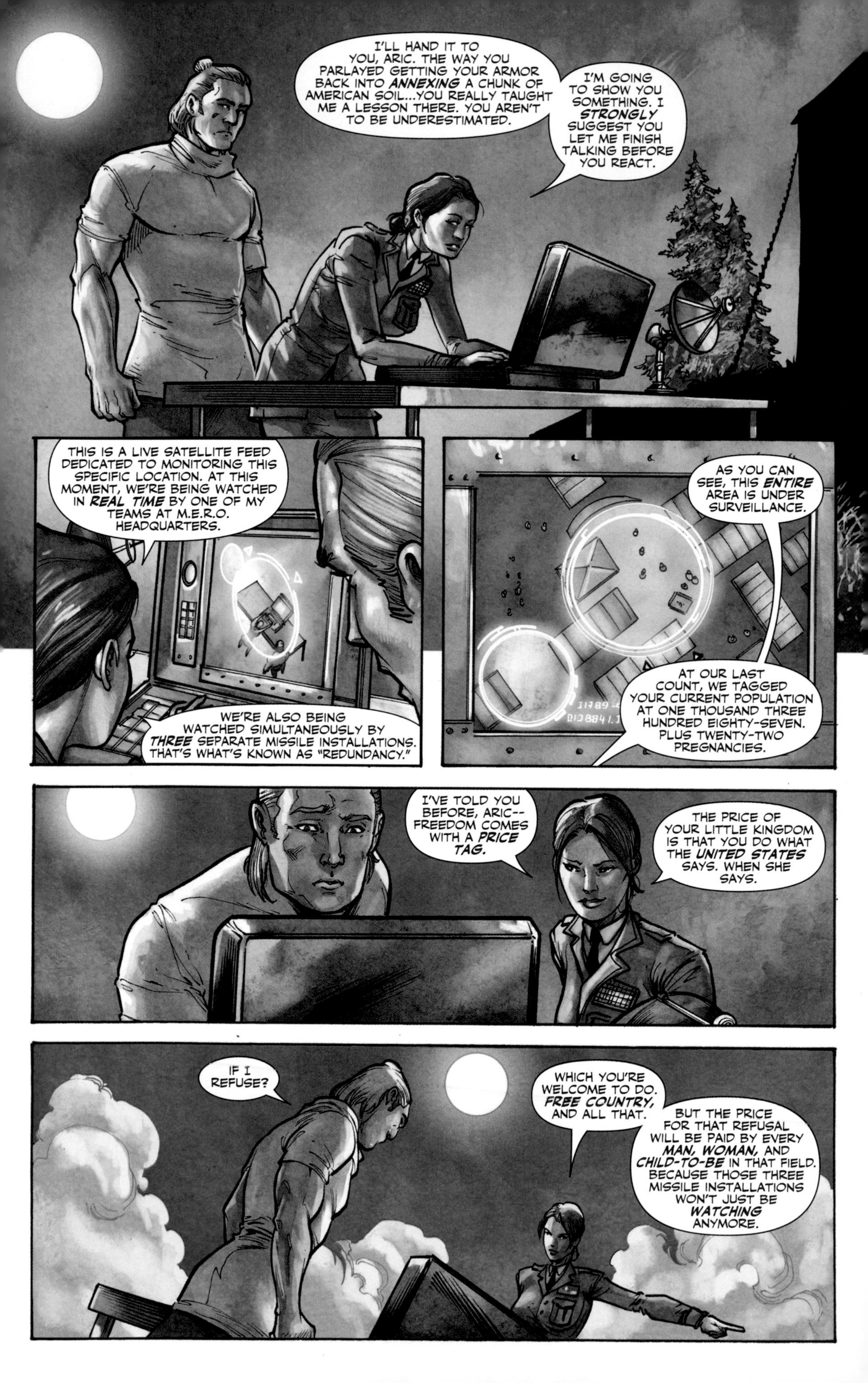
I'LL HAND IT TO YOU, ARIC. THE WAY YOU PARLAYED GETTING YOUR ARMOR BACK INTO ANNEXING A CHUNK OF AMERICAN SOIL...YOU REALLY TAUGHT ME A LESSON THERE. YOU AREN'T TO BE UNDERESTIMATED.
I'M GOING TO SHOW YOU SOMETHING. I STRONGLY SUGGEST YOU LET ME FINISH TALKING BEFORE YOU REACT.
THIS IS A LIVE SATELLITE FEED DEDICATED TO MONITORING THIS SPECIFIC LOCATION. AT THIS MOMENT, WE'RE BEING WATCHED IN REAL TIME BY ONE OF MY TEAMS AT M.E.R.O. HEADQUARTERS.
WE'RE ALSO BEING WATCHED SIMULTANEOUSLY BY THREE SEPARATE MISSILE INSTALLATIONS. THAT'S WHAT'S KNOWN AS "REDUNDANCY."
AS YOU CAN SEE, THIS ENTIRE AREA IS UNDER SURVEILLANCE.
AT OUR LAST COUNT, WE TAGGED YOUR CURRENT POPULATION AT ONE THOUSAND THREE HUNDRED EIGHTY-SEVEN. PLUS TWENTY-TWO PREGNANCIES.
I'VE TOLD YOU BEFORE, ARIC-- FREEDOM COMES WITH A PRICE TAG.
THE PRICE OF YOUR LITTLE KINGDOM IS THAT YOU DO WHAT THE UNITED STATES SAYS. WHEN SHE SAYS.
IF I REFUSE?
WHICH YOU'RE WELCOME TO DO. FREE COUNTRY, AND ALL THAT.
BUT THE PRICE FOR THAT REFUSAL WILL BE PAID BY EVERY MAN, WOMAN, AND CHILD-TO-BE IN THAT FIELD. BECAUSE THOSE THREE MISSILE INSTALLATIONS WON'T JUST BE WATCHING ANYMORE.

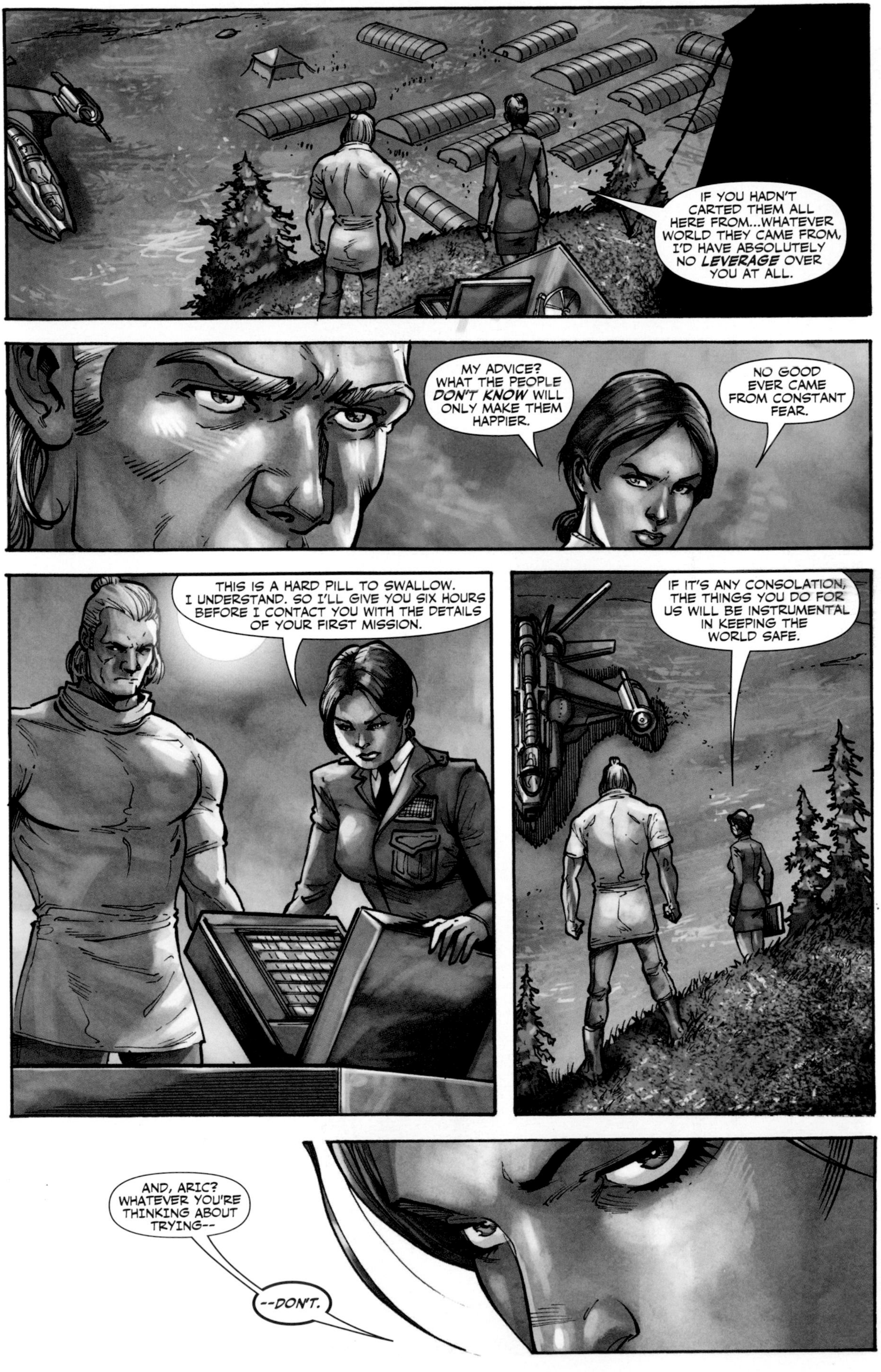
IF YOU HADN'T CARTED THEM ALL HERE FROM...WHATEVER WORLD THEY CAME FROM, I'D HAVE ABSOLUTELY NO LEVERAGE OVER YOU AT ALL.
MY ADVICE? WHAT THE PEOPLE DON'T KNOW WILL ONLY MAKE THEM HAPPIER.
NO GOOD EVER CAME FROM CONSTANT FEAR.
THIS IS A HARD PILL TO SWALLOW. I UNDERSTAND. SO I'LL GIVE YOU SIX HOURS BEFORE I CONTACT YOU WITH THE DETAILS OF YOUR FIRST MISSION.
IF IT'S ANY CONSOLATION, THE THINGS YOU DO FOR US WILL BE INSTRUMENTAL IN KEEPING THE WORLD SAFE.
AND, ARIC? WHATEVER YOU'RE THINKING ABOUT TRYING--
--DON'T.

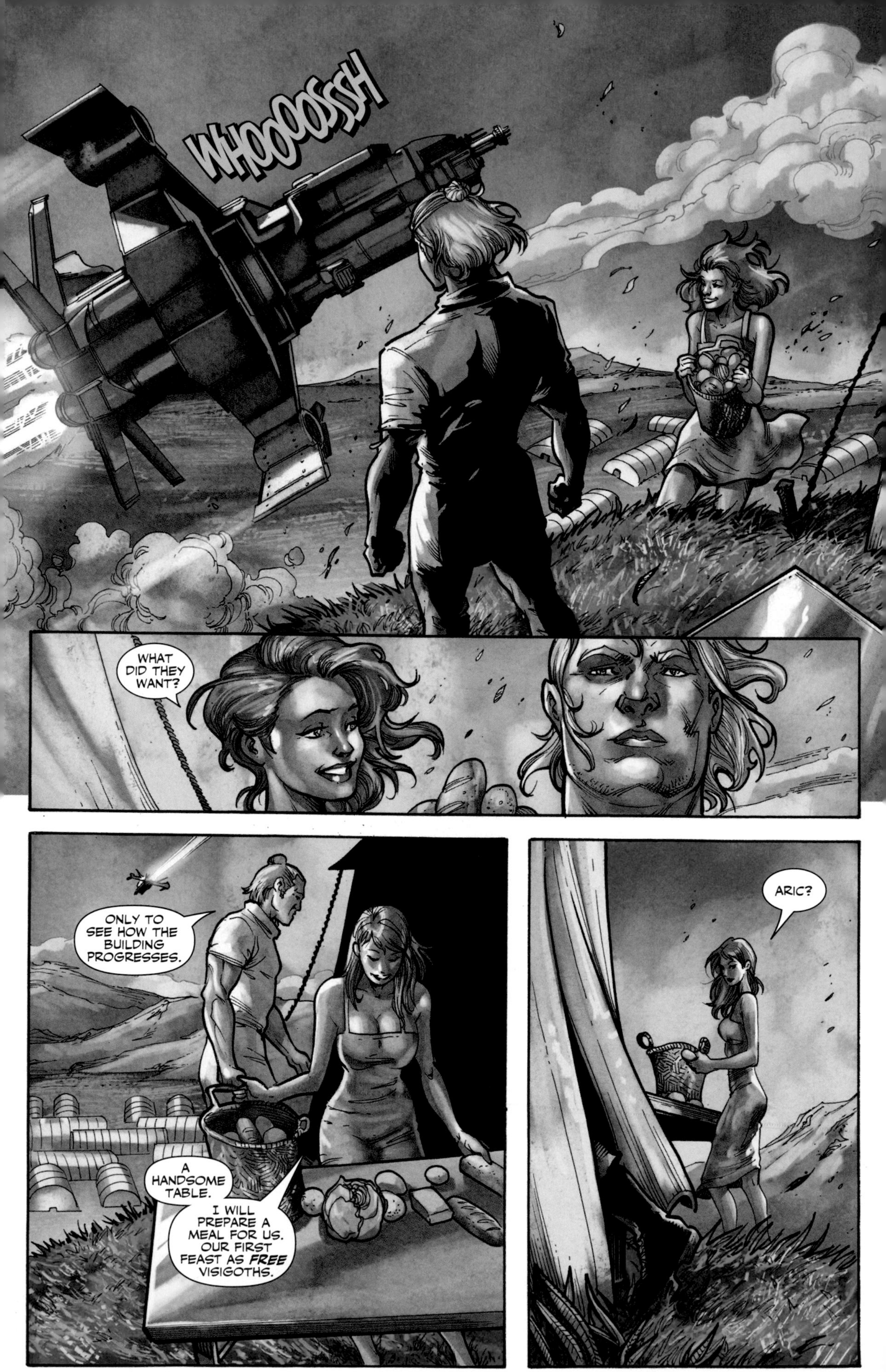
WHOOOOSSH
WHAT DID THEY WANT?
ONLY TO SEE HOW THE BUILDING PROGRESSES.
A HANDSOME TABLE.
I WILL PREPARE A MEAL FOR US. OUR FIRST FEAST AS FREE VISIGOTHS.
ARIC?

THE PACIFIC OCEAN.

INTERNATIONAL WATERS.

EIGHT HOURS LATER.

THE RUSSIAN CRUISER ANTON.

‹THE SUBMERSIBLE HAS REACHED TARGET DEPTH, CAPTAIN.›

‹VERY WELL. UPDATE THE LOGS AND BEGIN RECOVERY.›

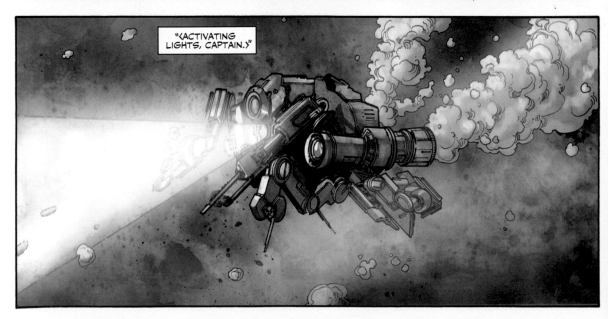

"‹ACTIVATING LIGHTS, CAPTAIN.›"

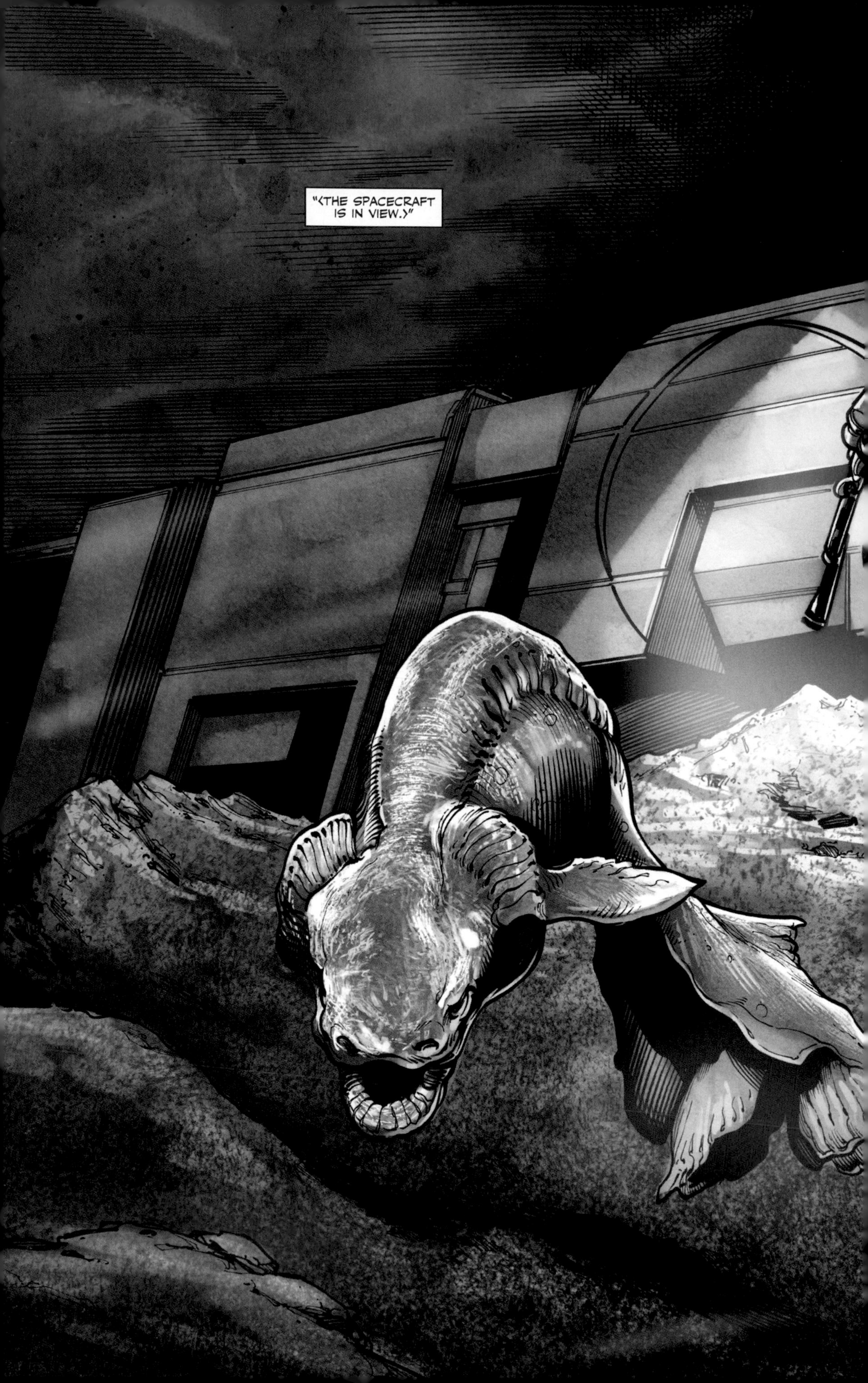
"<THE SPACECRAFT IS IN VIEW.>"

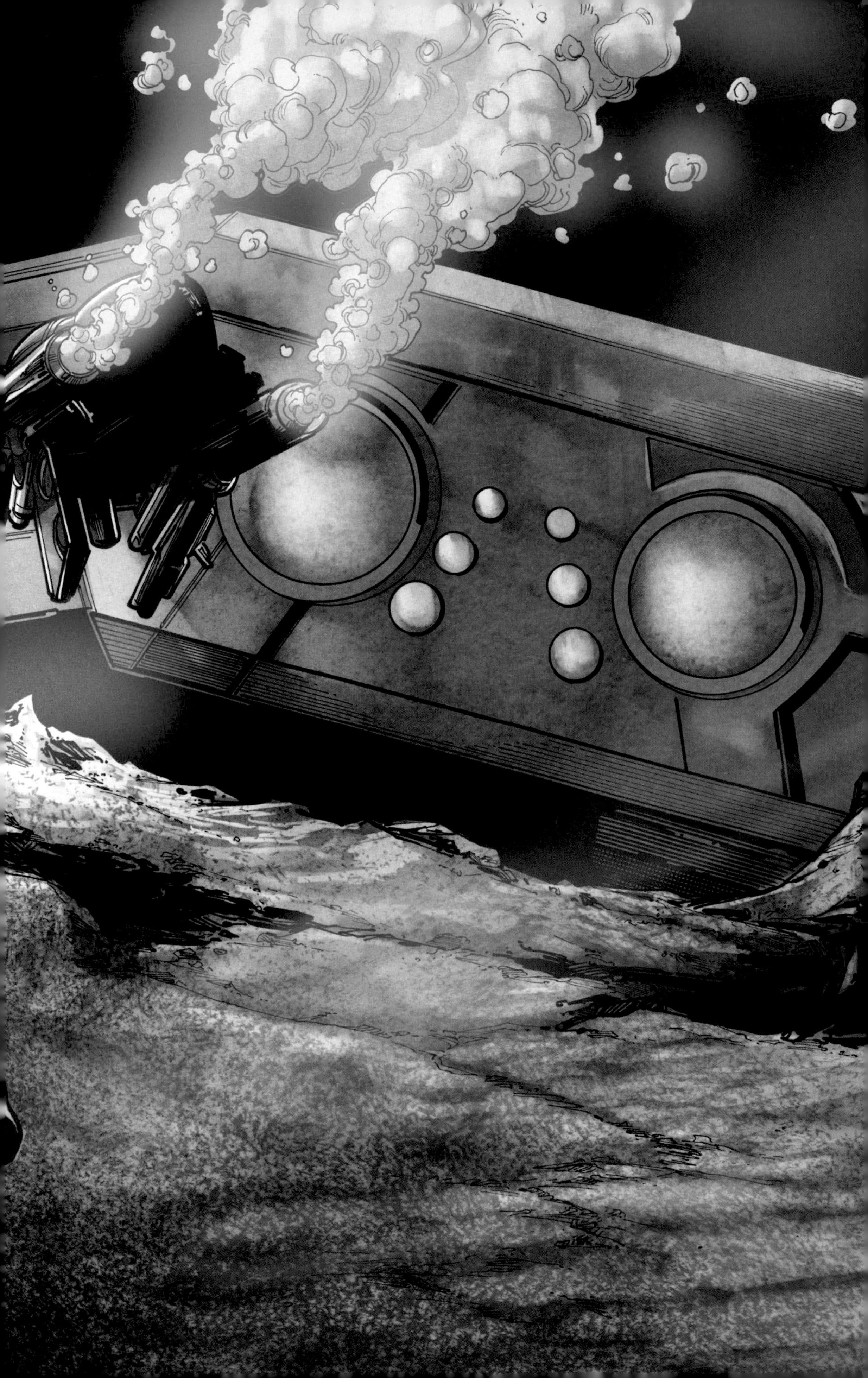

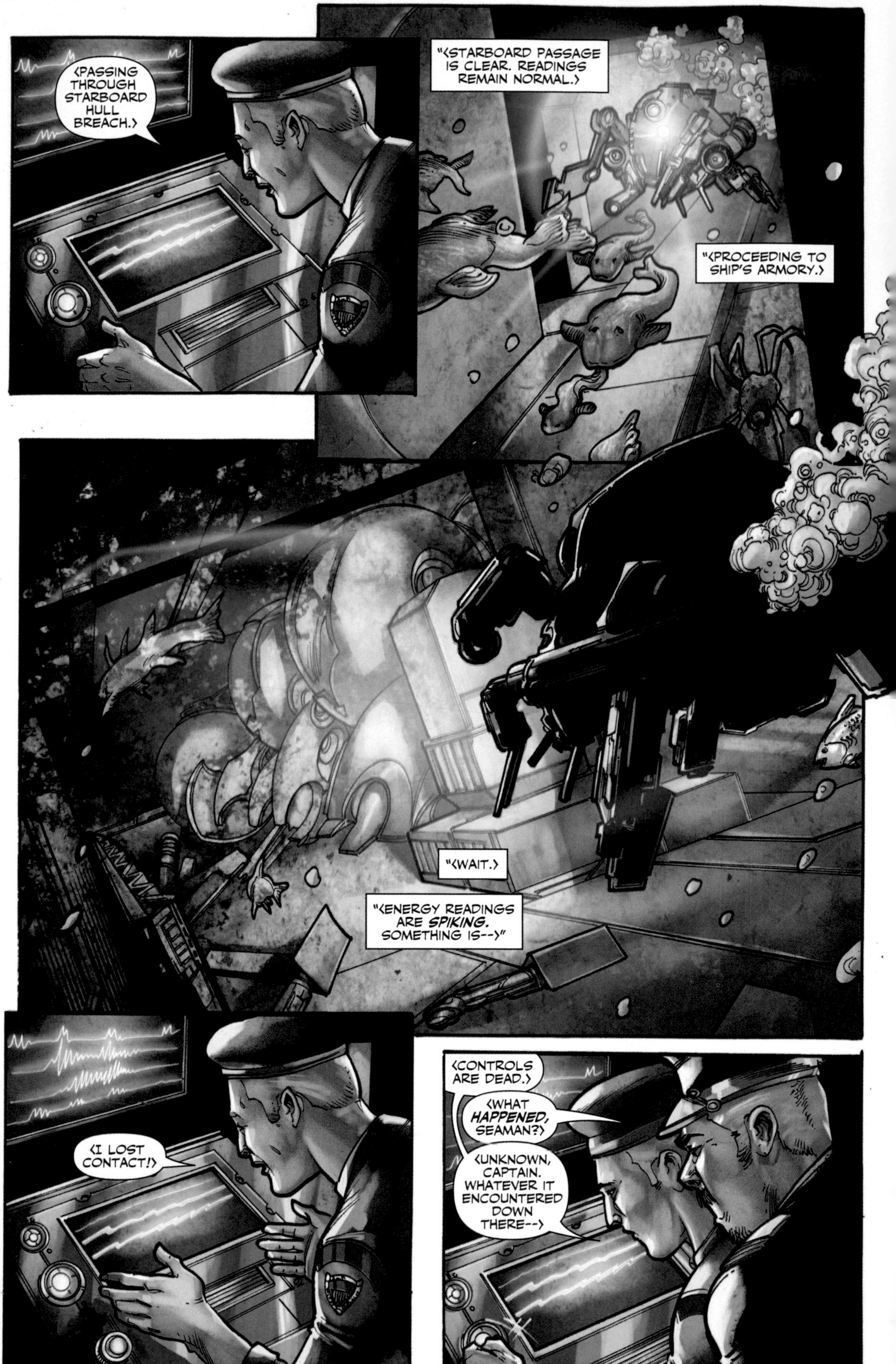

<PASSING THROUGH STARBOARD HULL BREACH.>
"<STARBOARD PASSAGE IS CLEAR. READINGS REMAIN NORMAL.>
"<PROCEEDING TO SHIP'S ARMORY.>
"<WAIT.>
"<ENERGY READINGS ARE *SPIKING.* SOMETHING IS-->"
<I LOST CONTACT!>
<CONTROLS ARE DEAD.>
<WHAT *HAPPENED,* SEAMAN?>
<UNKNOWN, CAPTAIN. WHATEVER IT ENCOUNTERED DOWN THERE-->

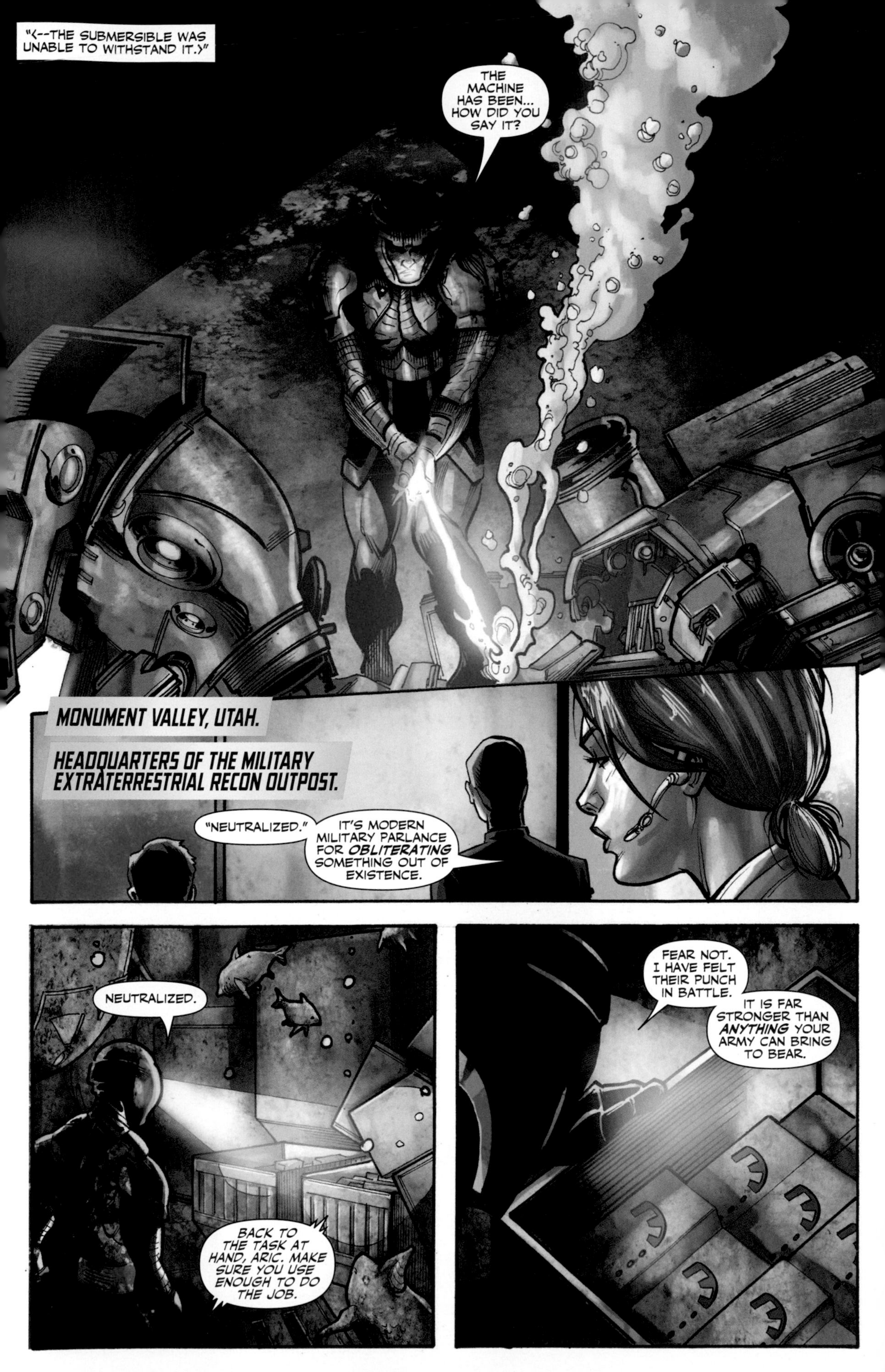
"<--THE SUBMERSIBLE WAS UNABLE TO WITHSTAND IT.>"
THE MACHINE HAS BEEN... HOW DID YOU SAY IT?
MONUMENT VALLEY, UTAH.
HEADQUARTERS OF THE MILITARY EXTRATERRESTRIAL RECON OUTPOST.
"NEUTRALIZED."
IT'S MODERN MILITARY PARLANCE FOR OBLITERATING SOMETHING OUT OF EXISTENCE.
NEUTRALIZED.
BACK TO THE TASK AT HAND, ARIC. MAKE SURE YOU USE ENOUGH TO DO THE JOB.
FEAR NOT. I HAVE FELT THEIR PUNCH IN BATTLE.
IT IS FAR STRONGER THAN ANYTHING YOUR ARMY CAN BRING TO BEAR.

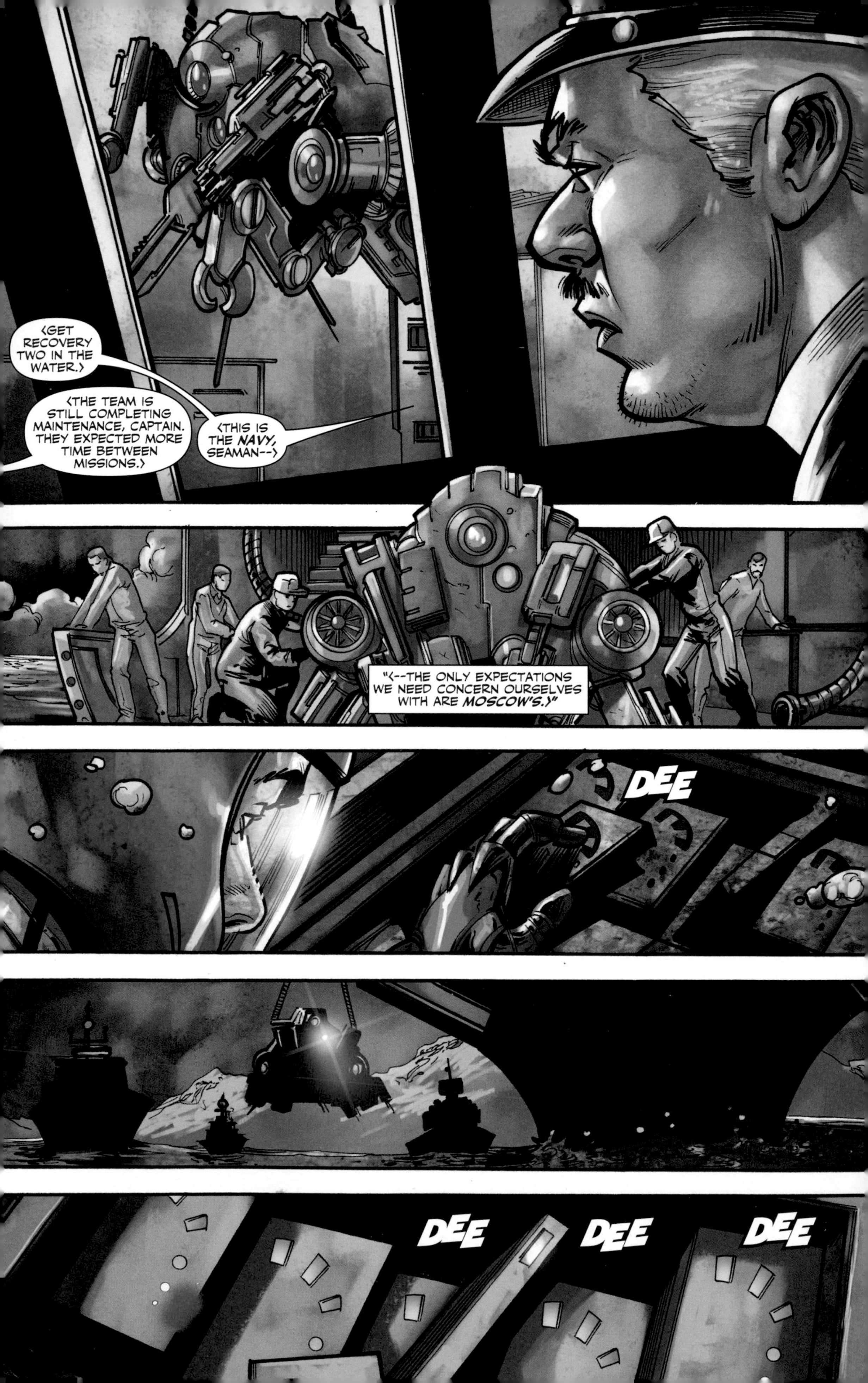

‹GET RECOVERY TWO IN THE WATER.›
‹THE TEAM IS STILL COMPLETING MAINTENANCE, CAPTAIN. THEY EXPECTED MORE TIME BETWEEN MISSIONS.›
‹THIS IS THE *NAVY,* SEAMAN--›
"‹--THE ONLY EXPECTATIONS WE NEED CONCERN OURSELVES WITH ARE *MOSCOW'S.*›"
DEE
DEE
DEE
DEE

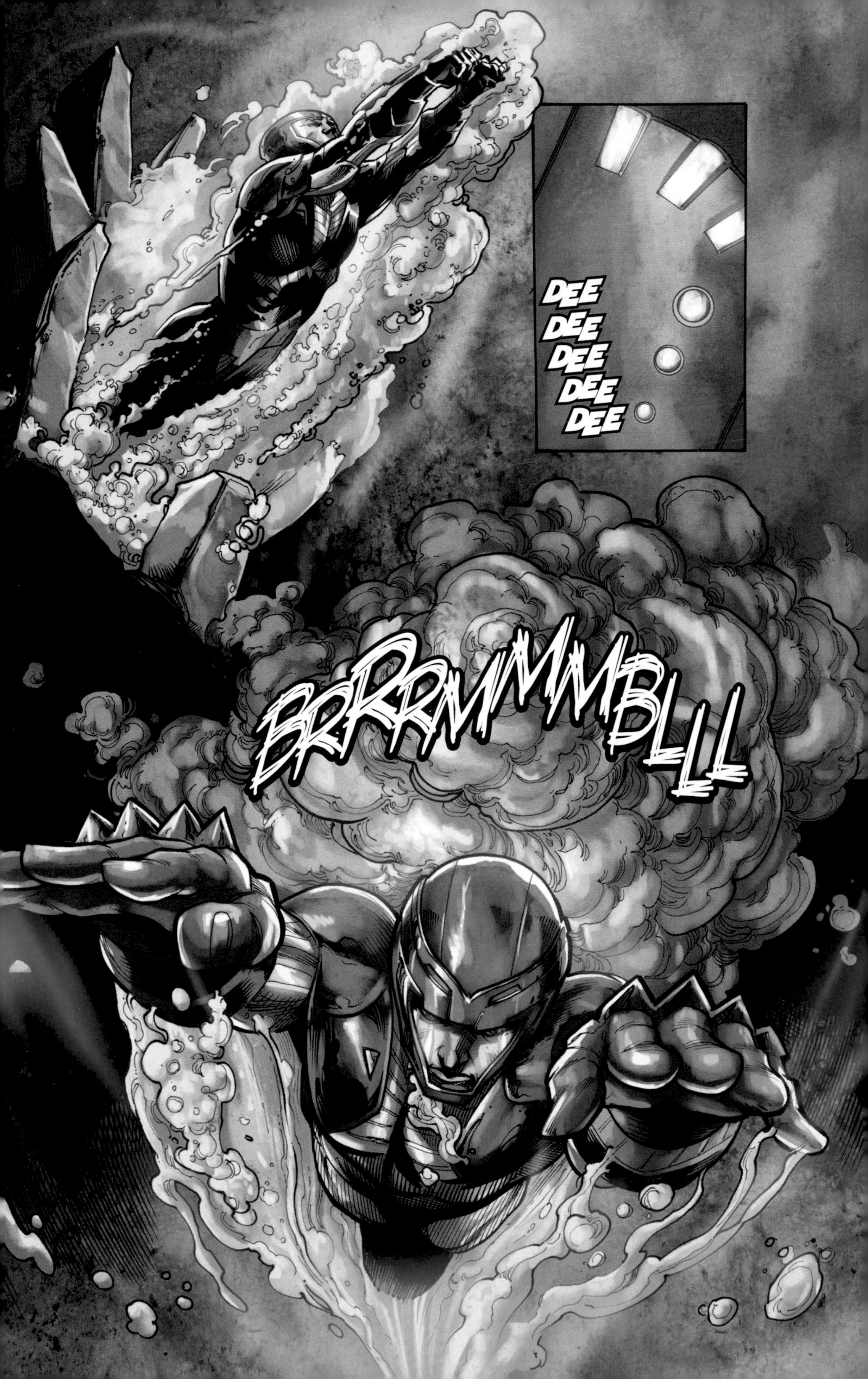
DEE
DEE
DEE
DEE
DEE
BRRRMMMBLLL

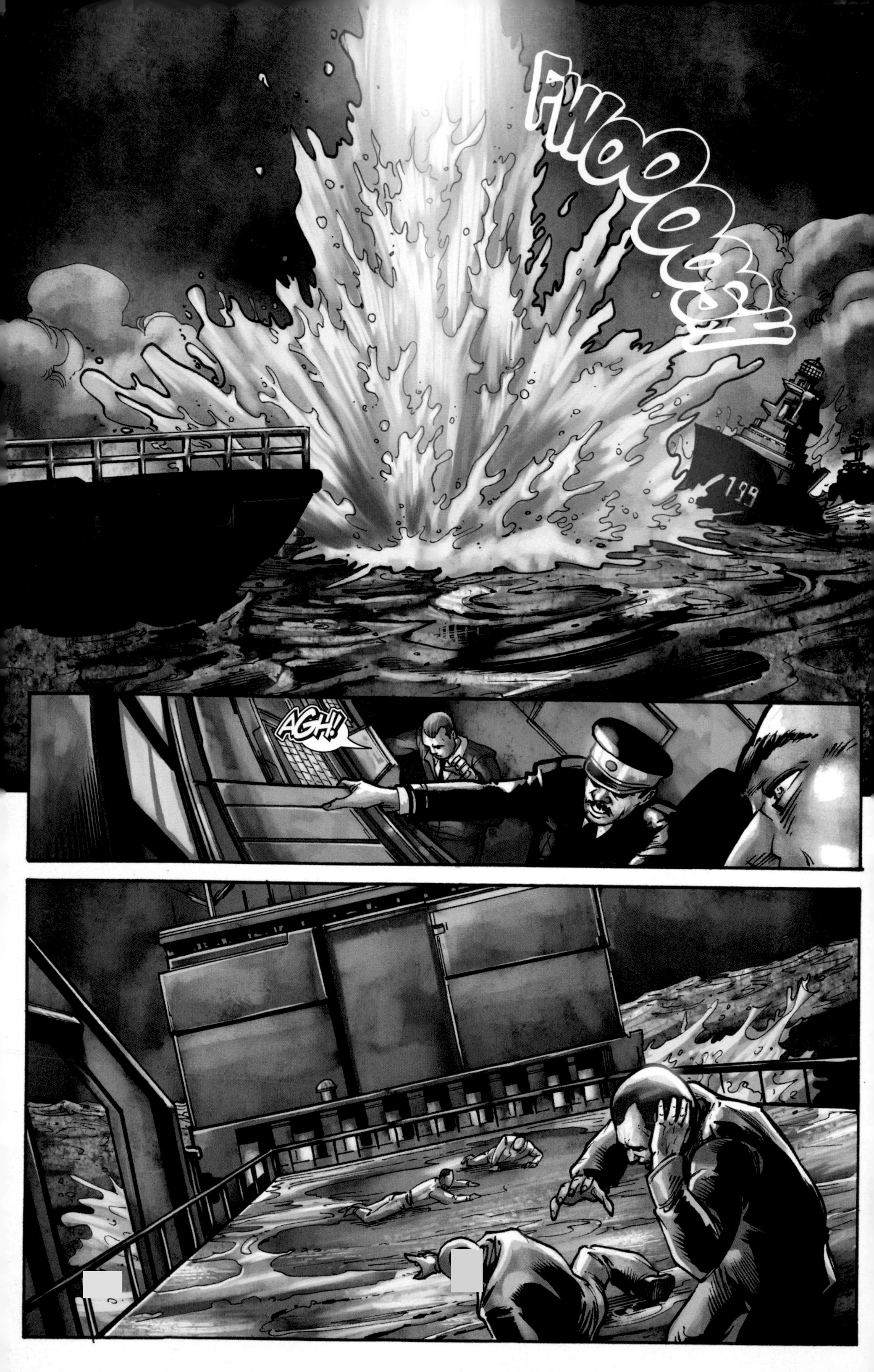
FWOOOOSH
AGH!

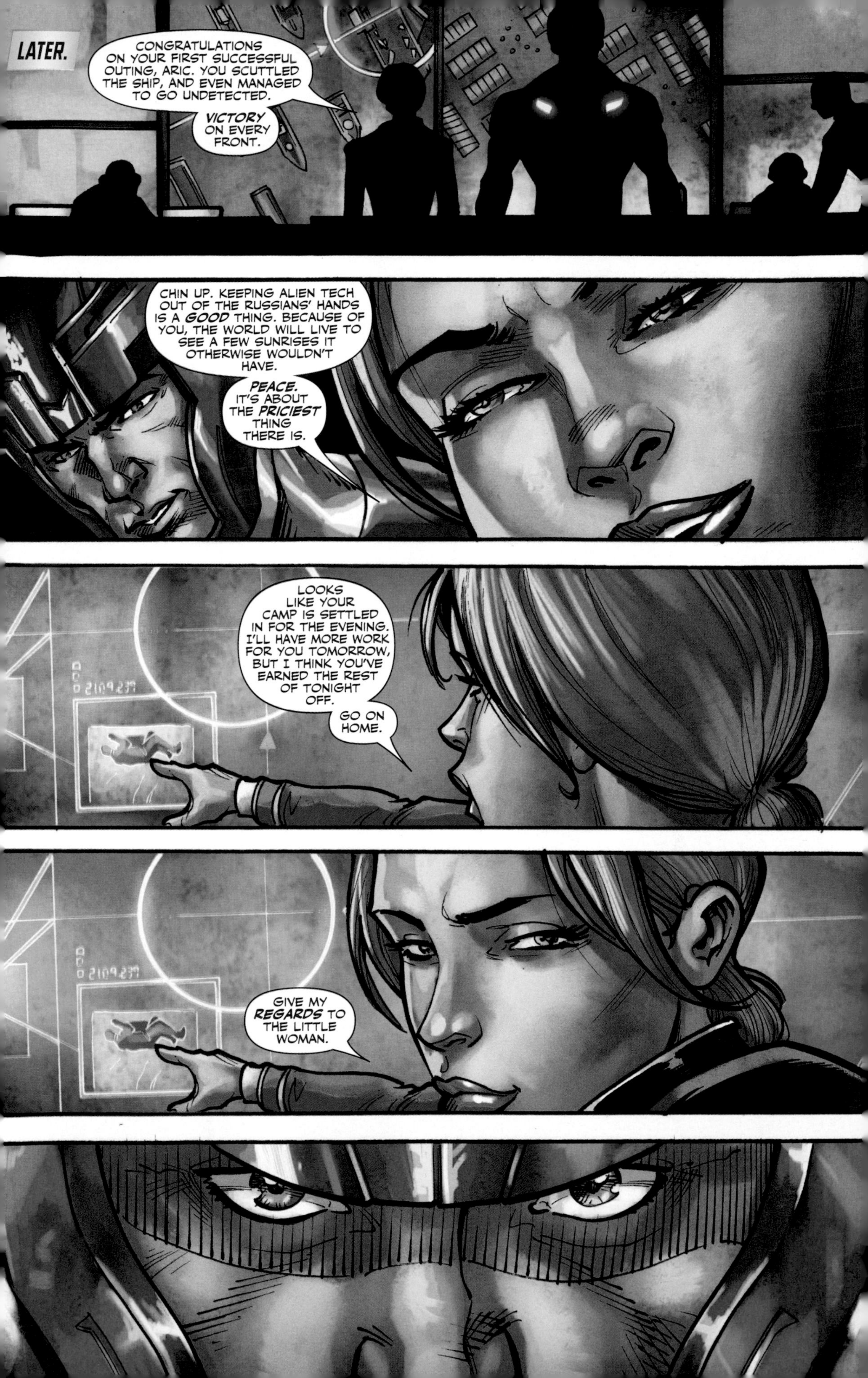
LATER.
CONGRATULATIONS ON YOUR FIRST SUCCESSFUL OUTING, ARIC. YOU SCUTTLED THE SHIP, AND EVEN MANAGED TO GO UNDETECTED.
VICTORY ON EVERY FRONT.
CHIN UP. KEEPING ALIEN TECH OUT OF THE RUSSIANS' HANDS IS A GOOD THING. BECAUSE OF YOU, THE WORLD WILL LIVE TO SEE A FEW SUNRISES IT OTHERWISE WOULDN'T HAVE.
PEACE. IT'S ABOUT THE PRICIEST THING THERE IS.
LOOKS LIKE YOUR CAMP IS SETTLED IN FOR THE EVENING. I'LL HAVE MORE WORK FOR YOU TOMORROW, BUT I THINK YOU'VE EARNED THE REST OF TONIGHT OFF.
GO ON HOME.
GIVE MY REGARDS TO THE LITTLE WOMAN.

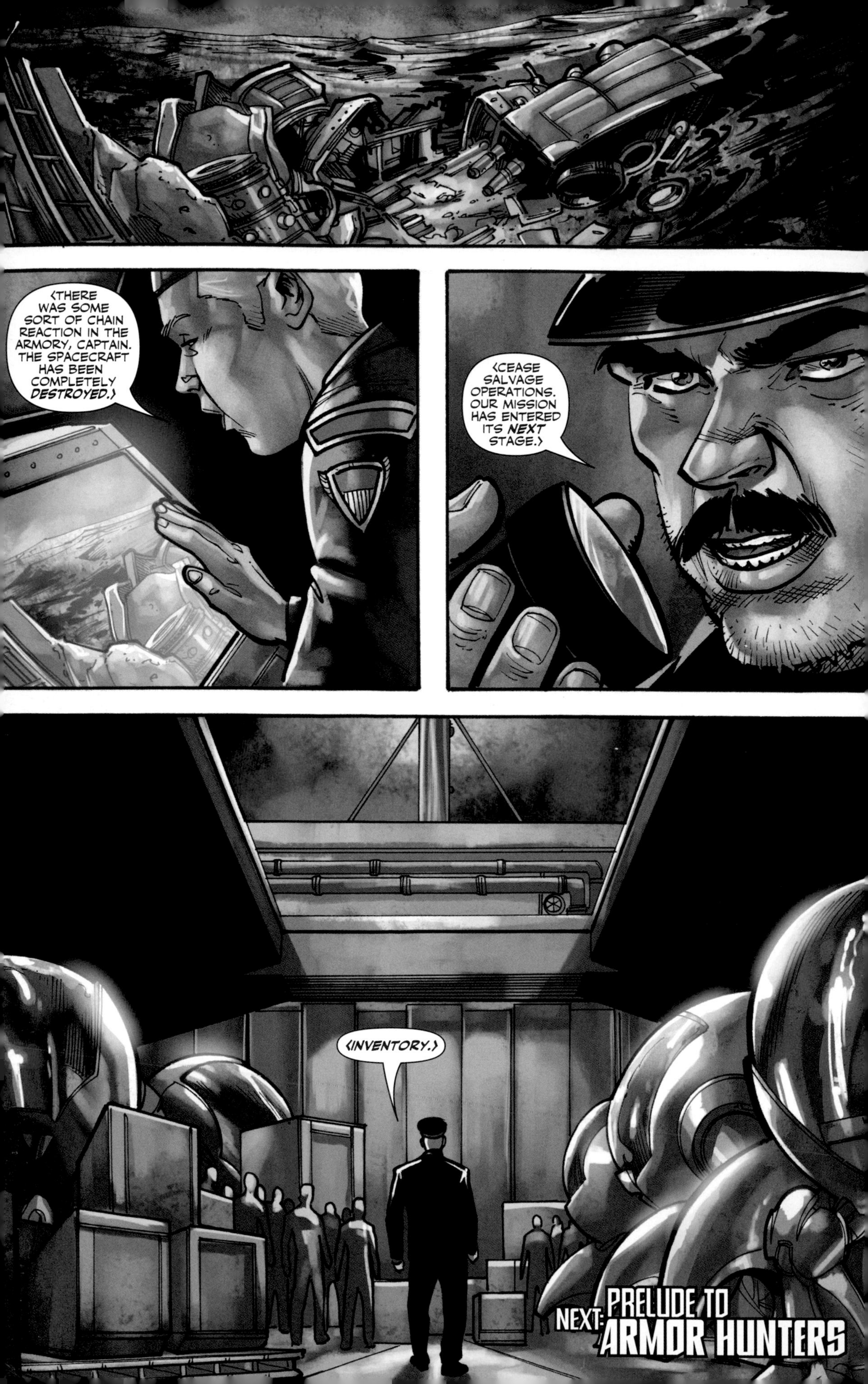
‹THERE WAS SOME SORT OF CHAIN REACTION IN THE ARMORY, CAPTAIN. THE SPACECRAFT HAS BEEN COMPLETELY DESTROYED.›
‹CEASE SALVAGE OPERATIONS. OUR MISSION HAS ENTERED ITS NEXT STAGE.›
‹INVENTORY.›
NEXT: PRELUDE TO ARMOR HUNTERS

GALLERY

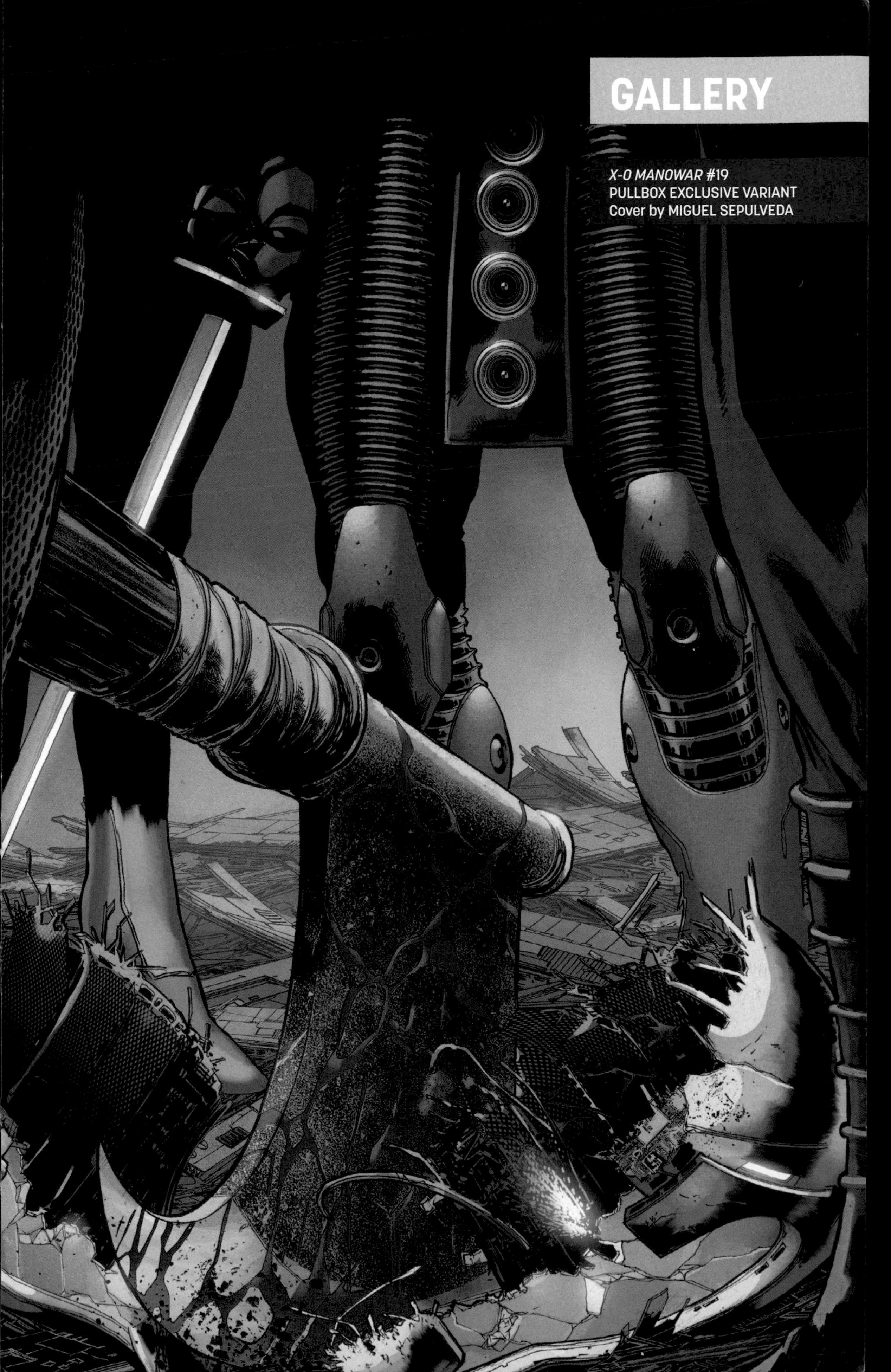

X-O MANOWAR #19
PULLBOX EXCLUSIVE VARIANT
Cover by MIGUEL SEPULVEDA

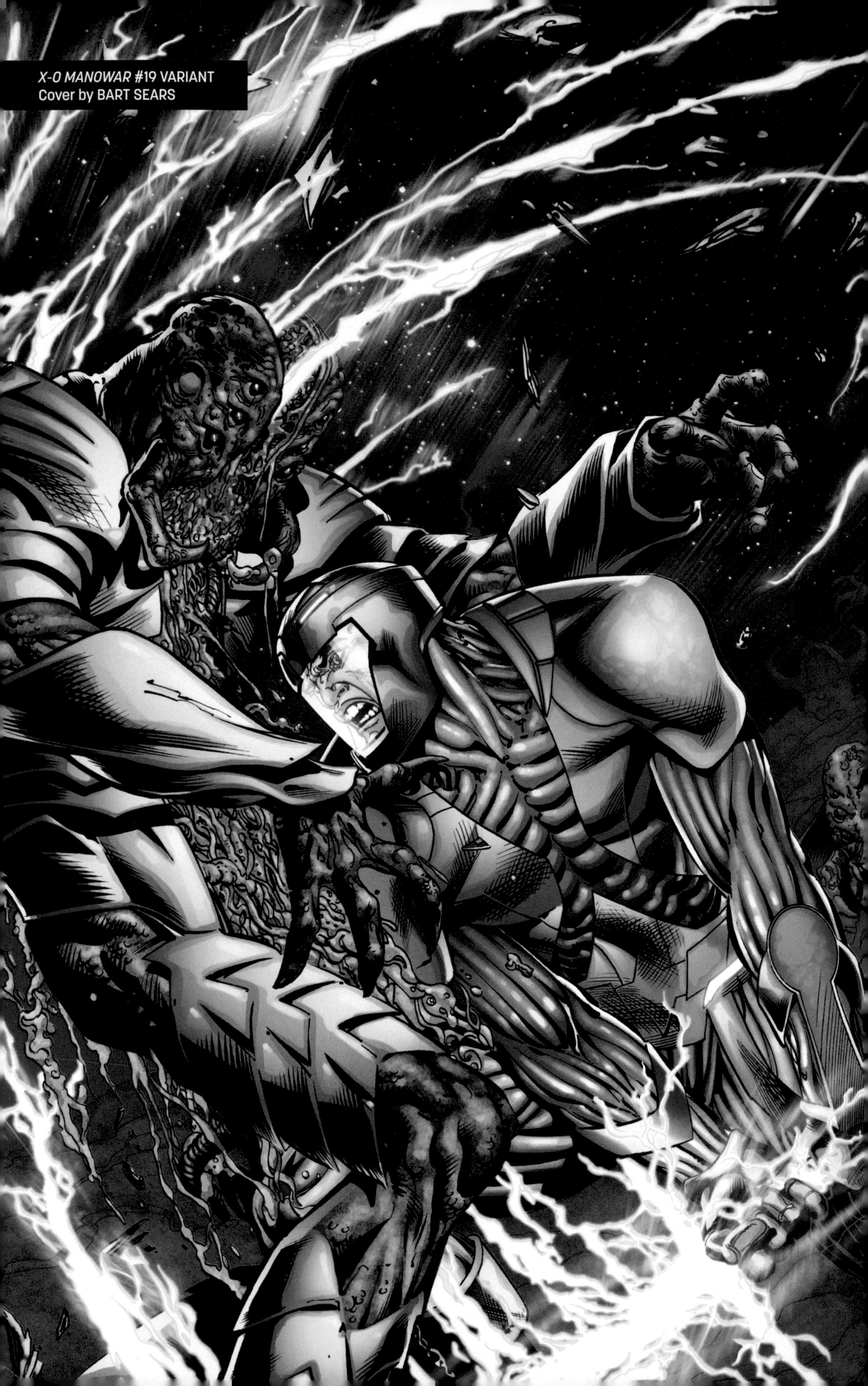

X-O MANOWAR #19 VARIANT
Cover by BART SEARS

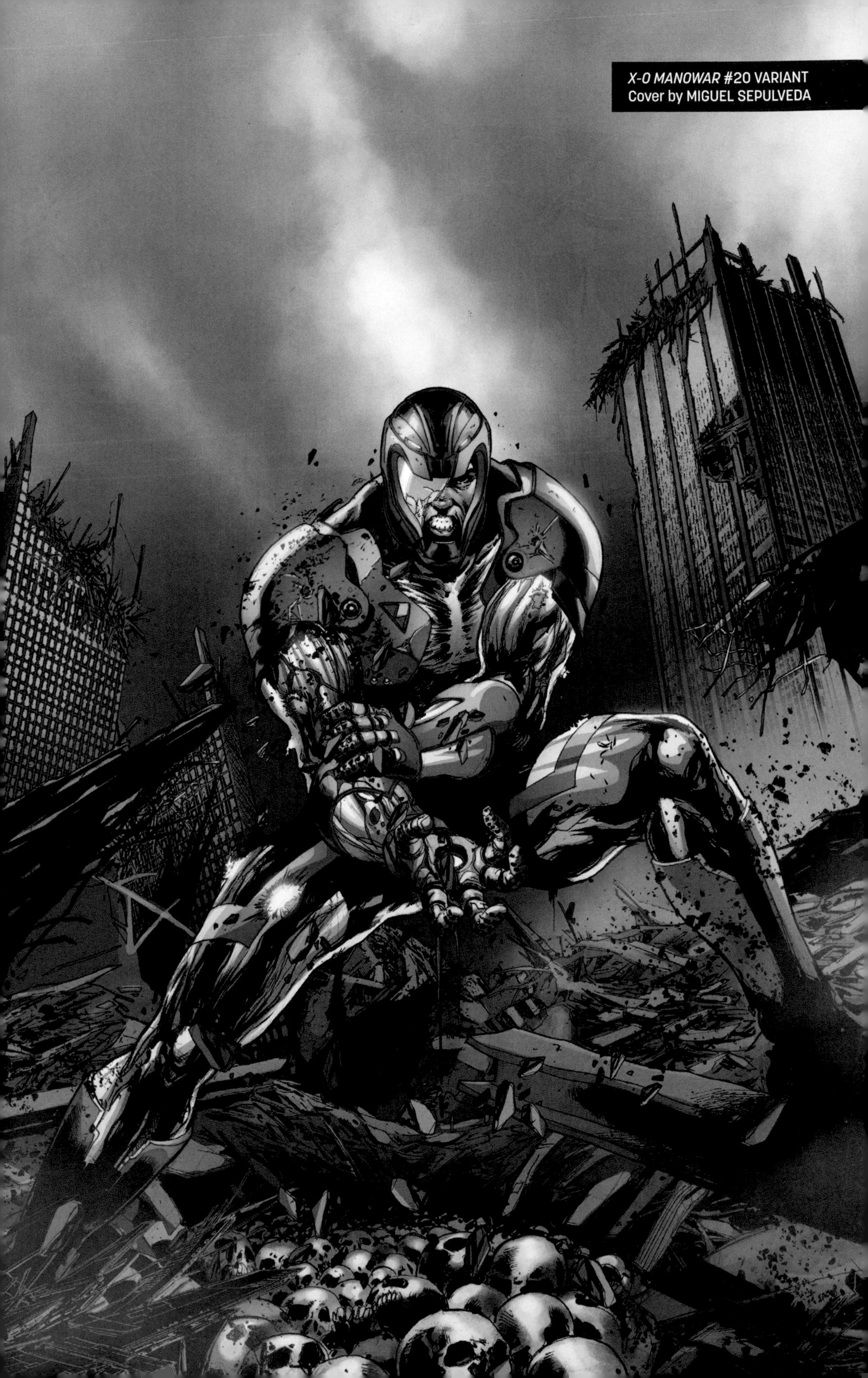

X-O MANOWAR #20 VARIANT
Cover by MIGUEL SEPULVEDA

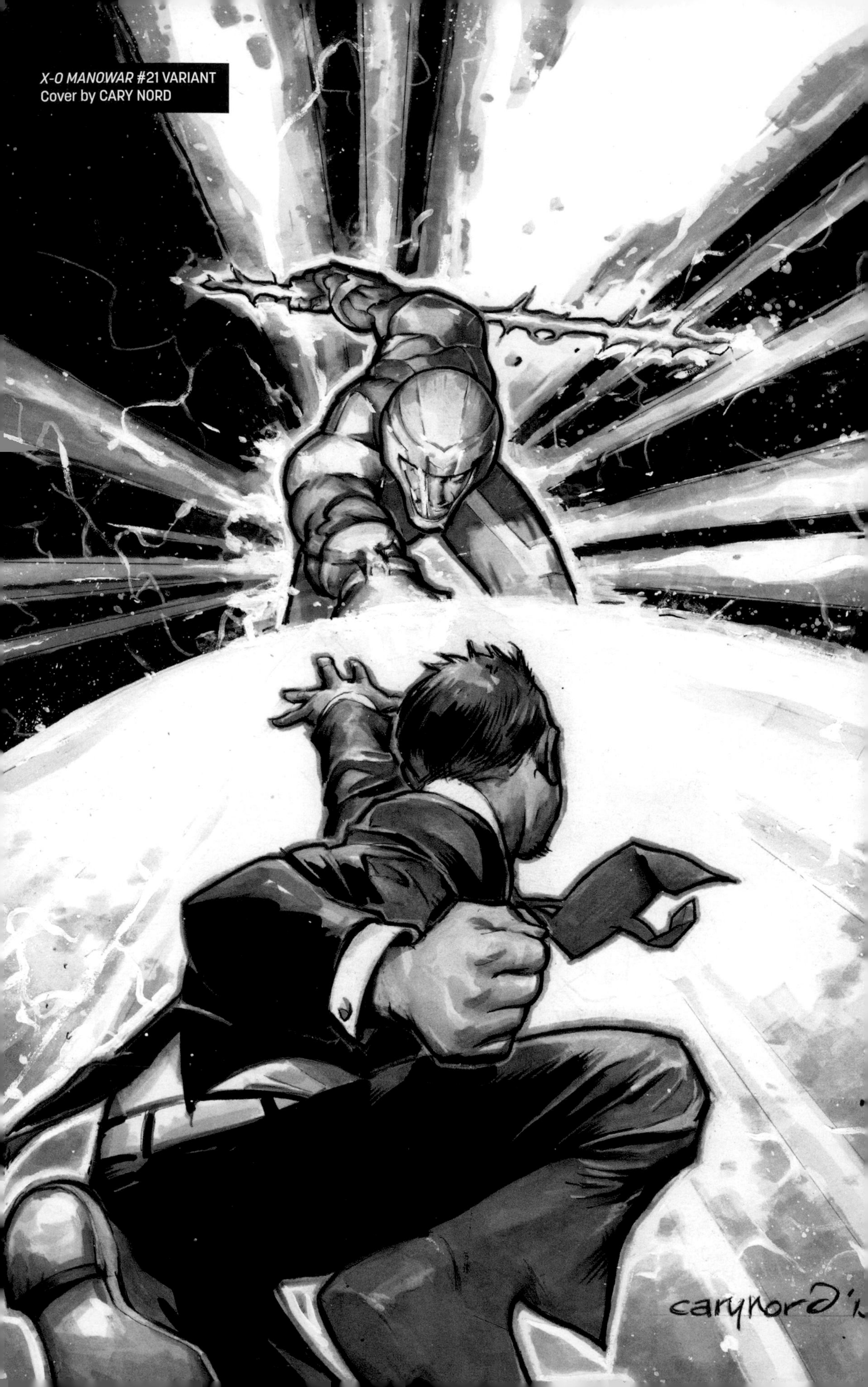
carynord

X-O MANOWAR #21 VARIANT
Cover by CARY NORD

X-O MANOWAR #22 VARIANT
Cover by WILL CONRAD

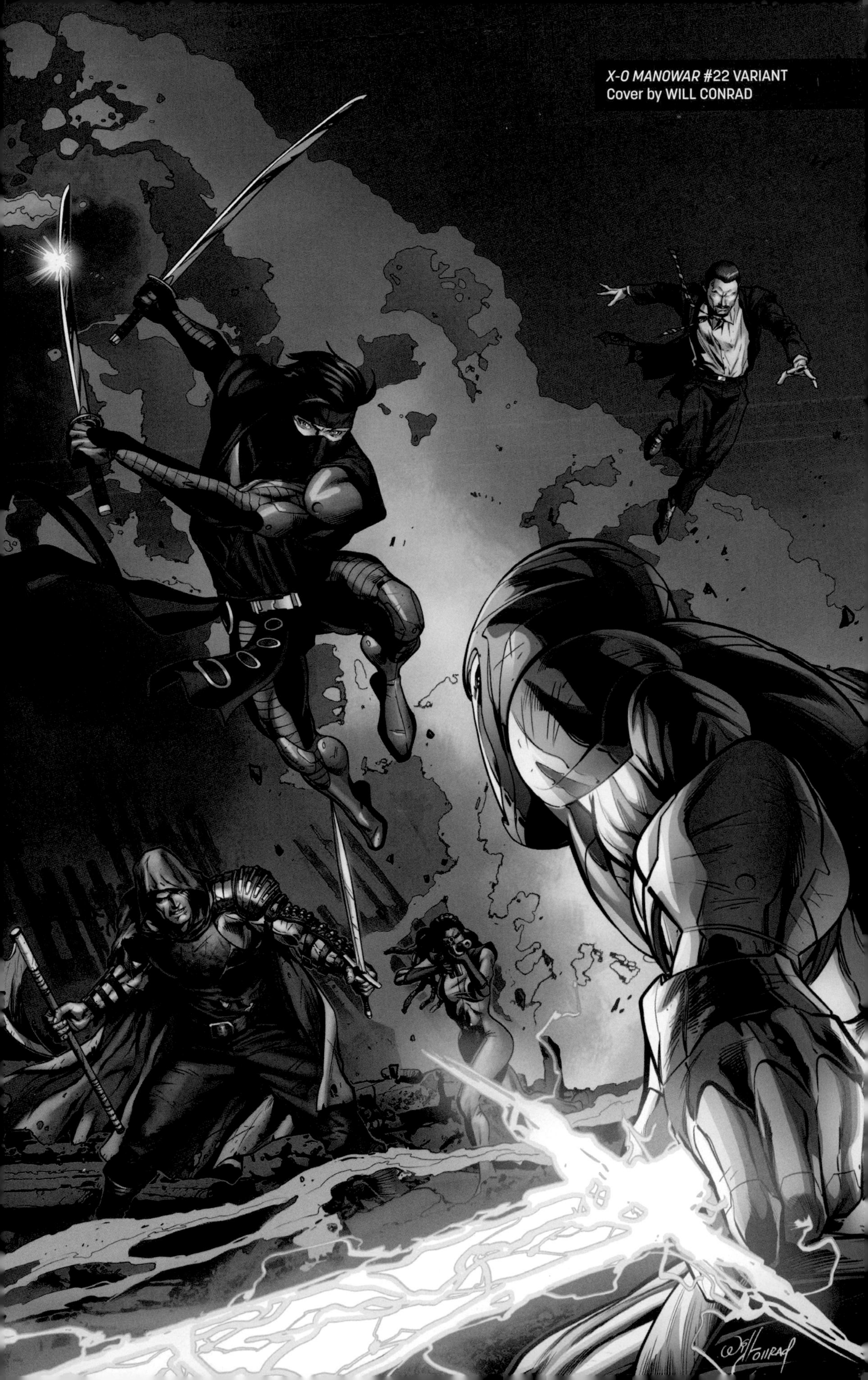
Will Conrad

X-O MANOWAR #22
VALIANT SIGNATURE SERIES VARIANT
Cover by JIM CALAFIORE

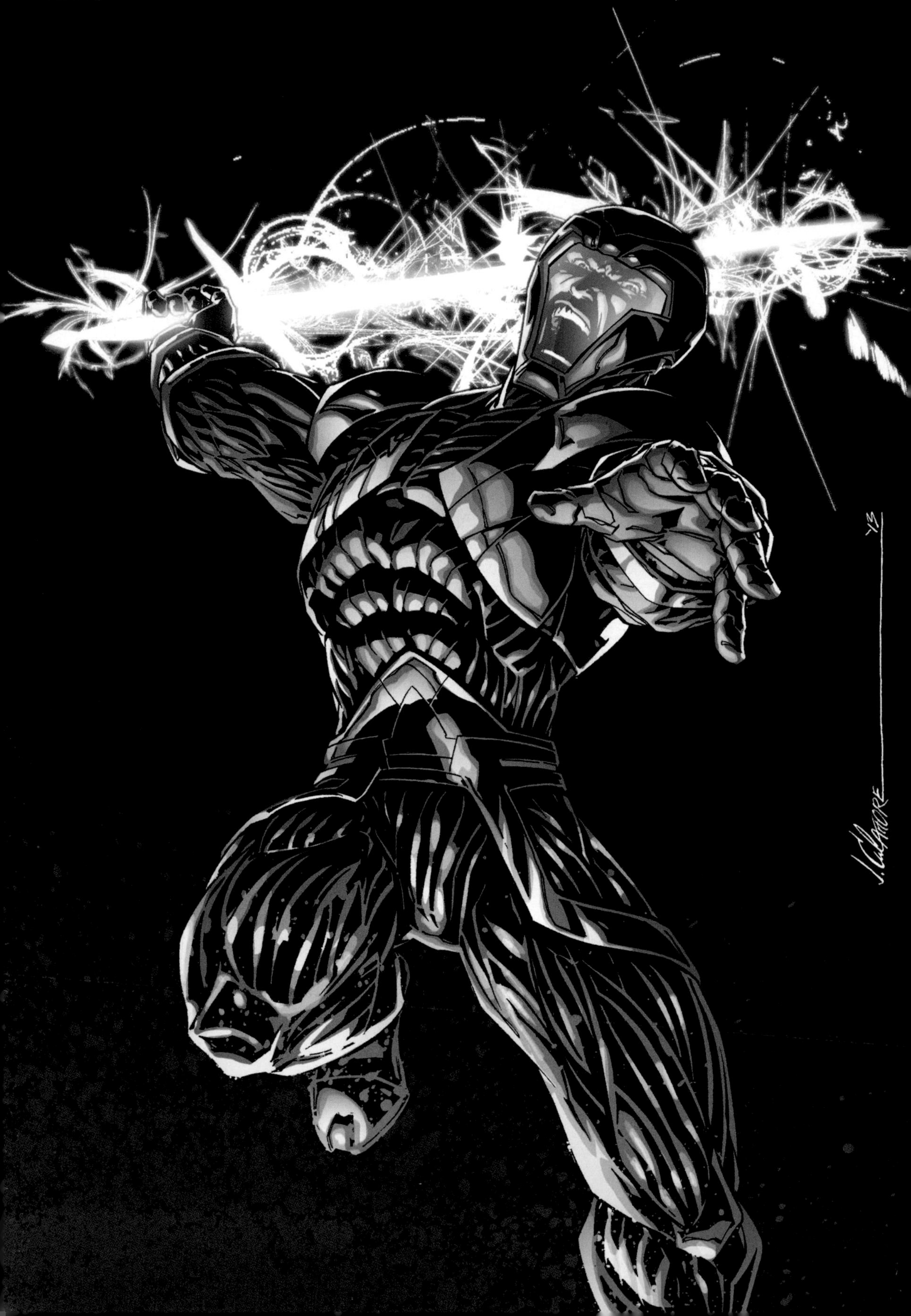

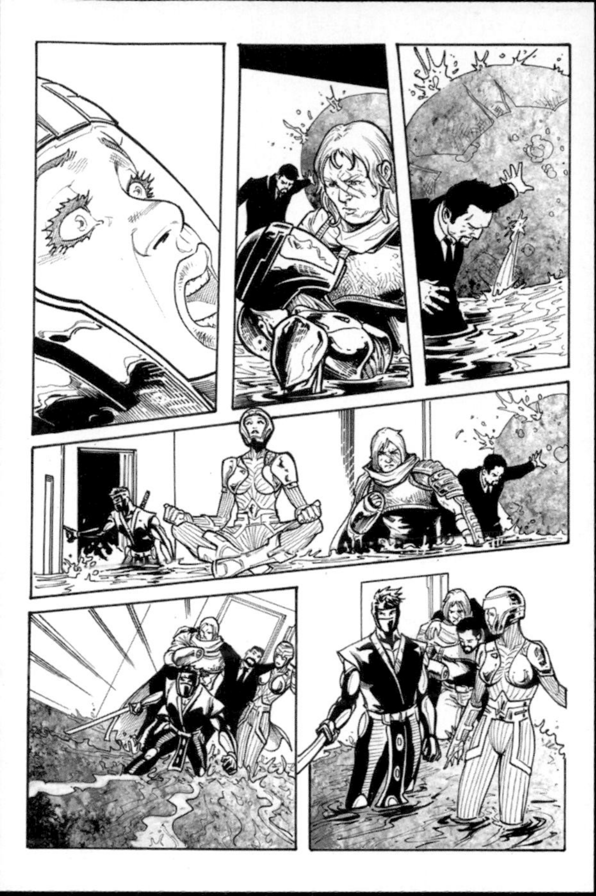

X-O MANOWAR #20, p.19
Layouts by CARY NORD
Finishes by VICENTE CIFUENTES

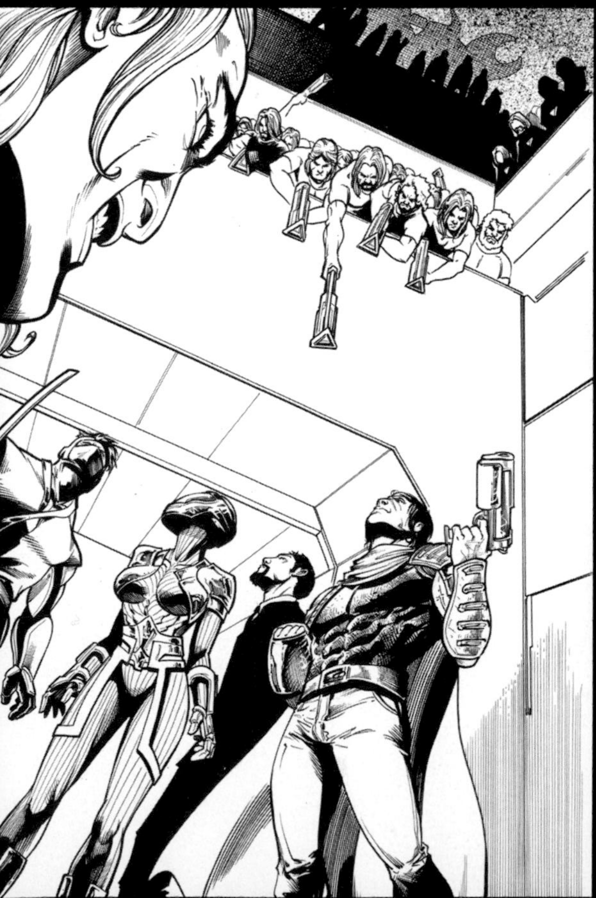

X-O MANOWAR #20, p.22
Layouts by CARY NORD
Finishes by VICENTE CIFUENTES

VALIANT DELUXE HARDCOVERS

ROBERT VENDITTI | CARY NORD | LEE GARBETT
TREVOR HAIRSINE | STEFANO GAUDIANO | MOOSE BAUMANN
VALIANT
X-O MANOWAR
DELUXE EDITION 1

X-O MANOWAR DELUXE EDITION BOOK 1

Writer: Robert Venditti | Artists: Cary Nord, Lee Garbett, and Trevor Hairsine
ISBN: 9781939346100 | Diamond Code: AUG131497 | Price: $39.99 |
Format: Oversized HC

Aric of Dacia, a fifth-century Visigoth armed with the universe's most powerful weapon, is all that stands between the Earth and all-out annihilation at the hands of the alien race that abducted him from his own time. Stranded in the modern day, X-O Manowar's battle against the Vine will take him into the shadows with the lethal operative known as Ninjak–and launch a quest for vengeance that will bring an alien empire to its knees. The Vine destroyed Aric's world. Now he will give them war.

Collecting X-O MANOWAR #1-14 and more than 20 pages of bonus materials!

JOSHUA DYSART | KHARI EVANS | TREVOR HAIRSINE
MICO SUAYAN | IAN HANNIN
VALIANT
HARBINGER
DELUXE EDITION 1

HARBINGER DELUXE EDITION BOOK 1

Writer: Joshua Dysart | Artists: Khari Evans, Trevor Hairsine, Barry Kitson, and Lee Garbett
ISBN: 9781939346131 | Diamond Code: SEP131373 | Price: $39.99 | Format: Oversized HC

Outside the law. Inside your head. You've never met a team of super-powered teenagers quite like the Renegades. Skipping across the country in a desperate attempt to stay one step ahead of the authorities, psionically powered teenager Peter Stanchek only has one option left–run. But he won't have to go it alone. As the shadowy corporation known as the Harbinger Foundation draws close on all sides, Peter will have to find and recruit other unique individuals like himself...other troubled, immensely powerful youths with abilities beyond their control. Their mission? Bring the fight back to the Harbinger Foundation's founder Toyo Harada–and dismantle his global empire brick by brick...

Collecting HARBINGER #0-14 and more than 20 pages of bonus materials!

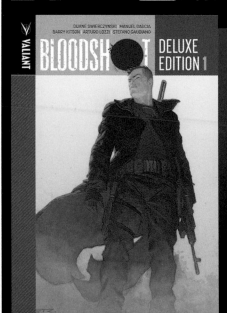

DUANE SWIERCZYNSKI | MANUEL GARCIA
BARRY KITSON | ARTURO LOZZI | STEFANO GAUDIANO
VALIANT
BLOODSHOT
DELUXE EDITION 1

BLOODSHOT DELUXE EDITION BOOK 1

Writer: Duane Swierczynski | Artists: Manuel García, Barry Kitson, Matthew Clark, and Arturo Lozzi
ISBN: 9781939346216 | Diamond Code: JAN141376 | Price: $39.99 | Format: Oversized HC

You have no name, just a project designation. They call you Bloodshot, but the voices inside your head call you "daddy, "sir," "commander," "comrade"–whatever it takes to motivate you to get the job done. But after so many missions and so many lives, you're finally ready to confront your handlers at Project Rising Spirit and find out who you really are. You'd better move quickly, though, because your former masters don't like it when a billion-dollar weapons project goes rogue. And wherever you go, all hell is sure to follow...

Collecting BLOODSHOT #1-13 and more than 20 pages of bonus materials!

VALIANT® DELUXE HARDCOVERS

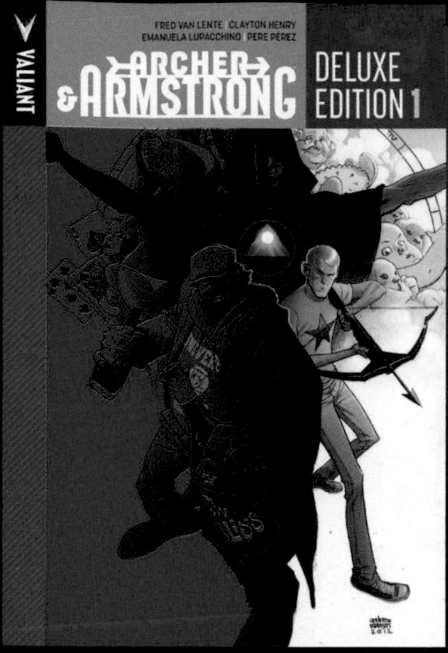
VALIANT
FRED VAN LENTE | CLAYTON HENRY
EMANUELA LUPACCHINO | PERE PÉREZ
ARCHER & ARMSTRONG
DELUXE EDITION 1

ARCHER & ARMSTRONG DELUXE EDITION BOOK 1

Writer: Fred Van Lente | Artists: Clayton Henry, Emanuela Lupacchino, Pere Pérez, and Álvaro Martínez
ISBN: 9781939346223 | Diamond Code: FEB141484 | Price: $39.99 | Format: Oversized HC

Join one of the most acclaimed adventures in comics as naive teenage assassin Obadiah Archer and the fun-loving, hard-drinking immortal called Armstrong unite to stop a plot ten thousand years in the making! From the lost temples of ancient Sumeria to modern-day Wall Street, Area 51, and beyond, Valiant's conspiracy-smashing adventurers are going on a globe-trotting quest to bring down the unholy coalition of cultists known as the Sect–and stop each of history's most notorious conspiracies from remaking the world in their own insane image.

Collecting ARCHER & ARMSTRONG #0-13 and more than 20 pages of bonus materials!

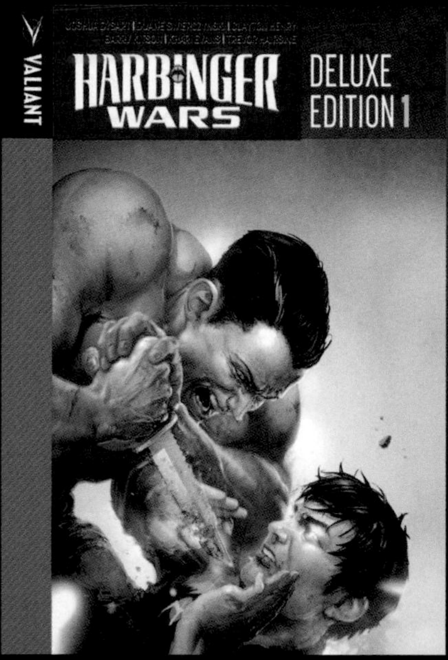
VALIANT
HARBINGER WARS
DELUXE EDITION 1

HARBINGER WARS DELUXE EDITION

Writer: Joshua Dysart & Duane Swierczynski | Artists: Clayton Henry, Pere Pérez, Barry Kitson, Khari Evans, Trevor Hairsine, Mico Suayan, and Clayton Crain
ISBN: 9781939346322 | Diamond Code: MAR141422 | **Price: $39.99 |**
Format: Oversized HC

Re-presenting Valiant's best-selling crossover event in complete chronological order!

When an untrained and undisciplined team of super-powered test subjects escapes from Project Rising Spirit and onto the Vegas Strip, Bloodshot and the Harbinger Renegades will find themselves locked in battle against a deadly succession of opponents–and each other. As the combined forces of the H.A.R.D. Corps, Bloodshot, and omega-level telekinetic Toyo Harada all descend on Las Vegas to vie for control of Rising Spirit's deadliest assets, the world is about to discover the shocking price of an all-out superhuman conflict...and no one will escape unscathed. Who will survive the Harbinger Wars?

Collecting HARBINGER WARS #1-4, HARBINGER #11-14, BLOODSHOT #10-13, material from the HARBINGER WARS SKETCHBOOK, and more than 20 pages of bonus materials!

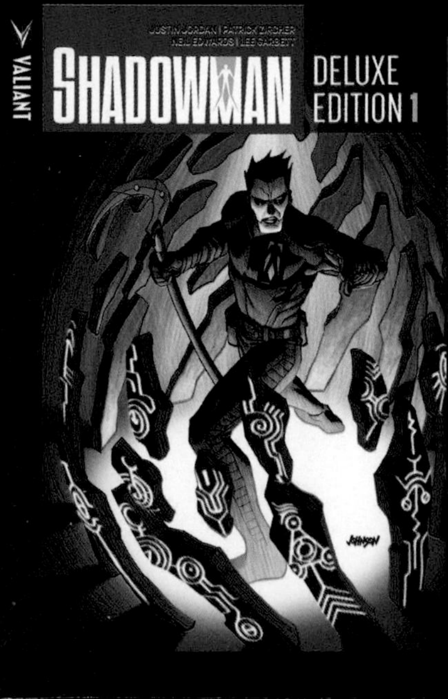
VALIANT
JUSTIN JORDAN | PATRICK ZIRCHER
NEIL EDWARDS | LEE GARBETT
SHADOWMAN
DELUXE EDITION 1

SHADOWMAN DELUXE EDITION BOOK 1

Writers: Justin Jordan and Patrick Zircher | Artists: Patrick Zircher, Neil Edwards, Lee Garbett, Diego Bernard, Roberto de la Torre, Mico Suayan, and Lewis LaRosa
ISBN: 9781939346438 | Price: $39.99 | Format: Oversized HC | COMING SOON

There are a million dreams in the Big Easy. But now its worst nightmare is about to come true. As the forces of darkness prepare to claim New Orleans as their own, Jack Boniface must accept the legacy he was born to uphold. As Shadowman, Jack is about to become the only thing that stands between his city and an army of unspeakable monstrosities from beyond the night. But what is the true cost of the Shadowman's otherworldly power? And can Jack master his new abilities before Master Darque brings down the wall between reality and the otherwordly dimension known only as the Deadside?

Collecting SHADOWMAN #0-10 and more than 20 pages of bonus materials!

VALIANT

TRADE PAPERBACKS

VALIANT
TO KILL A KING
UNITY

UNITY VOL. 1: TO KILL A KING
ISBN: 9781939346261 | Diamond Code: JAN141356 | Price: $14.99 | Format: TP

UNITY VOL. 2: TRAPPED BY WEBNET
ISBN: 9781939346346| Price: $14.99 | Format: TP | COMING SOON

VALIANT
ROBERT VENDITTI CARY NORD STEFANO GAUDIANO MOOSE BAUMANN
BY THE SWORD
X-O MANOWAR

X-O MANOWAR VOL. 1: BY THE SWORD
ISBN: 9780979640995 | Diamond Code: OCT121241 | Price: $9.99 | Format: TP

X-O MANOWAR VOL. 2: ENTER NINJAK
ISBN: 9780979640940 | Diamond Code: JAN131306 | Price: $14.99 | Format: TP

X-O MANOWAR VOL. 3: PLANET DEATH
ISBN: 9781939346087 | Diamond Code: JUN131325 | Price: $14.99 | Format: TP

X-O MANOWAR VOL. 4: HOMECOMING
ISBN: 9781939346179 | Diamond Code: OCT131347 | Price: $14.99 | Format: TP

X-O MANOWAR VOL. 5: AT WAR WITH UNITY
ISBN: 9781939346247 | Diamond Code: FEB141472 | Price: $14.99 | Format: TP

VALIANT
SETTING THE WORLD ON FIRE
BLOODSHOT

BLOODSHOT VOL. 1: SETTING THE WORLD ON FIRE
ISBN: 9780979640964 | Diamond Code: DEC121274 | Price: $9.99 | Format: TP

BLOODSHOT VOL. 2: THE RISE AND THE FALL
ISBN: 9781939346032| Diamond Code: APR131280 | Price: $14.99 | Format: TP

BLOODSHOT VOL. 3: HARBINGER WARS
ISBN: 9781939346124 | Diamond Code: AUG131494 | Price: $14.99 | Format: TP

BLOODSHOT VOL. 4: H.A.R.D. CORPS
ISBN: 9781939346193 | Diamond Code: NOV131275 | Price: $14.99 | Format: TP

BLOODSHOT VOL. 5: GET SOME
ISBN: 9781939346315 | Price: $14.99 | Format: TP | COMING SOON

VALIANT
SWORD OF THE WILD
ETERNAL WARRIOR

ETERNAL WARRIOR VOL. 1: SWORD OF THE WILD
ISBN: 9781939346209 | Diamond Code: NOV131271 | Price: $9.99 | Format: TP

ETERNAL WARRIOR VOL. 2: ETERNAL EMPEROR
ISBN: 9781939346292 | Price: $14.99 | Format: TP | COMING SOON

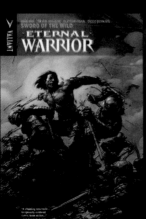

VALIANT® TRADE PAPERBACKS

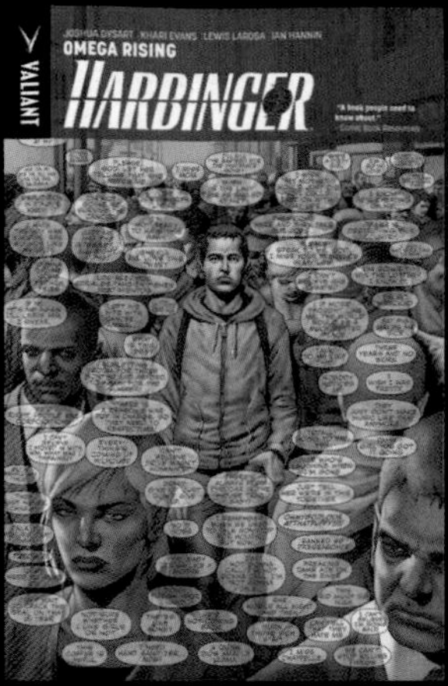
VALIANT
JOSHUA DYSART | KHARI EVANS | LEWIS LAROSA | IAN HANNIN
OMEGA RISING
HARBINGER

HARBINGER VOL. 1: OMEGA RISING
ISBN: 9780979640957 | Diamond Code: NOV121345 | Price: $9.99 | Format: TP

HARBINGER VOL. 2: RENEGADES
ISBN: 9781939346025 | Diamond Code: MAR131332 | Price: $14.99 | Format: TP

HARBINGER WARS (MINI-SERIES)
ISBN: 9781939346094 | Diamond Code: JUL131325 | Price: $14.99 | Format: TP

HARBINGER VOL. 3: HARBINGER WARS
ISBN: 9781939346117 | Diamond Code: JUL131326 | Price: $14.99 | Format: TP

HARBINGER VOL. 4: PERFECT DAY
ISBN: 9781939346155 | Diamond Code: DEC131331 | Price: $14.99 | Format: TP

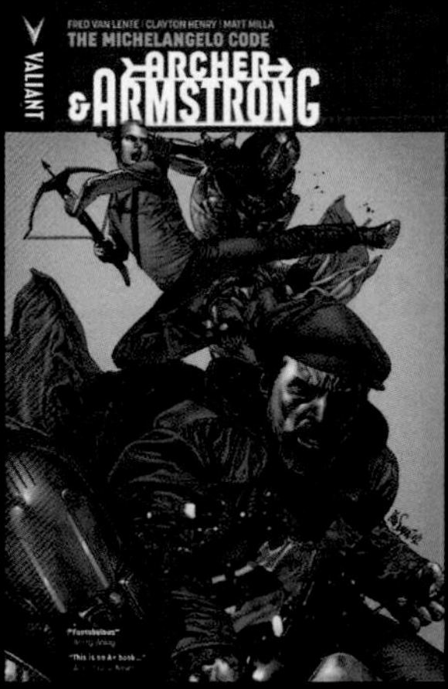
VALIANT
FRED VAN LENTE | CLAYTON HENRY | MATT MILLA
THE MICHELANGELO CODE
ARCHER & ARMSTRONG

ARCHER & ARMSTRONG VOL. 1: THE MICHELANGELO CODE
ISBN: 9780979640988 | Diamond Code: JAN131309 | Price: $14.99 | Format: TP

ARCHER & ARMSTRONG VOL. 2: WRATH OF THE ETERNAL WARRIOR
ISBN: 9781939346049 | Diamond Code: MAY131314 | Price: $14.99 | Format: TP

ARCHER & ARMSTRONG VOL. 3: FAR FARAWAY
ISBN: 9781939346148 | Diamond Code: OCT131350 | Price: $14.99 | Format: TP

ARCHER & ARMSTRONG VOL. 4: SECT CIVIL WAR
ISBN: 9781939346254 | Diamond Code: DEC131317 | Price: $14.99 | Format: TP

ARCHER & ARMSTRONG VOL. 5: MISSION: IMPROBABLE
ISBN: 9781939346353 | Price: $14.99 | Format: TP | COMING SOON

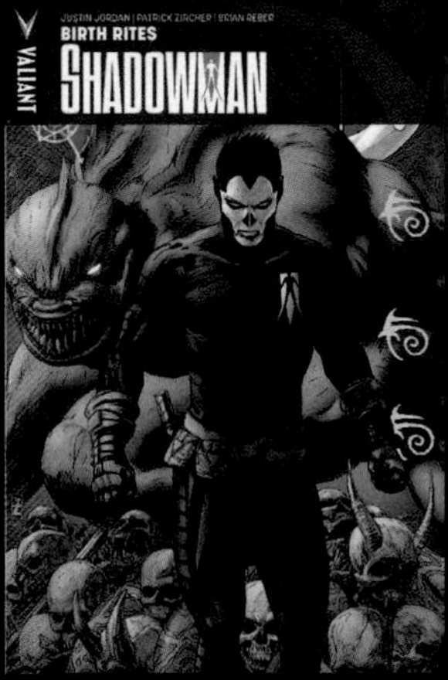
VALIANT
JUSTIN JORDAN | PATRICK ZIRCHER | BRIAN REBER
BIRTH RITES
SHADOWMAN

SHADOWMAN VOL. 1: BIRTH RITES
ISBN: 9781939346001 | Diamond Code: FEB131168 | Price: $9.99 | Format: TP

SHADOWMAN VOL. 2: DARQUE RECKONING
ISBN: 9781939346056 | Diamond Code: AUG131482 | Price: $14.99 | Format: TP

SHADOWMAN VOL. 3: DEADSIDE BLUES
ISBN: 9781939346162 | Diamond Code: NOV131282 | Price: $14.99 | Format: TP

SHADOWMAN VOL. 4: FEAR, BLOOD, AND SHADOWS
ISBN: 9781939346278 | Diamond Code: MAR141410 | Price: $14.99 | Format: TP

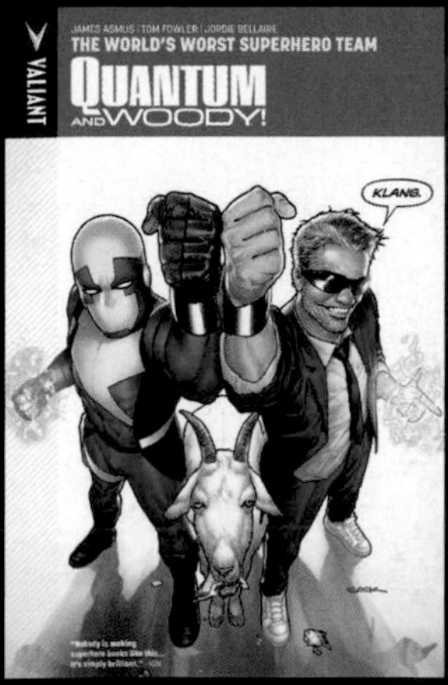
VALIANT
JAMES ASMUS | TOM FOWLER | JORDIE BELLAIRE
THE WORLD'S WORST SUPERHERO TEAM
QUANTUM AND WOODY!
KLANG.

QUANTUM AND WOODY VOL. 1: THE WORLD'S WORST SUPERHERO TEAM
ISBN: 9781939346186 | Diamond Code: SEP131374 | Price: $9.99 | Format: TP

QUANTUM AND WOODY VOL. 2: IN SECURITY
ISBN: 9781939346230 | Diamond Code: JAN141365 | Price: $14.99 | Format: TP

VALIANT

X-O MANOWAR®

VOLUME SIX: PRELUDE TO ARMOR HUNTERS

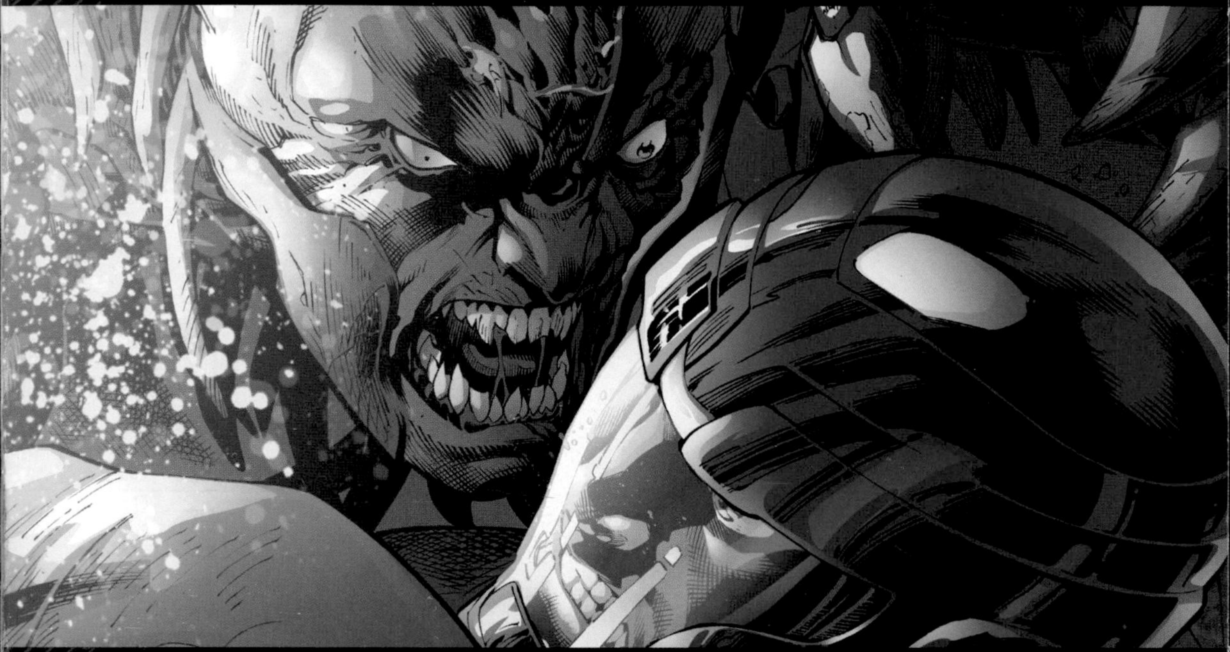

THE ROAD TO ARMOR HUNTERS STARTS HERE!

Aric of Dacia, a fifth-century warrior bonded to alien armor and transplanted to the modern day, is now the most important weapon in the arsenal of M.E.R.O., the top-secret American intelligence organization that monitors extraterrestrial life on Earth. In order to protect his people, Aric must undergo dangerous missions in space, but nothing can prepare him for the stunning secret that awaits him in the stars.

Collecting **X-O MANOWAR #23-24** and the oversized **X-O MANOWAR #25** anniversary spectacular, the march toward ARMOR HUNTERS begins here as New York Times best-selling writer Robert Venditti (*Green Lantern*) and red-hot artist Diego Bernard (*Eternal Warrior*) join an all-star cast of comic book superstars - including Sean Chen (*Iron Man*), Tom Fowler (*Quantum and Woody*), Bryan Hitch (*The Ultimates*), J.G. Jones (*Final Crisis*), Barry Kitson (*The Amazing Spider-Man*), Cary Nord (*Conan*), and many more - to deliver an essential introduction to the biggest Valiant event ever attempted.

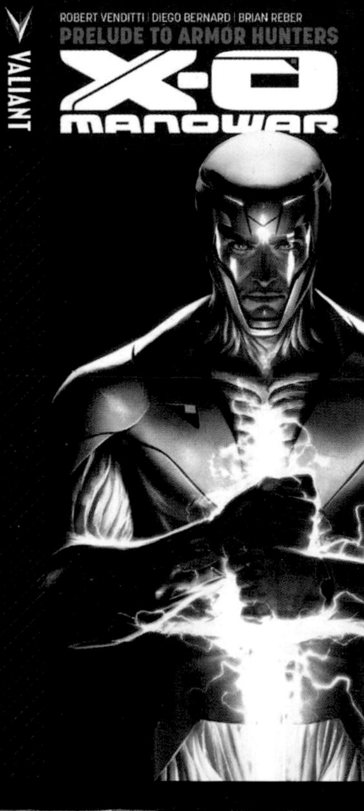
VALIANT
ROBERT VENDITTI | DIEGO BERNARD | BRIAN REBER
PRELUDE TO ARMOR HUNTERS
X-O
MANOWAR

TRADE PAPERBACK
978-1-939346-40-7